2023
SUN SIGN
BOOK

Forecasts by
Alice DeVille

Cover design by Kevin R. Brown
GettyImages.com/803108768/© MimaCZ
GettyImages.com/1133041125/© Nel_Dragon
Interior illustration on page 19 by the Llewellyn Art Department

© 2022 by Llewellyn Publications
ISBN: 978-0-7387-6400-9
Llewellyn is a registered trademark of Llewellyn Worldwide Ltd.
2143 Wooddale Drive, Woodbury, MN 55125-2989
www.llewellyn.com
Printed in the United States of America

Contents

2022

SEPTEMBER
S	M	T	W	T	F	S
				1	2	3
4	5	6	7	8	9	10
11	12	13	14	15	16	17
18	19	20	21	22	23	24
25	26	27	28	29	30	

OCTOBER
S	M	T	W	T	F	S
						1
2	3	4	5	6	7	8
9	10	11	12	13	14	15
16	17	18	19	20	21	22
23	24	25	26	27	28	29
30	31					

NOVEMBER
S	M	T	W	T	F	S
		1	2	3	4	5
6	7	8	9	10	11	12
13	14	15	16	17	18	19
20	21	22	23	24	25	26
27	28	29	30			

DECEMBER
S	M	T	W	T	F	S
				1	2	3
4	5	6	7	8	9	10
11	12	13	14	15	16	17
18	19	20	21	22	23	24
25	26	27	28	29	30	31

2023

JANUARY
S	M	T	W	T	F	S
1	2	3	4	5	6	7
8	9	10	11	12	13	14
15	16	17	18	19	20	21
22	23	24	25	26	27	28
29	30	31				

FEBRUARY
S	M	T	W	T	F	S
			1	2	3	4
5	6	7	8	9	10	11
12	13	14	15	16	17	18
19	20	21	22	23	24	25
26	27	28				

MARCH
S	M	T	W	T	F	S
			1	2	3	4
5	6	7	8	9	10	11
12	13	14	15	16	17	18
19	20	21	22	23	24	25
26	27	28	29	30	31	

APRIL
S	M	T	W	T	F	S
						1
2	3	4	5	6	7	8
9	10	11	12	13	14	15
16	17	18	19	20	21	22
23	24	25	26	27	28	29
30						

MAY
S	M	T	W	T	F	S
	1	2	3	4	5	6
7	8	9	10	11	12	13
14	15	16	17	18	19	20
21	22	23	24	25	26	27
28	29	30	31			

JUNE
S	M	T	W	T	F	S
				1	2	3
4	5	6	7	8	9	10
11	12	13	14	15	16	17
18	19	20	21	22	23	24
25	26	27	28	29	30	

JULY
S	M	T	W	T	F	S
						1
2	3	4	5	6	7	8
9	10	11	12	13	14	15
16	17	18	19	20	21	22
23	24	25	26	27	28	29
30	31					

AUGUST
S	M	T	W	T	F	S
		1	2	3	4	5
6	7	8	9	10	11	12
13	14	15	16	17	18	19
20	21	22	23	24	25	26
27	28	29	30	31		

SEPTEMBER
S	M	T	W	T	F	S
					1	2
3	4	5	6	7	8	9
10	11	12	13	14	15	16
17	18	19	20	21	22	23
24	25	26	27	28	29	30

OCTOBER
S	M	T	W	T	F	S
1	2	3	4	5	6	7
8	9	10	11	12	13	14
15	16	17	18	19	20	21
22	23	24	25	26	27	28
29	30	31				

NOVEMBER
S	M	T	W	T	F	S
			1	2	3	4
5	6	7	8	9	10	11
12	13	14	15	16	17	18
19	20	21	22	23	24	25
26	27	28	29	30		

DECEMBER
S	M	T	W	T	F	S
					1	2
3	4	5	6	7	8	9
10	11	12	13	14	15	16
17	18	19	20	21	22	23
24	25	26	27	28	29	30
31						

2024

JANUARY
S	M	T	W	T	F	S
	1	2	3	4	5	6
7	8	9	10	11	12	13
14	15	16	17	18	19	20
21	22	23	24	25	26	27
28	29	30	31			

FEBRUARY
S	M	T	W	T	F	S
				1	2	3
4	5	6	7	8	9	10
11	12	13	14	15	16	17
18	19	20	21	22	23	24
25	26	27	28	29		

MARCH
S	M	T	W	T	F	S
					1	2
3	4	5	6	7	8	9
10	11	12	13	14	15	16
17	18	19	20	21	22	23
24	25	26	27	28	29	30
31						

APRIL
S	M	T	W	T	F	S
	1	2	3	4	5	6
7	8	9	10	11	12	13
14	15	16	17	18	19	20
21	22	23	24	25	26	27
28	29	30				

MAY
S	M	T	W	T	F	S
			1	2	3	4
5	6	7	8	9	10	11
12	13	14	15	16	17	18
19	20	21	22	23	24	25
26	27	28	29	30	31	

JUNE
S	M	T	W	T	F	S
						1
2	3	4	5	6	7	8
9	10	11	12	13	14	15
16	17	18	19	20	21	22
23	24	25	26	27	28	29
30						

JULY
S	M	T	W	T	F	S
	1	2	3	4	5	6
7	8	9	10	11	12	13
14	15	16	17	18	19	20
21	22	23	24	25	26	27
28	29	30	31			

AUGUST
S	M	T	W	T	F	S
				1	2	3
4	5	6	7	8	9	10
11	12	13	14	15	16	17
18	19	20	21	22	23	24
25	26	27	28	29	30	31

Meet Alice DeVille

Alice DeVille is known internationally as an astrologer, consultant, and writer. She has been writing articles for the Llewellyn annuals since 1998. Her contributions have appeared in Llewellyn's *Sun Sign Book*, *Moon Sign Book*, and *Herbal Almanac*. Alice discovered astrology in her late teens when she was browsing the book section of a discount department store and found a book that had much more astrology detail in it than simple Sun sign descriptions. Bells of recognition went off immediately. She purchased the book and knew she had to have more.

Alice is a former analyst for the USDA Forest Service in Washington, DC. She later held credentials as a Realtor for twenty-two years in the Commonwealth of Virginia and earned real estate appraisal credentials and certifications in diverse real estate specialties. Her knowledge of feng shui led to the development of numerous workshops and seminars including those that provided Realtors with tips to enhance selling homes and working with buyers.

Alice specializes in relationships of all types that call for solid problem-solving advice to get to the core of issues and give clients options for meeting critical needs. Her clients seek solutions in business practices, career and change management, real estate, relationships, and training. Numerous websites and publications have featured her articles, including StarIQ, Astral Hearts, Llewellyn, Meta Arts, Inner Self, and ShareItLiveIt. Quotes from her work on relationships have appeared in books, publications, training materials, calendars, planners, audio tapes, and world-famous quotes lists. Often cited is "Each relationship you have with another reflects the relationship you have with yourself." Alice's Llewellyn material on relationships has appeared in *Something More* by Sarah Ban Breathnach and *Through God's Eyes* by Phil Bolsta and on Oprah's website.

Alice is available for writing books and articles for publishers, newspapers, and magazines, as well as conducting workshops and doing radio or TV interviews. For information, contact her at DeVilleAA@aol.com or alice.deville27@gmail.com.

How to Use This Book

by Kim Rogers-Gallagher

Hi there! Welcome to the 2023 edition of *Llewellyn's Sun Sign Book*. This book centers on Sun sign astrology—that is, the set of general attributes and characteristics that those of us born under each of the twelve particular Sun signs share. You'll find descriptions of your sign's qualities tucked into your sign's chapter, along with the type of behavior you tend to exhibit in different life situations—with regard to relationships, work situations, and the handling of money and possessions, for example. Oh, and there's a section that's dedicated to good old-fashioned fun, too, including what will bring you joy and how to make it happen.

There's a lot to be said for Sun sign astrology. First off, the Sun's sign at the time of your birth describes the qualities, talents, and traits you're here to study this time around. If you believe in reincarnation, think of it as declaring a celestial major for this lifetime. Sure, you'll learn other things along the way, but you've announced to one and all that you're primarily interested in mastering this one particular sign. Then, too, on a day when fiery, impulsive energies are making astrological headlines, if you're a fiery and/or impulsive sign yourself—like Aries or Aquarius, for example—it's easy to imagine how you'll take to the astrological weather a lot more easily than a practical, steady-handed sign like Taurus or Virgo.

Obviously, astrology comes in handy, for a variety of reasons. Getting to know your "natal" Sun sign (the sign the Sun was in when you were born) can most certainly give you the edge you need to ace the final and move on to the next celestial course level—or basically to succeed in life, and maybe even earn a few bonus points toward next semester. Using astrology on a daily basis nicely accelerates the process.

Now, there are eight other planets and one lovely Moon in our neck of the celestial woods, all of which also play into our personalities. The sign that was on the eastern horizon at the moment of your birth—otherwise known as your *Ascendant*, or *rising sign*—is another indicator of your personality traits. Honestly, there are all kinds of cosmic factors, so if it's an in-depth, personal analysis you're after, a professional astrologer is the only way to go—especially if you're curious about relationships, past lives, future trends, or even the right time to schedule an important life event. Professional astrologers calculate your birth chart—again, the "natal" chart—based on the date, place, and exact time of your birth—which allows for a far more personal and specific reading. In the meantime, however, in addition to reading up on your Sun sign, you can use the tables on pages 8 and 9 to find the sign of your Ascendant. (These tables, however, are approximate and tailored to those of us born in North America, so if the traits of your Ascendant don't sound familiar, check out the sign directly before or after.)

There are three sections to each sign chapter in this book. As I already mentioned, the first section describes personality traits, and while it's fun to read your own, don't forget to check out the other Sun signs. (Oh, and do feel free to mention any rather striking behavioral similarities to skeptics. It's great fun to watch a Scorpio's reaction when you tell them they're astrologically known as "the sexy sign," or a Gemini when you thank them for creating the concept of multitasking.)

The second section is entitled "The Year Ahead" for each sign. Through considering the movements of the slow-moving planets (Jupiter, Saturn, Uranus, Neptune, Pluto), the eclipses, and any other outstanding celestial movements, this segment will provide you with the big picture of the year—or basically the broad strokes of what to expect, no matter who you are or where you are, collectively speaking.

The third section includes monthly forecasts, along with rewarding days and challenging days, basically a heads-up designed to alert you to potentially easy times as well as potentially tricky times.

At the end of every chapter you'll find an Action Table, providing general information about the best time to indulge in certain activities. Please note that these are only suggestions. Don't hold yourself back or rush into anything your intuition doesn't wholeheartedly agree with—and again, when in doubt, find yourself a professional.

Well, that's it. I hope that you enjoy this book, and that being aware of the astrological energies of 2023 helps you create a year full of fabulous memories!

Kim Rogers-Gallagher has written hundreds of articles and columns for magazines and online publications and has two books of her own, *Astrology for the Light Side of the Brain* and *Astrology for the Light Side of the Future.* She's a well-known speaker who's been part of the UAC faculty since 1996. Kim can be contacted at KRGPhoenix313@yahoo.com for fees regarding readings, classes, and lectures.

Ascendant Table

Your Sun Sign	6–8 am	8–10 am	10 am–Noon	Noon–2 pm	2–4 pm	4–6 pm
Aries	Taurus	Gemini	Cancer	Leo	Virgo	Libra
Taurus	Gemini	Cancer	Leo	Virgo	Libra	Scorpio
Gemini	Cancer	Leo	Virgo	Libra	Scorpio	Sagittarius
Cancer	Leo	Virgo	Libra	Scorpio	Sagittarius	Capricorn
Leo	Virgo	Libra	Scorpio	Sagittarius	Capricorn	Aquarius
Virgo	Libra	Scorpio	Sagittarius	Capricorn	Aquarius	Pisces
Libra	Scorpio	Sagittarius	Capricorn	Aquarius	Pisces	Aries
Scorpio	Sagittarius	Capricorn	Aquarius	Pisces	Aries	Taurus
Sagittarius	Capricorn	Aquarius	Pisces	Aries	Taurus	Gemini
Capricorn	Aquarius	Pisces	Aries	Taurus	Gemini	Cancer
Aquarius	Pisces	Aries	Taurus	Gemini	Cancer	Leo
Pisces	Aries	Taurus	Gemini	Cancer	Leo	Virgo

Your Time of Birth

Your Sun Sign	Your Time of Birth					
	6–8 pm	8–10 pm	10 pm–Midnight	Midnight–2 am	2–4 am	4–6 am
Aries	Scorpio	Sagittarius	Capricorn	Aquarius	Pisces	Aries
Taurus	Sagittarius	Capricorn	Aquarius	Pisces	Aries	Taurus
Gemini	Capricorn	Aquarius	Pisces	Aries	Taurus	Gemini
Cancer	Aquarius	Pisces	Aries	Taurus	Gemini	Cancer
Leo	Pisces	Aries	Taurus	Gemini	Cancer	Leo
Virgo	Aries	Taurus	Gemini	Cancer	Leo	Virgo
Libra	Taurus	Gemini	Cancer	Leo	Virgo	Libra
Scorpio	Gemini	Cancer	Leo	Virgo	Libra	Scorpio
Sagittarius	Cancer	Leo	Virgo	Libra	Scorpio	Sagittarius
Capricorn	Leo	Virgo	Libra	Scorpio	Sagittarius	Capricorn
Aquarius	Virgo	Libra	Scorpio	Sagittarius	Capricorn	Aquarius
Pisces	Libra	Scorpio	Sagittarius	Capricorn	Aquarius	Pisces

How to use this table: 1. Find your Sun sign in the left column.

2. Find your approximate birth time in a vertical column.

3. Line up your Sun sign and birth time to find your Ascendant.

This table will give you an approximation of your Ascendant. If you feel that the sign listed as your Ascendant is incorrect, try the one either before or after the listed sign. It is difficult to determine your exact Ascendant without a complete natal chart.

Astrology Basics

Natal astrology is done by freeze-framing the solar system at the moment of your birth, from the perspective of your birth place. This creates a circular map that looks like a pie sliced into twelve pieces. It shows where every heavenly body we're capable of seeing was located when you arrived. Basically, it's your astrological tool kit, and it can't be replicated more than once in thousands of years. This is why we astrologers are so darn insistent about the need for you to either dig your birth certificate out of that box of ancient paperwork in the back of your closet or get a copy of it from the county clerk's office where you were born. Natal astrology, as interpreted by a professional astrologer, is done exactly and precisely for you and no one else. It shows your inherent traits, talents, and challenges. Comparing the planets' current positions to their positions in your birth chart allows astrologers to help you understand the celestial trends at work in your life—and most importantly, how you can put each astrological energy to a positive, productive use.

Let's take a look at the four main components of every astrology chart.

Planets

The planets represent the needs or urges we all experience once we hop off the Evolutionary Express and take up residence inside a human body. For example, the Sun is your urge to shine and be creative, the Moon is your need to express emotions, Mercury is in charge of how you communicate and navigate, and Venus is all about who and what you love—and more importantly, how you love.

Signs

The sign a planet occupies is like a costume or uniform. It describes how you'll go about acting on your needs and urges. If you have Venus in fiery, impulsive Aries, for example, and you're attracted to a complete stranger across the room, you won't wait for them to come to you. You'll walk over and introduce yourself the second the urge strikes you. Venus in intense, sexy Scorpio, however? Well, that's a different story. In this case, you'll keep looking at a prospective beloved until they finally give in, cross the room, and beg you to explain why you've been staring at them for the past couple of hours.

Houses

The houses represent the different sides of our personalities that emerge in different life situations. For example, think of how very different you act when you're with an authority figure as opposed to how you act with a lover or when you're with your BFF.

Aspects

The aspects describe the distance from one planet to another in a geometric angle. If you were born when Mercury was 90 degrees from Jupiter, for example, this aspect is called a square. Each unique angular relationship causes the planets involved to interact differently.

Meet the Planets

The planets represent energy sources. The Sun is our source of creativity, the Moon is our emotional warehouse, and Venus describes who and what we love and are attracted to—not to mention why and how we go about getting it and keeping it.

Sun

The Sun is the head honcho in your chart. It represents your life's mission—what will give you joy, keep you young, and never fail to arouse your curiosity. Oddly enough, you weren't born knowing the qualities of the sign the Sun was in when you were born. You're here to learn the traits, talents, and characteristics of the sign you chose—and rest assured, each of the twelve is its own marvelous adventure! Since the Sun is the Big Boss, all of the other planets, including the Moon, are the Sun's staff, all there to help the boss by helping you master your particular area of expertise. Back in the day, the words from a song in a recruitment commercial struck me as a perfect way to describe our Sun's quest: "Be all that you can be. Keep on reaching. Keep on growing. Find your future." The accompanying music was energizing, robust, and exciting, full of anticipation and eagerness. When you feel enthused, motivated, and stimulated, that's your Sun letting you know you're on the right path.

Moon

If you want to understand this lovely silver orb, go outside when the Moon is nice and full, find yourself a comfy perch, sit still, and have a nice long look at her. The Moon inspires us to dream, wish, and sigh, to reminisce, ruminate, and remember. She's the Queen of Emotions, the astrological purveyor of feelings and reactions. In your natal chart, the condition of the Moon—that is, the sign and house she's in and the connections she makes with your other planets—shows how you'll deal with whatever life tosses your way—how you'll respond, how you'll cope, and how you'll pull it all together to move on after a crisis. She's where your instincts and hunches come from, and the source of every gut feeling and premonition. The Moon describes your childhood home, your relationship with your mother, your attitude toward childbearing and children in general, and what you're looking for in a home. She shows what makes you feel safe, warm, comfy, and loved. On a daily basis, the Moon describes the collective mood.

Mercury

Next time you pass by a flower shop, take a look at the FTD logo by the door. That fellow with the wings on his head and his feet is Mercury, the ancient Messenger of the Gods. He's always been a very busy guy. Back in the day, his job was to shuttle messages back and forth between the gods and goddesses and we mere mortals—obviously, no easy feat. Nowadays, however, Mercury is even busier. With computers, cell phones, social media, and perhaps even the occasional human-to-human interaction to keep track of—well, he must be just exhausted. In a nutshell, he's the astrological energy in charge of communication, navigation, and travel, so he's still nicely represented by that winged image. He's also the guy in charge of the five senses, so no matter what you're aware of right now, be it taste, touch, sound, smell, or sight—well, that's because Mercury is bringing it to you, live. At any rate, you'll hear about him most when someone mentions that Mercury is retrograde, but even though these periods have come to be blamed for all sorts of problems, there's really no cause for alarm. Mercury turns retrograde (or, basically, appears to move backwards from our perspective here on Earth) every three months for three weeks, giving us all a chance for a do-over—and who among us has never needed one of those?

Venus

So, if it's Mercury that makes you aware of your environment, who allows you to experience all kinds of sensory sensations via the five senses? Who's in charge of your preferences in each department? That delightful task falls under the jurisdiction of the lovely lady Venus, who describes the physical experiences that are the absolute best—in your book, anyway. That goes for the music and art you find most pleasing, the food and beverages you can't get enough of, and the scents you consider the sweetest of all—including the collar of the shirt your loved one recently wore. Touch, of course, is also a sense that can be quite delightful to experience. Think of how happy your fingers are when you're stroking your animal companion's fur, or the delicious feel of cool bed sheets when you slip between them after an especially tough day. Venus brings all those sensations together in one wonderful package, working her magic through love of the romantic kind, most memorably experienced through intimate physical interaction with an "other." Still, your preferences in any relationship also fall under Venus's job description.

Mars

Mars turns up the heat, amps up the energy, and gets your show on the road. Whenever you hear yourself grunt, growl, or grumble—or just make any old "rrrrr" sound in general—your natal Mars has just made an appearance. Adrenaline is his business and passion is his specialty. He's the ancient God of War—a hot-headed guy who's famous for having at it with his sword first and asking questions later. In the extreme, Mars is often in the neighborhood when violent events occur, and accidents, too. He's in charge of self-assertion, aggression, and pursuit, and one glance at his heavenly appearance explains why. He's the Red Planet, after all—and just think of all the expressions about anger and passion that include references to the color red or the element of fire: "Grrr!" "Seeing red." "Hot under the collar." "All fired up." "Hot and heavy." You get the idea. Mars is your own personal warrior. He describes how you'll react when you're threatened, excited, or angry.

Jupiter

Santa Claus. Luciano Pavarotti with a great big smile on his face as he belts out an amazing aria. Your favorite uncle who drinks too much, eats too much, and laughs far too loud—yet never fails to go well above and beyond the call of duty for you when you need him. They're all perfect examples of Jupiter, the King of the Gods, the giver of all things good, and the source of extravagance, generosity, excess, and benevolence in our little corner of the Universe. He and Venus are the heavens' two most popular planets—for obvious reasons. Venus makes us feel good. Jupiter makes us feel absolutely over-the-top excellent. In Jupiter's book, if one is good, it only stands to reason that two would be better, and following that logic, ten would be just outstanding. His favorite words are "too," "many," and "much." Expansions, increases, and enlargements—or basically, just the whole concept of growth—are all his doing. Now, unbeknownst to this merry old fellow, there really is such a thing as too much of a good thing—but let's not pop his goodhearted bubble. Wherever Jupiter is in your chart, you'll be prone to go overboard, take it to the limit, and push the envelope as far as you possibly can. Sure, you might get a bit out of control every now and then, but if envelopes weren't ever pushed, we'd never know the joys of optimism, generosity, or sudden, contagious bursts of laughter.

Saturn

Jupiter expands. Saturn contracts. Jupiter encourages growth. Saturn, on the other hand, uses those rings he's so famous for to restrict growth. His favorite word is "no," but he's also very fond of "wait," "stop," and "don't even think about it." He's ultra-realistic and quite pessimistic, a cautious, careful curmudgeon who guards and protects you by not allowing you to move too quickly or act too recklessly. He insists on preparation and doesn't take kindly when we blow off responsibilities and duties. As you can imagine, Saturn is not nearly as popular as Venus and Jupiter, mainly because none of us like to be told we can't do what we want to do when we want to do it. Still, without someone who acted out his part when you were too young to know better, you might have dashed across the street without stopping to check for traffic first, and—well, you get the point. Saturn encourages frugality, moderation, thoughtfulness, and self-restraint, all necessary habits to learn if you want to play nice with the other grown-ups. He's also quite fond of building things, which necessarily starts with solid foundations and structures that are built to last.

Uranus

Say hello to Mr. Unpredictable himself, the heavens' wild card—to say the very least. He's the kind of guy who claims responsibility for lightning strikes, be they literal or symbolic. Winning the lottery, love at first sight, accidents, and anything seemingly coincidental that strikes you as oddly well-timed are all examples of Uranus's handiwork. He's a rebellious, headstrong energy, so wherever he is in your chart, you'll be defiant, headstrong, and quite unwilling to play by the rules, which he thinks of as merely annoying suggestions that far too many humans adhere to. Uranus is here to inspire you to be yourself—exactly as you are, with no explanations and no apologies whatsoever. He motivates you to develop qualities such as independence, ingenuity, and individuality—and with this guy in the neighborhood, if anyone or anything gets in the way, you'll 86 them. Period. Buh-bye now. The good news is that when you allow this freedom-loving energy to guide you, you discover something new and exciting about yourself on a daily basis—at least. The tough but entirely doable part is keeping him reined in tightly enough to earn your daily bread and form lasting relationships with like-minded others.

Neptune

Neptune is the uncontested Mistress of Disguise and Illusion in the solar system, beautifully evidenced by the fact that this ultra-feminine energy has been masquerading as a male god for as long as gods and goddesses have been around. Just take a look at the qualities she bestows: compassion, spirituality, intuition, wistfulness, and nostalgia. Basically, whenever your subconscious whispers, it's in Neptune's voice. She activates your antennae and sends you subtle, invisible, and yet highly powerful messages about everyone you cross paths with, no matter how fleeting the encounter. I often picture her as Glinda the Good Witch from *The Wizard of Oz*, who rode around in a pink bubble, singing happy little songs and casting wonderful, helpful spells. Think "enchantment"—oh, and "glamour," too, which, by the way, was the old-time term for a magical spell cast upon someone to change their appearance. Nowadays, glamour is often thought of as a rather idealized and often artificial type of beauty brought about by cosmetics and airbrushing, but Neptune is still in charge, and her magic still works. When this energy is wrongfully used, deceptions, delusions and fraud can result—and since she's so fond of ditching reality, it's easy to become a bit too fond of escape hatches like drugs and alcohol. Still, Neptune inspires romance, nostalgia, and sentimentality, and she's quite fond of dreams and fantasies, too—and what would life be like without all of that?

Pluto

Picture all the gods and goddesses in the heavens above us living happily in a huge mansion in the clouds. Then imagine that Pluto's place is at the bottom of the cellar stairs, and on the cellar door (which is in the kitchen, of course) a sign reads "Keep out. Working on Darwin Awards." That's where Pluto would live—and that's the attitude he'd have. He's in charge of unseen cycles—life, death, and rebirth. Obviously, he's not an emotional kind of guy. Whatever Pluto initiates really has to happen. He's dark, deep, and mysterious—and inevitable. So yes, Darth Vader does come to mind, if for no other reason than because of James Earl Jones's amazing, compelling voice. Still, this intense, penetrating, and oh-so-thorough energy has a lot more to offer. Pluto's in charge of all those categories we humans aren't fond of—like death and decay, for example—but on the less drastic side, he also inspires recycling, repurposing, and reusing. In your chart, Pluto represents a place where you'll be ready to go big or go home, where investing all or nothing is a given. When a crisis comes up—when you need to be totally committed and totally authentic to who you really are to get through it—that's when you'll meet your Pluto. Power struggles and mind games, however—well, you can also expect those pesky types of things wherever Pluto is located.

A Word about Retrogrades

"Retrograde" sounds like a bad thing, but I'm here to tell you that it isn't. In a nutshell, retrograde means that from our perspective here on Earth, a planet appears to be moving in reverse. Of course, planets don't ever actually back up, but the energy of retrograde planets is often held back, delayed, or hindered in some way. For example, when Mercury—the ruler of communication and navigation—appears to be retrograde, it's tough to get from point A to point B without a snafu, and it's equally hard to get a straight answer. Things just don't seem to go as planned. But it only makes sense. Since Mercury is the planet in charge of conversation and movement, when he's moving backward—well, imagine driving a car that only had reverse. Yep. It wouldn't be easy. Still, if that's all you had to work with, you'd eventually find a way to get where you wanted to go. That's how all retrograde energies work. If you have retrograde planets in your natal chart, don't rush them. These energies may need a bit more time to function well for you than other natal planets, but if you're patient, talk about having an edge! You'll know these planets inside and out. On a collective basis, think of the time when a planet moves retrograde as a chance for a celestial do-over.

Signs of the Zodiac

The sign a planet is "wearing" really says it all. It's the costume an actor wears that helps them act out the role they're playing. It's the style, manner, or approach you'll use in each life department—whether you're being creative on a canvas, gushing over a new lover, or applying for a management position. Each of the signs belongs to an element, a quality, and a gender, as follows.

Elements

The four elements—fire, earth, air, and water—describe a sign's aims. Fire signs are spiritual, impulsive energies. Earth signs are tightly connected to the material plane. Air signs are cerebral, intellectual creatures, and water signs rule the emotional side of life.

Qualities

The three qualities—cardinal, fixed, and mutable—describe a sign's energy. Cardinal signs are tailor-made for beginnings. Fixed energies are solid, just as they sound, and are quite determined to finish what they start. Mutable energies are flexible and accommodating but can also be scattered or unstable.

Genders

The genders—masculine and feminine—describe whether the energy attracts (feminine) or pursues (masculine) what it wants.

The Twelve Signs

Here's a quick rundown of the twelve zodiac signs.

Aries

Aries planets are hotheads. They're built from go-getter cardinal energy and fast-acting fire. Needless to say, Aries energy is impatient, energetic, and oh-so-willing to try anything once.

Taurus

Taurus planets are aptly represented by the symbol of the bull. They're earth creatures, very tightly connected to the material plane, and fixed—which means they're pretty much immovable when they don't want to act.

Sequence	Sign	Glyph	Ruling Planet	Symbol
1	Aries	♈	Mars	Ram
2	Taurus	♉	Venus	Bull
3	Gemini	♊	Mercury	Twins
4	Cancer	♋	Moon	Crab
5	Leo	♌	Sun	Lion
6	Virgo	♍	Mercury	Virgin
7	Libra	♎	Venus	Scales
8	Scorpio	♏	Pluto	Scorpion
9	Sagittarius	♐	Jupiter	Archer
10	Capricorn	♑	Saturn	Goat
11	Aquarius	♒	Uranus	Water Bearer
12	Pisces	♓	Neptune	Fish

Gemini

As an intellectual air sign that's mutable and interested in anything new, Gemini energy is eternally curious—and quite easily distracted. Gemini planets live in the moment and are expert multitaskers.

Cancer

Cancer is a water sign that runs on its emotions, and since it's also part of the cardinal family, it's packed with the kind of start-up energy that's perfect for raising a family and building a home.

Leo

This determined, fixed sign is part of the fire family. As fires go, think of Leo planets as bonfires of energy—and just try to tear your eyes away. Leo's symbol is the lion, and it's no accident. Leo planets care very much about their familial pride—and about their personal pride.

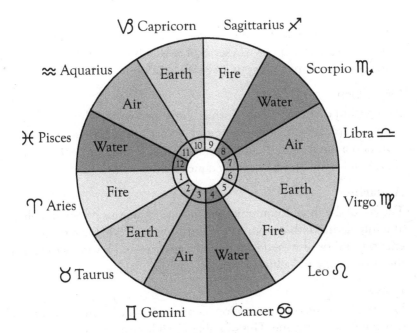

Virgo

Virgo is mutable and therefore easily able to switch channels when necessary. It's part of the earth family and connected to the material world (like Taurus). Virgo energy loves to work, organize, and sort, but most of all, to fix what's broken.

Libra

This communicative air sign runs on high. It's cardinal, so when it comes to making connections, Libra is second to none. Libra planets are people pleasers and the honorary cruise directors of the zodiac, and are as charming and accommodating as the day is long.

Scorpio

Scorpio is of the water element and a highly emotional creature. Scorpio energy is fixed, too, so feelings are tough to shake and obsessions are easy to come by. Planets in this sign are devoted and determined and can be absolutely relentless.

Sagittarius

Sagittarius has all the fire of Aries and Leo but, due to its mutable nature, tends to be distracted, spreading its energy among projects and interests. Think of Sagittarius energy as a series of red-hot brush fires, firing up and dying down and firing up again in a new location.

Capricorn

As the third earth sign, Capricorn is concerned with reality and practicality, complete with all the rules and regulations it takes to build and maintain a life here on Planet Number Three. Capricorn energy takes charge and assumes responsibility quite easily.

Aquarius

The last of the three communicative air signs, Aquarius prefers mingling and interacting with a group via friendships. Freedom-loving Aquarius energy won't be restricted—not for long, anyway—and is willing to return the favor, in any and all relationships.

Pisces

Watery Pisces runs on its emotions—and even more so on its intuition, which is second to none. This mutable, flexible sign is aptly represented by the constant fluctuating movements of its symbol, the two fish.

Aspects

Astrological aspects describe the relationships between planets and important points in a horoscope chart. Basically, they're the mathematical angles that measure the distance between two or more planets. Planets in square aspect are 90 degrees apart, planets in opposition are 180 degrees apart, and so forth. Each of these aspect relationships seems to link energies in a very different way. For example, if two planets are in square aspect, think of what you know about "squaring off," and you'll understand exactly how they're interacting. Think of aspects as a way of describing the type of conversation going on between celestial bodies.

Here's a brief description of the five major aspects.

Conjunction

When two planets are within a few degrees of each other, they're joined at the hip. The conjunction is often called the aspect of "fusion," since the energies involved always act together.

Sextile
Planets in sextile are linked by a 60-degree angle, creating an exciting, stimulating astrological "conversation." These planets encourage, arouse, and excite each other.

Square
The square aspect is created by linking energies in a 90-degree angle—which tends to be testy and sometimes irritating but always action-oriented.

Trine
The trine is the "lazy" aspect. When planets are in this 120-degree angle, they get along so well that they often aren't motivated to do much. Trines make things easy—too easy, at times—but they're also known for being quite lucky.

Opposition
Oppositions exist between planets that are literally opposite one another. Think about seesaws and playing tug of war, and you'll understand how these energies get along. Sure, it can be a power struggle at times, but balance is the key.

2023 at a Glance

Energy-oriented Mars begins 2023 retrograde in fast-talking Gemini and wastes little time resuming direct motion on January 12, much to the relief of those with something to say and communication contracts in the works. All of this year's Mercury retrograde transits occur in grounded earth signs ready to show another side of their signature qualities. Mercury in Capricorn starts off the year already retrograde and goes direct on January 18. The Messenger of the Gods will be retrograde three additional times this year, in April, August, and December. Uranus, another planet that starts the year in retrograde motion, moves direct on January 22. Uranus blasts its way through Taurus, hanging on to its reputation for disrupting the lives of earthlings this year, especially those with fixed signs in their birth charts. Venus, the love and beauty planet, is stable until July 22, when it takes a retrograde break in Leo and gives late-born members of this regal sign a challenge or two to work on in the love department. Jupiter begins the year in assertive Aries and zips through all 30 degrees of this sign by May 16, when the Great Benefactor turns over the reins to asset-driven Taurus. It moves retrograde on September 4, putting certain lucrative deals on hold until after December 30.

The gatekeeping taskmaster known as Saturn keeps a steady pace going as it wraps up its two-and-a-half-year cycle in Aquarius and doesn't shift gears until it hands over the gavel to the multi-directional sign Pisces on March 7. Saturn stays in direct motion until June 17, when it uses the psychic sign's intuitive powers and the convenient retrograde opportunity to look at deeper views of life and new ways to handle responsibility before going direct on November 4. Neptune continues to monitor confusion, illusions, and nightmares from its home base in Pisces in late degrees of the sign, making the most impact on late-born Pisces dreamers. The six-month hiatus ends on December 6 and the glamour planet comes out of hiding to take a look at the shape of things—the economy, creative juices, and your sentimental heart.

Pluto in Capricorn continues to advance toward completing its cycle in this sign and gives us a few teaser moments from March 23 to June 11 when it steps into Aquarius to try on new clothes, wondering how well the mantle fits before taking over in November 2024. Break loose from a few pieces of baggage you're unable to shed during the Pluto retrograde cycle that runs from May 1 to October 10 this year. Look for impact from four eclipses in 2023 when two new signs enter the picture. The eclipses occur in Aries on April 20, in Scorpio on May 5, in Libra on October 14, and in Taurus on October 28. Manifest prosperity and joyful experiences!

2023 SUN SIGN BOOK

Forecasts by
Alice DeVille

Aries

The Ram
March 20 to April 20

♈

Element: Fire

Quality: Cardinal

Polarity: Yang/masculine

Planetary Ruler: Mars

Meditation: I build
on my strengths

Gemstone: Diamond

Power Stones: Bloodstone,
carnelian, ruby

Key Phrase: I am

Glyph: Ram's head

Anatomy: Head, face, throat

Colors: Red, white

Animal: Ram

Myths/Legends: Artemis,
Jason and the Golden Fleece

House: First

Opposite Sign: Libra

Flower: Geranium

Keyword: Initiative

The Aries Personality

Strengths, Talents, and the Creative Spark

With your high-energy attitude, you're ready to forge a new pathway in 2023, Aries. Jupiter is in your sign this year, meaning that whatever you undertake turns to gold. Potential opportunities include changing careers or applying for a new job. Enjoy your status as the leader of the zodiac and look for ways to demonstrate how well your fast-thinking mind assimilates innovation. Be ready to act when inspiration strikes. Gather support among your peers by creating scenarios that snap bored colleagues right out of a rut and into the richly rewarding world of innovation. Come up with best-in-class solutions that offer expertise and a progressive path to accomplishing your mission.

You seldom let others preach a wet blanket monologue suggesting "you'll never be happy in your work" or "you aren't good enough to find work you love." With your lively fire-sign drive, you thrive on nonstop action. Can't isn't one of your frequently used words. Using high-powered enthusiasm, you silence any negative self-talk by searching for organizations and people who share your philosophy and have compatible goals. If you don't do that before accepting a position, you know that your tenure will be short-lived and you will bolt quickly if you feel your talents are misplaced. Your objective is to design the big picture, motivating others to use skills wisely and meeting critical deadlines to achieve goals.

Mars is your ruler, Aries. With your superb initiative and abundant energy, you develop plans, show your management style, and implement strategies in record time. You can hold your own in an argument, getting antsy when redundancy threatens the flow of discussions or skews the timeline. To you, too much trivia is a time-waster. You'll have words with key players, seldom masking your anger or settling on inferior decisions. Those who know you admire your straightforward approach to addressing issues and appreciate your unwillingness to play games or waste their time.

Intimacy and Personal Relationships

Why do the same old thing over and over again? Adventure calls your name when you are searching for the perfect partner to share a new pastime or form of entertainment. Travel could be part of your ideal vision to stimulate exciting moods and create special moments, and you make an ideal traveling companion. Individuals who enjoy trying new ventures, attending sports events, cheering for the best NASCAR driver, or applauding the star performers at a stage show bring enjoyment to your world and become favorite friends. Your sociable nature puts you in the company of potential mates from all walks of life. One of them could capture your heart and move to the top of the pedestal once you feel the level of trust and understanding is mutual.

Fire sign members Leo and Sagittarius often make ideal partners, along with conversational Gemini and your opposite sign, Libra, a fascinating air sign whose attraction can be mesmerizing. You have intense passion in common with Scorpios. Ideally, you're on a quest to discover the intricate mind, habits, and loving qualities a potential partner owns. As you get to know someone, you soak up every bit of the admiration your loved one demonstrates and offer loyalty and romance in return. Your passionate spirit longs to share affection and devotion with a compatible partner, who should be patient and understanding when you blow off steam. Although you are quick to anger, your significant other won't have to wait long to make up and bask in the loving feelings. Jupiter in Aries this year may accelerate the search for a soul mate.

Values and Resources

Although sharing the limelight is not your strong suit, you can be very successful in professional arenas when you present your creative ideas and recruit a team who enjoys pooling resources and getting the job done. Your strong plan of action includes steps to accomplish goals, take innovative and daring risks, and meet deadlines. You value freedom in managing your workload. Even if you're not the boss, you like to operate independently until you figure out a strategy, always mindful of deadlines and the anticipated outcome. Efficiency, ownership of your brand or projects, and a positive self-image mean the world to you. Aries often possess astute mechanical ability and excel at developing or executing blueprints for construction projects, home renovation, or equipment modification. Many of your sign enjoy driving a sporty car or a decked-out motor home.

Blind Spots and Blockages

Impulsiveness is your Achilles' heel, and it leads you down one or more dead-end paths if you're not paying attention. An adrenaline rush comes up spontaneously when you're fired up. In your desire to get on with things, you act rashly and sometimes have to go back to reinvent the wheel or start a project from scratch when concepts don't mesh and lead to more questions than logical outcomes. Professionalism takes a hit if you don't keep to a timeline. Avoid feeding too many new ideas to your subordinates or cluttering plans with too many sidebars, losing sight of the goal and mission. You can be very bossy or pushy in relationships, not only with romantic partners but also with family, colleagues, and friends. Those of you who fall in love easily without knowing much about your potential partner run the risk of choosing a sparring partner with whom you clash at every turn. Even if you enjoy intimate moments, the exhaustion of constantly making up, apologizing, and meeting differing opinions at every turn leaves you disillusioned about making a relationship permanent. Find a partner who loves you for your inner warmth and displays it often.

Goals and Success

As Aries is the first sign in the zodiac, it's difficult to think of you without identifying your prized trait of initiative and applauding your performance when you deliver the goods. You may not know everything about the work when you get an assignment, but your curiosity and fearless commitment open the mental and physical toolboxes you need to accomplish the goal. When an idea lights up your life, you run with it and challenge yourself to make it better, clearer, and sought after by experts in related fields. You want things to happen, and your to-do list works because you push yourself to set priorities and make the valuable contacts that get the answers and resources you need. Along the way, you stop to assess what assets you possess and make improvements to them that bring you acclaim.

Aries Keywords for 2023
Liberating, listening, locating

The Year Ahead for Aries

What's your plan for expressing your unique individuality in 2023 through your passionate spirit and your work? As the year begins, key houses in your chart show significant planetary activity. With expansive Jupiter in your solar first house of individuality and Pluto making a final sweep through your solar tenth house of career, you're initiating new, liberating relationships and saying goodbye to facets of your career or important projects that call for closure. Any planets that appear in your solar first house accentuate your Aries traits and add depth to your personality. On April 20, the first Solar Eclipse of the year takes place in Aries and your solar first house, where it is sure to make an impact on prominent goals. Since August of 2022, Mars has occupied your solar third house of communication, contracts, and transportation in Gemini, where it went retrograde on October 30, 2022, slowing down progress in negotiating agreements, buying real estate, and purchasing essential goods. The planet of distribution systems is going direct in motion on January 12, ridding you of the burden of inertia that affected purchases related to equipping homes, businesses, educational institutions, and medical facilities. Mercury, the messenger planet, has been retrograde in Capricorn since December 29, 2022, in your solar tenth house, and moves direct on January 18, opening the door for smoother communication, better listening, and a resumption of plans that have been on hold. On January 22, Uranus in Taurus makes a station to go direct in your solar second house of income and resources, where it has been retrograde since August 2022.

Jupiter

Although Pisces was the main driver of Jupiter's activity in 2022, you had a considerable preview of what life would be like when the planet of expansion occupied Aries and your solar first house for a number of months last year. It was setting you up for greater visibility and highlighted ways to deliver the goods. Some of you received promotions, awards, grants, and personal recognition. While in Pisces and your complex twelfth house, the benevolent planet gave you opportunities to lay out your plans for this year, to line up key players, identify options for a career change or locate a better work environment, and find ways to fulfill your dreams. Now you're the lucky one with Jupiter in your sign speeding through your solar first house, affecting every degree of Aries and completing its cycle in Aries on May 17 before you can catch your next breath. This prominent appearance in your sign gives you a chance to set the tone you desire in launching new enterprises, securing a raise, and improving your health. Although you'll have to keep an eye on your weight, a regular exercise program and skipping the second helpings will help. When Jupiter begins a rapid trip through Taurus, it pauses for a few months by going retrograde on September 4 and turning direct in

Taurus on December 30. Jupiter in Taurus occupies your solar second house for seven months in 2023 and gives you clues for increasing your net worth and your salary, adding to your savings accounts, and contributing more to a retirement fund. Those of you born between March 21 and April 7 see the most action while Jupiter is in Taurus.

Saturn

Saturn, the planet of discipline and restriction, continues to occupy your solar eleventh house, where it has monopolized your time related to organizational affiliations, professional groups, friendships, and humanitarian initiatives while in Aquarius since December 2020. This journey has been both demanding and rewarding, bringing more responsibility than you ever imagined—sometimes resulting in you having to cover two positions at a time due to turnover or calling for overtime hours to get the job done when unforeseen delays in the work flow affected your timeline goals. Your hard work has paid off, and you have been richly rewarded with promotions, raises, and awards. While still in Aquarius, Saturn most affects Aries born between April 12 and 20. You may have to wrap up a project in the first few months of the year that involves analyzing your employer's funds and making accounting recommendations for funding the company operations. Over the last two and a half years, you have had a chance to identify new goals and assess what you have to do to bring fulfillment and greater liberation your way.

Complexity in the nature of your work and reframing of your personal goals seem to dovetail with the entry of Saturn into Pisces, which occurs on March 7 when this demanding planet enters your solar twelfth house of changing your inner core, healing, meditation, and seclusion. During the remaining months of 2023, Saturn most affects those of you born between March 20 and 29. You'll be able to break out of a rut, enjoy a less frantic pace, take time off before starting a new job, or make plans to travel and have some much deserved fun. Those of you who are experiencing health problems set appointments with medical professionals and make arrangements to stabilize your health. You'll have the company of transiting Neptune in Pisces in this house giving you the incentive to enjoy a few psychic visions.

Uranus

Since May 2018, you've had a taste of disruption in your solar second house of earned income, developmental opportunities, financial outlook, resources, and values during a seven-year passage of Uranus in Taurus in this sector of your chart. The year starts out with Uranus in retrograde motion and going direct on January 22, which most likely sends a few challenges your way or creates delays in financial transactions. If you applied for a new position, your actual start date may be pushed ahead to later in the year. Uranus transits produce unexpected circumstances, so some Aries may experience layoffs or receive unanticipated promotions or bonuses. If you are job hunting, wait until after Uranus goes direct to interview, making use of the waiting time by researching interesting prospects. A lottery win often occurs when Uranus visits the second house—a big win or lots of little ones. The unpredictable planet will move into retrograde motion on August 28 and go direct on January 27, 2024. This year, those of you born between April 4 and 15 experience the most activity from Uranus in the second house of income and money matters. Aries who have planets in the second house of their birth chart could experience erratic situations with employment, job seeking, loan applications, purchase of goods, and self-improvement programs.

Neptune

While still in dreamy Pisces, the final water sign in the zodiac, slow-moving Neptune will continue its journey through your solar twelfth house, which began in April 2011. This passage can be quite inspirational as you make discoveries about your inner mind, develop new perceptions about your intuitive talent, and heal from emotional or physical conditions. Those of you who need surgery or critical medical treatment have the most success when locating the ideal dates that your natal chart suggests and coordinating them with the availability of doctors and surgeons. Neptune in the twelfth house often stirs up creativity and vision and is an ideal transit for actors, dramatists, musicians, and writers eager to produce noteworthy material. When Saturn enters this same house in Pisces on March 7, your commitment to these goals may become firmer than ever when you realize you want to allocate the time to see your dreams come true. Those of you in the beauty industry may receive recognition for developing a new fragrance or creating a new hairstyle that catches on in the public eye. The year can bring news of others' illnesses, property losses, or employment setbacks. You could have a busy schedule with hospital visits, supplementing another's living expenses, contributing to worthy charities, and helping with tuition for children or other relatives. For some, confusing revelations may expose your well-kept secrets and keep you on guard to deal with the fallout. Those of you born between April 12 and 19 see the most activity from Neptune this year.

Pluto

This year, Pluto in Capricorn, the sole outer planet still occupying your solar tenth house of authority, career, ambition, status in life, people in high places, and reputation, completes a cycle in this sign that began here in January 2008. No doubt you have seen executives come and go, career highs and advancements, the realization of goals, and honors for the excellent work you performed on behalf of your organization and colleagues. Transformation is strongly associated with Pluto's energy, which slowly but surely brought you greater insight into what drives your soul and gives you some of that passionate spark that makes you succeed in your aspirations and plans. Congratulate yourself on any burdens you eliminated. You still have time to liberate excess baggage that limits your options, since Pluto is going to make a brief entry into Aquarius starting on March 23. On May 1 it turns retrograde in the first degree of Aquarius and then returns to Capricorn on June 11 to complete the remaining months of its cycle, which officially ends in November 2024. Aries most affected by this Pluto-in-Capricorn windup are those born between April 16 and 20. Those Aries born between March 20 and 22 feel the impact of a brief harmonious teaser when Pluto occupies Aquarius from March 23 through June 11. Consider options about emerging goals, professional groups you might like to join, and friendships you value.

How Will This Year's Eclipses Affect You?

In 2023 a total of four eclipses occur: two Solar (New Moon) Eclipses and two Lunar (Full Moon) Eclipses, which create intense periods that start to manifest a few months before their actual occurrence. Two of the eclipse signs are changing this year. The first eclipse occurs in your solar first house, the second in your solar eighth house, the third in your solar seventh house, and the final eclipse in your solar second house. Eclipses unfold in cycles involving all twelve signs of the zodiac, and usually occur in pairs about two weeks apart. Don't fear eclipses—think of them as growth opportunities that allow you to release old and outworn patterns. They often stimulate unexpected surprises and windfalls. The

closer an eclipse is to a planet or point in your birth chart, the greater the importance of the eclipse in your life. Those of you born with a planet at the same degree as an eclipse are likely to see a high level of activity in the house where the eclipse occurs.

The first Solar Eclipse of 2023 takes place on April 20 in your sign and your solar first house of appearance, assertiveness, character, image, individuality, personality, and passion. You'll be challenged to work on your goals, develop projects, and keep promises about taking better care of yourself if you have become too intense about checking all the boxes in your work world and letting downtime slide. Engage qualified consultants if you need help managing key areas of your life.

Two weeks later, on May 5, the first Lunar Eclipse of the year takes place in Scorpio and your solar eighth house of partnership ventures, joint funds and debts, investments, estates, wills, sex, birth, death, and regeneration. This eclipse brings opportunities to review your financial net worth and collaborate with your partner to pay it down, initiating a solid savings plan that meets your mutual goals. You or a partner could apply for a second job or consider supplemental work to escalate goals to reduce what you owe. A partner's raise or windfall is a strong possibility that manifests and helps with money management.

On October 14, the second Solar Eclipse of 2023 takes place in your opposite sign of Libra and your solar seventh house of business and personal partners, spouses, collaborators, roommates, doctors, lawyers, therapists, advisors, consultants, enemies, and the public. When this eclipse hits, you could be surprised by what you discover about the nature of personal or professional relationships. You benefit most from strengthening bonds, communicating harmoniously, and fulfilling mutual goals. If challenges emerge, address them and seek peaceful solutions to eliminate growing tension.

The year's final eclipse on October 28 is a Lunar Eclipse in Taurus and your solar second house of money, resources, how you spend your money, and what you value. Even though you are wary of the presence of Uranus in Taurus in this house, you could be feeling relieved after paying down a chunk of debt during the year. Since Uranus is conjunct this eclipse degree, you are wise to be on the lookout for sudden repairs to your home, vehicle, or electronic equipment or for unanticipated shakeups in your employment zone. Maintain cheerfulness as you navigate new directions and celebrate the successes you earn along the way.

Aries | January

Overall Theme

Several planets shift direction this month, allowing you to resume plans you tabled last year due to unforeseen circumstances or family issues. Jupiter in Aries and your solar first house for the next several months lets you build confidence in your goals and share your optimistic enthusiasm for achieving successful outcomes.

Relationships

Savor the warm memories of the holiday season by dining with friends and sharing highlights with them. Accept invitations from close associates on the 21st or 24th. Enjoy outings with romantic partners and set aside time for a special date night around the 8th. Treat children to a favorite entertainment venue, and celebrate the excitement of their responsiveness to fun and games.

Success and Money

Enjoy special sales and spend holiday cash gifts on the 2nd. Take the time to review your 2023 budget; listen to your partner and discuss planned expenses. One of your power days is the 21st, which coincides with activities that benefit friends and group collaborations.

Pitfalls and Potential Problems

Watch for erratic shifts in energy when Mars goes direct on the 12th and a Mercury station to move direct on the 18th liberates a holding pattern but cautions you to look for a better day to execute plans. Steer clear of arguments with family members on the Cancer Full Moon of January 6. An intimate partner could oppose a proposal to travel on the 14th.

Rewarding Days

2, 8, 21, 24

Challenging Days

4, 6, 14, 18

Aries | February

Overall Theme

Note that there are no planets in retrograde motion this month. Take advantage of this rare absence of chaos by setting aside quality time to work on career objectives, develop strategic organizational goals, and locate resources you need to get the job done. Jupiter and Mars are on friendly terms and highlight quality communication and sought-after agreement in negotiating favorable contract terms.

Relationships

February dates that favor romance are the 10th and the 22nd. You and a loved one may celebrate Valentine's Day early due to work obligations. Unattached Aries may spot a pair of irresistible eyes across a crowded room on the 17th and find a reason to facilitate an introduction.

Success and Money

Collaborative efforts pay off when clear details surface and put stakeholders in a trusting, positive mindset from the 10th through the 18th. Celebrate with a power lunch on the 18th that involves professional contacts whose talents you have come to value. Accept an invitation to dinner with a good friend on the 20th.

Pitfalls and Potential Problems

Keep the peace at home base on the 3rd, when a family member is cranky and seems to lack the focus to concentrate on your message. Curb the tendency to overspend for a Valentine's Day gift on the Leo Full Moon of the 5th. You could easily overlook quality if the price of a gift is too good to be true, especially on the 8th.

Rewarding Days
10, 17, 18, 22

Challenging Days
3, 5, 8, 25

Aries | March

Overall Theme

The month starts out on a productive note when Mercury and Saturn in late Aquarius form a conjunction in your solar eleventh house of group affiliations. Just as efficiency peaks on a project you're finalizing, Neptune in Pisces could stimulate the discovery of misleading information that throws a monkey wrench into your well-intended plans to complete the work.

Relationships

Your best day for family harmony is the 2nd, when lunar aspects favor warmth and rapport along with straightforward communication. That loving feeling dissipates on the 3rd, when a snide remark piques sensitive feelings and triggers hostile exchanges. Relatives at distant locations announce plans to visit or extend an invitation to you. Listen when friends claim center stage at an engaging brunch date on the 19th.

Success and Money

Networks generate productive feedback on the 9th, which is also a compatible date for travel related to partnership ventures. When an unexpected windfall puts you in a generous mood on the 22nd, you are inspired to spend extra cash on the items on your family's wish list.

Pitfalls and Potential Problems

Your work environment could be overrun with challenges on the Virgo Full Moon of March 7, when style differences bring discussions to a halt. Neptune triggers confusion over details that no one bothered to verify. A solution looks briefly optimistic until a new stream of objections overwhelms the team and tables action until the 15th.

Rewarding Days

2, 15, 19, 22

Challenging Days

3, 5, 7, 25

Aries | April

Overall Theme

The whole gamut of relationships with members of your family seems to overwhelm your personal space this month. The energy revolves around your significant other, matters of intimacy, siblings and cousins, those who live at home base, and children, whether they are your own or individuals you teach or coach.

Relationships

The Libra Full Moon on the 6th brings up sore spots between you and your partner, especially if you have been arguing over spending habits and one of you went overboard in making a purchase. It could be chilly in the bedroom until warmth and rapport resume. A friend you recruited to join a special interest group bails out unexpectedly.

Success and Money

On the 21st you could win a cash award at a drawing. Treat companions to a tasty meal. Neighbors host a community party on the 23rd, creating goodwill and extending hospitality to residents new to the area. The dish you bring draws raves and more invitations from attendees. You meet a new contact and listen to an interesting career offer through a relative around the April 20th Solar Eclipse in your sign.

Pitfalls and Potential Problems

Disagreements flare among professional associates on the 14th, when egos clash and impede decision-making, delaying a deadline for a high-interest project. Mercury goes retrograde on the 21st in Taurus and your solar second house, alerting you to watch financial transactions. Children under your care could be hard to control on the 27th, with crying, squabbling, and hissy fits.

Rewarding Days

17, 21, 23, 25

Challenging Days

6, 8, 14, 27

Aries | May

Overall Theme

Mother's Day is May 14, the same date on which Mercury moves direct. Double-check appointments and dates for when bills are due this month. Save time for relaxation. Make it happen on the 13th by taking calming walks, seeing an inspiring movie, indulging in a favorite dessert, and taking a nap when the spirit moves you.

Relationships

Loving gestures pop up this month via spontaneous expression from contacts on the 10th and 13th. Nothing says loving like honoring your mother and other special women who are mothers on the 14th, when Mother's Day floods your thoughts with cherished memories. Family members give you reason to welcome their presence on the 23rd.

Success and Money

Enjoy listening to compliments on your performance around the 9th, when your boss acknowledges a job well done. The Taurus New Moon on the 19th ushers in a prosperous vibe and leads to attractive bargains if you are shopping for practical goods and services.

Pitfalls and Potential Problems

The Lunar Eclipse on May 5 in Scorpio and your solar eighth house opposes still-retrograde Mercury in Taurus and your solar second house. Don't negotiate major contracts or purchases until after the 9th. Pluto moved into early Aquarius on March 23 and turns retrograde this month on May 1 in your solar eleventh house. Examine any painful issues involving friends and associates and look for ways to heal differences.

Rewarding Days

9, 13, 19, 23

Challenging Days

1, 5, 25, 31

Aries | June

Overall Theme

Communication, negotiations, and local travel occupy your mind this month as you make time to finalize vacation plans, schedule enjoyable recreation and entertainment with loved ones, and spend time with your significant other putting more sparkle into romantic interludes.

Relationships

Treat your partner to a Friday night date on the 2nd to unwind from the demanding workweek both of you experienced. Count on visits or invitations from siblings and cousins who are eager to share celebratory news with you and want to reconnect through mutual recreational interests.

Success and Money

On the 11th you could be tapped to deliver an important speech at a social event that showcases your talent and puts you in the spotlight for future events. Spend extra cash on your home decorating projects around the 15th to make it presentable for company. Extra guests arrive bearing gifts on the 17th.

Pitfalls and Potential Problems

Relatives at a distance may voice disappointment over being left out of a get-together on your turf. Saturn turns retrograde in Pisces on June 17th, possibly affecting entertainment plans due to weather conditions. Neptune in Pisces goes retrograde on the 30th, reminding you to take security precautions by sharing private information discreetly.

Rewarding Days

2, 11, 15, 28

Challenging Days

4, 7, 22, 30

Aries | July

Overall Theme
Your ruling planet, Mars, is moving through your solar fifth house in Leo through July 10, along with transiting Venus in Leo. That combination is perfect for meeting a romantic partner, getting engaged, or setting a wedding date. Start celebrating when the Moon is in Sagittarius on the 1st, and make it a memorable holiday weekend.

Relationships
Camaraderie with family members gets a boost on the 17th when the New Moon in Cancer creates the momentum for hosting a festive gathering. Enjoy the celebration and surprising information that others share. Look to your boss or those in charge at the workplace for compliments and a vote of confidence toward the end of the month.

Success and Money
Performance achievements net you a bonus or raise around the 11th, when Mercury moves into Leo and favors your professional activity and reputation. If you're looking for opportunities to spend your windfall, you'll find lots of temptation while scoping out bargains on the 9th through the 12th.

Pitfalls and Potential Problems
Avoid humorless types on the Capricorn Full Moon of July 3. A party could break up early over someone who drinks too much and says all the wrong embarrassing things. On the 5th miscommunications occur over project details in a group setting, until a dilemma-liberating facilitator steps in to save the day. Venus turns retrograde on the 22nd conjunct Mercury, and the atmosphere could easily turn volatile when the Uranus square the next day interacts to provoke a hothead.

Rewarding Days
1, 10, 17, 30

Challenging Days
5, 19, 22, 23

Aries | August

Overall Theme
Lunations drive the energy that prevails at this time. The month begins and ends with a Full Moon in two different signs: in Aquarius on the 1st in your solar eleventh house and in Pisces on the 30th in your solar twelfth house. The New Moon in Leo on the 16th highlights your social and romantic activity. The first half of August favors travel and vacations.

Relationships
August 13 favors family fun and is a good day to travel to an adventurous destination. If you're meeting up with other relatives who live in another location, be sure the sleeping accommodations meet the needs of each age group and that recreational offerings include swimming, boating, games, and sports venues.

Success and Money
Rapport with your work team reflects a cooperative spirit and a positive attitude that gets the job done and strengthens the reputation of the group. The last week of the month highlights outstanding accomplishments that show how invested the group is in meeting and exceeding deadlines. You get credit for your role in demonstrating leadership.

Pitfalls and Potential Problems
Another of this year's earth-sign Mercury retrograde periods starts on August 23 in Virgo and contributes to delays in starting projects, obtaining a loan, or enjoying some stress-free time off. Keep an eye out, as accommodations may be changed without warning. Uranus in Taurus goes retrograde on the 28th in your solar second house, generating a mix-up over the cost of goods and services. Check paperwork and reservation details in advance.

Rewarding Days
4, 13, 18, 27

Challenging Days
1, 10, 17, 23

Aries | September

Overall Theme

When Venus goes direct on September 3 in Leo and your solar fifth house of romance, don't be surprised if you locate the contact information you misplaced for a special someone you met in July. Make up for lost time by extending an invitation for an entertainment event or a meal in a place that stimulates conversation and has a hospitable vibe.

Relationships

Harmony looks good on several fronts. At home base, family members show warmth, rapport, and unity. You and your significant other bask in the glow of loving vibes, enjoying mutual interests and letting your eyes smile in appreciation of the love and intimacy you feel. Authority figures at your workplace bombard you with praise while simultaneously increasing your workload with high-priority tasks.

Success and Money

The New Moon in Virgo in your solar sixth house on the 14th shines a light on new acquisitions in the form of contracts, grants, new hires, or installation of upgraded equipment. You gain new insight about medical issues and find a competent doctor to treat problem areas. Investments in your retirement portfolio pay dividends that make a difference in your bottom line.

Pitfalls and Potential Problems

On September 4, Jupiter goes retrograde for several months in Taurus and your solar second house. Be sure you're not starting a long trip or a complicated project on that date. Mercury turns direct in Virgo on September 15. You're likely to find missing items, receive lost mail, and decipher vague messages around that time.

Rewarding Days

9, 16, 18, 23

Challenging Days

4, 7, 12, 19

Aries | October

Overall Theme

Relationships and interactions with a variety of people occupy your time in October. The last Solar Eclipse of 2023 falls on October 14 in Libra and your solar seventh house, highlighting personal and business connections and how you're dealing with them. To address security needs, the final Lunar Eclipse of the year falls on October 28 in earthy Taurus and your solar second house of income, money, and resources.

Relationships

Matters connected to coworkers and productivity shine on the 11th. You could hear good news about your health on that day as well—listen and ask questions. Look for kudos and applause from your boss around the 20th acknowledging the quality of your work. Invite siblings for a meal on the 4th, when the conversation is lively and the food is sensational.

Success and Money

You could seal the deal on the 9th, when stakeholders meet to discuss final details of a business proposal. Aries who are involved in a heated romance make beautiful music on the 5th. A reconciliation could be in the works for estranged parties around the 26th. *Sorry* is a magic word.

Pitfalls and Potential Problems

Pluto goes direct on the 10th in Capricorn and your solar tenth house. Note the old attitudes that make an exit in your life shortly after the planet of transformation stations to move forward. Watch your wallet on the October 28th Lunar Eclipse in Taurus. Patience pays off.

Rewarding Days

4, 11, 20, 24

Challenging Days

1, 7, 16, 28

Aries | November

Overall Theme

It's not too early to focus on the lively party scene that will be unfolding over the next two months. On the 4th, look for an early invitation that brings an odd assortment of partygoers together, with mixed reactions from attendees over the food and the fare. Confer with your partner if it's your turn to host the family gathering this year, and start making plans that elevate guests' spirits.

Relationships

Positive vibes stir at home base, with family members expressing excitement over holiday celebrations. Newly hired people at your workplace will show gratitude at your generous invitation to attend your Thanksgiving feast. On the 17th, your boss may distribute holiday bonuses or grant an extra day off to grateful employees.

Success and Money

Use extra cash from work accomplishments to splurge on lavish fare for your Thanksgiving meal. On the November 13th New Moon in Scorpio, you learn that your retirement portfolio has a larger balance than expected. Enjoy the windfall by keeping the same mix of funds that enhanced prosperity.

Pitfalls and Potential Problems

Saturn stations to move direct on the 4th, which is a welcome shift after months of delays but could affect the flow of plans you have on that date. On the 23rd, Thanksgiving Day, listen to weather reports, which may be harsh. Be sure out-of-town guests arrive by the 22nd to avoid travel delays.

Rewarding Days

2, 7, 17, 22

Challenging Days

4, 11, 23, 27

Aries | December

Overall Theme

Take advantage of a bargain fare and a pre-holiday getaway with your partner for some relaxing R&R during the first half of the month. Return before the 12th and avoid any run-ins with Mercury when it turns retrograde on the 13th. A charitable donation you make in response to a crisis in another country contributes meals and medicine to meet the critical needs of affected citizens.

Relationships

Cooperative ventures shine. You and your love interest get cozy exchanging endearing words on the 7th. Business partners and consultants provide advice that allows you to successfully seal a pending deal or sign a contract by December 15. Doctors modify a health regimen that brings relief to a lingering ailment.

Success and Money

Schedule medical tests and exams on the 5th for best results. You and your partner finalize plans for holiday entertaining on the 22nd. Choose a thoughtful gift for someone you admire, and invite the lucky person for a meal and a welcome celebration. A generous year-end bonus puts a smile on your face and the option to fund modest planned upgrades for your home.

Pitfalls and Potential Problems

Even though you may not be at your job on a Saturday, the recent hard work, intense pressure, and long hours could push all the wrong buttons on the 16th, when the lunar energy conflicts with hard aspects to Venus, Uranus, and Neptune. Avoid taking anger and frustrations out on others.

Rewarding Days

5, 14, 18, 22

Challenging Days

3, 12, 16, 26

Aries Action Table

These dates reflect the best—but not the only—times for success and ease in these activities, according to your Sun sign.

	JAN	FEB	MAR	APR	MAY	JUN	JUL	AUG	SEP	OCT	NOV	DEC
Move	8			23						4		
Romance		10				2			16			7
Seek counseling/coaching	21		19		13			6			17	
Ask for a raise		17			9		30	27			7	
Vacation			15							24		
Get a loan				21		11	17		18			22

Taurus

The Bull
April 20 to May 21

☉

Element: Earth

Quality: Fixed

Polarity: Yin/feminine

Planetary Ruler: Venus

Meditation: I trust myself and others

Gemstone: Emerald

Power Stones: Diamond, blue lace agate, rose quartz

Key Phrase: I have

Glyph: Bull's head

Anatomy: Throat, neck

Color: Green

Animal: Cattle

Myths/Legends: Isis and Osiris, Ceridwen, Bull of Minos

House: Second

Opposite Sign: Scorpio

Flower: Violet

Keyword: Conservation

The Taurus Personality

Strengths, Talents, and the Creative Spark

As the first member of the earth element, Taurus resonates to resource-fulness and the income-oriented second house of earning power, money you have at your disposal, how you want to spend your assets, what goods and services you treasure, personal development, material possessions, and the people who sell you related services, including those in the banking, self-improvement, and teaching industries. Personal affiliation with money represents a part of your life that often attracts satisfying, lucrative work and makes a bold statement in your chart. Born under the sign of the Bull, you are both an earth sign and the first of four fixed signs. With a notably strong will, you have the passion and determination to succeed. Once you commit to a plan and hone the vision, you demonstrate decisiveness, one of your strongest characteristics.

Under the rulership of Venus, Taurus displays the qualities of grace, sensibility, altruistic leanings, and resourcefulness. Your gifts are many, and you rely on balance and harmony to make your talents shine at their highest levels. Normally you seek and attract lucrative work. When it doesn't meet your goals, you move on to another venue using the finely honed skills and diplomacy you've perfected. Very few individuals are able to convince you to change your mind. If you don't see a need to, you keep your thoughts intact. In your quest for continuous improvement, you work through obstacles to bolster performance and achieve goals. Many of you like to work with your hands and thrive in careers that showcase your artistic talent in baking, clothing and hair design, floral arrangement, gardening, healing arts, and music. You enjoy the finer things in life and work diligently to make sure you are surrounded by them.

Intimacy and Personal Relationships

In the department of love and affection, adoration means placing your loved one on a pedestal, offering a continuous flow of devotion. It may take you longer than most to declare your intentions, but once you do, the loved one seldom doubts the depth of your feelings. You could write a book on courting a prospective partner with your endless romantic gestures—the flowers, wine, music, candlelight dinners, and elegant accommodations at fancy inns and restaurants. This sign loves lots of hugs and kisses (especially on the neck). They like to spoil their partners with unexpected gifts and entertainment venues. Taurus also appreciates impeccable manners and likes partners who wear subtle but sensual aftershave—never the overpowering, cloying type. Possessiveness can get in the way of advancing the relationship when one of the partners needs more breathing room. Taurus enjoys amicable relationships with friends, relatives, and work colleagues, putting a priority on loyalty and shared values. Your Achilles' heel is staying too long in a relationship where the flames have fizzled and you have missed the obvious signs along the way. Ideal mates are the earth signs Virgo and Capricorn or the water signs Cancer and Pisces. Your opposite sign, Scorpio, often has magnetic allure.

Values and Resources

A leader who values organization captures your attention when you're applying for a job. You search for the ideal workplace that fits the career you desire, preferring structure and reliable routines, along with autonomy to tackle your work and showcase your talent. You want to shine when you throw your energy into a project. Doing your homework and researching copious facets of designated tasks is right in your wheelhouse in your quest to turn in a quality product. You're a reliable worker who savors the material comforts of the work environment, keeps the physical space orderly, and manages expenditures carefully. You do well handling money, and in your climb up the ladder of success, you may hold jobs in the banking, mortgage, or real estate industries. Positions that range from cashier to CEO are perfect picks to build valuable experience in your unfolding career path. Your discriminating taste in fine foods and appreciation for presentation techniques may lead you to seek a degree in culinary arts and food services management. Those of you with an artistic flair excel in performing arts, clothing design, music, and home decorating.

Blind Spots and Blockages

It's hard for you to admit that being a habitual workaholic interferes with the quality of your business and personal relationships. That's because you don't recognize that inflexibility takes a toll on the life balance necessary to cultivate meaningful alliances and keep love and play in motion in lieu of a round-the-clock work style. You dote on your children, expect a lot from them, and want them to take education seriously. You'll pay for the best schools and insist on discipline to score high grades. By focusing on perfection, you sometimes undermine their confidence. Add praise for their efforts and build self-esteem. Do the same with employees. Although you provide monetary compensation or recommend performance awards, nothing speaks louder than a public word of praise. Make it a point this year, while Uranus is still barreling through your sign, to call a truce with excessive patterns of stubbornness by listening without judgment to what others have to say before you engage in unyielding verbal combat.

Goals and Success

Security is your driver, and nothing makes you more content than holding a job that makes excellent use of your talents and pays a generous salary. Commitment is a strong Taurus quality, and you take pride in seeing a job through to completion, regardless of the challenges you encounter along the way. You're motivated to be at the top of your game to excel in providing quality work and outstanding services. You're much more comfortable having a plan that defines your goals and allows you to move at a reasonable pace, rather than racing rapidly to the finish line only to have to redo some of the steps along the way. Inevitably you choose a path in life that gives you access to fulfillment of all your senses in the form of a substantial paycheck, so you can easily afford to acquire your personal preferences and satisfy the desires of the loved ones you enjoy pampering. Your lifestyle includes beautiful surroundings, the perfect romantic partner, magnificent music, a luxury car, and a well-stocked refrigerator filled with the finest foods to satisfy your expensive taste buds.

Taurus Keywords for 2023
Advantage, appreciation, assessment

The Year Ahead for Taurus

After experiencing firsthand the shock value of Uranus, the planet of sudden blowups, in your sign since May 2018, you know what it's like to have a roller coaster rumbling through your solar first house. You've been getting rid of things, losing items you valued, and rethinking relationships, many of which have outlived their importance in your space, and you don't like it. Taking a multilevel inventory on the emotional, intellectual, physical, and spiritual planes is not a course of action that fits your style, because you revere the status quo and don't want to start over. This transit hits so close to home in 2023 for Taurus individuals born in May in the middle date range, as Uranus starts off the year in retrograde motion, going direct on January 22. Mars has been retrograde, too, in Gemini and your solar second house of income, money, and resources since October 30, 2022, and resumes direct motion on January 12. Research sales to purchase items that you put on hold late last year and enjoy the bargain prices.

The four 2023 Mercury retrograde periods will fall in earth signs. On January 18, Mercury resumes direct motion in Capricorn and your ninth house of long-distance travel, foreign cultures, and higher learning. Perhaps you'll pack your bags and take the alluring cruise that was put on hold last year. Once again Saturn in Aquarius occupies your solar tenth house of achievements, authority figures, and responsibility. The planet of restriction clears away any holdover tasks as the new year begins, and quietly moves into Pisces and your solar eleventh house for the next two and a half years, allowing you to work on group initiatives and humanitarian goals. An effort you started last year receives a significant increase in funds that will help others recover from financial and emotional hardships. Take advantage of inspiring opportunities to make the world a better place for those in need of hope.

Jupiter

In 2023 Jupiter starts out full of ambition and passion in Aries and your solar twelfth house, and puts the wheels in motion to deliver much needed services and compassion to those whose lives have been altered by the lingering effects of the pandemic. Your favorite charities may be the beneficiaries of your time and money as you work tirelessly to aid worthy causes through fundraisers or volunteer programs that help those who suffered from fire, storm damage, and other natural disasters such as widespread illness. Healing is in the wind for those of you who have experienced medical setbacks or need recovery from surgery. While in the twelfth house, Jupiter stimulates your creative mind and amplifies your interest in metaphysics, writing, and dreams. Take advantage of downtime to develop breakthrough ideas and create a framework that brings you success and opens the door for new networks. All members of Taurus benefit from this transit of Jupiter that creates opportunities to accelerate planning strategies. On May 16, Jupiter says goodbye to Aries and aloha to your sign, eager to leave a trail of optimistic expansion. Although the perks are good, you'll have to watch your waistline due to the increased number of social invitations. When Jupiter begins its rapid trip through Taurus, it pauses for a few months by going retrograde on September 4 and turning direct in Taurus on December 30. Jupiter in Taurus occupies your solar first house for the last seven months of 2023. Those of you born between April 20 and May 7 see the most action while Jupiter is in Taurus. Work on your cherished goals and watch your dreams come true.

Saturn

With the planet of restriction lingering in your solar tenth house of career, ambition, authority figures, government, maturity, and standards of excellence, Saturn in Aquarius is ready to cash in on the accomplishments resulting from hard work and discipline. Saturn has been on duty in Aquarius since December 2020, pushing you to internalize changing work conditions designed to promote health and environmental safety, efficiency, and better business practices. Taurus, you don't like change, but that is what you'll get this year, along with a different version of red tape. You'll accept the challenge but could end up working far too many hours. If you're offered a transfer, you just might take it. Make adjustments to stay healthy—some of you undertake a personal assessment of the organization and may decide to leave for greener pastures that permit better life balance. Those of you born between May 13 and 21 see the most action while Saturn remains in Aquarius. Modify your personal goals or accept a new job after Saturn moves into compatible Pisces on March 7, when this demanding planet enters your solar eleventh house of groups, friendships, associations, goals, and wishes. During the remaining months of 2023, Saturn most affects those of you born between April 20 and 29. You'll welcome a change to begin a new venture, break out of energy-sucking ruts, set a new pace, take a refreshing break before starting a new job, or vacation with loved ones. You'll have the company of transiting Neptune in Pisces in this house, giving you the incentive to enjoy and implement your dreams, join new networks, and savor an intuitive vision.

Uranus

The year starts out with Uranus in retrograde motion in Taurus and going direct on January 22, shaking up the energy in your solar first house of action, assertiveness, enterprise, individuality, passion, and possibilities. When a planet like Uranus, the great disrupter, thrashes its way through your solar first house in your own sign, Taurus, you can expect bizarre encounters with quirky personalities, unanticipated routines, perplexing challenges, and sudden mood swings. This pattern has been around you since May 2018. Plans you expected to finalize may have resulted in delays that affected personal or financial matters. If you thought you were going to start a new position in 2023, your actual start date may have been delayed. Uranus transits produce unexpected circumstances, changes in attitude, and sometimes surprising windfalls such as bonuses or job promotions. The dilemma for you is that you feel powerless when you lose control of your domain. Uranus transits may seem to change conditions in your outer world, but the real change is the internal shift that is taking place inside you, and that will startle those who know you well. This year, those of you born between May 5 and 16 experience the most activity from Uranus in your solar first house of personal expression.

Neptune

While Neptune moves through your solar eleventh house of goals, groups, professional resources, and friendships this year, your predictable Taurus personality may engage in reasonable risk-taking that takes contacts by surprise. Instead of encountering your usual driven and hard-to-change attitude, your friends glimpse the laid-back side of you that exudes a calm approach to problem-solving rather than your workaholic intensity. Since the compassionate planet arrived in this house in April 2011, Neptune has been dropping hints for you to get in touch with your inner dreams and include more of your intuitive insight in your collaborative dealings. Mysterious Neptune has a way of casting a spell on you when you become enamored of a new spiritual interest, line of work, or charitable cause. When you actually tap into your psychic gifts, you get that strong feeling in your solar plexus that you have discovered your true purpose. Saturn in Pisces shows up in this same house in March to help you validate your feelings and reframe the way you express responsibility. Taurus individuals born between May 13 and 21 see the most activity from Neptune this year. Dream big.

Pluto

Since late January 2008, Pluto, the planet of psychological depth, has been firmly planted in Capricorn and your solar ninth house, the area of your chart that relates to advanced education, foreign countries and cultures, your higher mind, in-laws, philosophy, publishing, religion, relocation, and long-distance travel. During this long passage, you may have experienced blocks in these areas or recognized that people in your circle are undergoing challenges connected with these themes. This transformative planet allows hidden elements to surface as the year unfolds. People at a distance may divulge secrets to you, often involving details of their personal or professional lives such as unfaithfulness, pending divorces, business failures, organizational closures, or an inability to meet deadlines. A buildup of stress could erode your confidence and cause you to explode over trivial things when you're really blaming yourself for matters over which you have no control. Release what is blocking your subconscious mind through contemplation, meditation, prayer, and yoga. Temperance is the key—if you lose it, you destroy your resolve to manage everyday life and meet setbacks with grace and an astute array of solutions. Get to the heart of your fears.

Pluto will make a brief entry into Aquarius on March 23. It will turn retrograde on May 1 in the first degree of Aquarius and return to Capricorn on June 11 to complete the remaining months of its cycle, which officially ends in November 2024. Taurus individuals most affected by this Pluto-in-Capricorn windup are those born between May 18 and 21. Those born between April 20 and 22 feel the impact of a brief teaser when Pluto occupies Aquarius from March 23 through June 11. Enjoy a few hints about upcoming changes to long-range goals, organizational authority, and career aspirations during this Pluto-in-Aquarius cycle. You can expect change this year driven by Pluto's ability to uncover hidden baggage and help you release what's stuck in your psyche that you no longer need to protect. Welcome healing new directions.

How Will This Year's Eclipses Affect You?

In 2023 a total of four eclipses occur: two Solar (New Moon) Eclipses and two Lunar (Full Moon) Eclipses, which create intense periods that start to manifest a few months before their actual occurrence. Two of the eclipse signs are changing this year. The first eclipse occurs in your solar twelfth house, the second in your solar seventh house, the third in your solar sixth house, and the final eclipse in your solar first house. Eclipses unfold in cycles involving all twelve signs of the zodiac, and usually occur in pairs about two weeks apart. Don't fear eclipses—think of them as growth opportunities that allow you to release old and outworn patterns. They often stimulate unexpected surprises and windfalls. The

closer an eclipse is to a planet or point in your birth chart, the greater the importance of the eclipse in your life. Those of you born with a planet at the same degree as an eclipse are likely to see a high level of activity in the house where the eclipse occurs.

The first Solar Eclipse of 2023 takes place on April 20 in Aries and your solar twelfth house of introspection, activity behind the scenes, healing your mind and body, mystical moments, psychic impressions, secrets, and recovery. You deserve some quality downtime to reflect on next steps and plan for your future. Take care of any lingering effects of illness you experienced in the recent past, and tend to others in your circle who may be ill. Work on your resume if you are contemplating a job change. Consult quality experts if you need help sorting out key areas of your life.

Two weeks later, on May 5, the first Lunar Eclipse of the year takes place in Scorpio and your solar seventh house of personal and business partners, collaborators, cooperators, roommates, legal or medical professionals, therapists, open enemies, and the public. This eclipse brings opportunities to review the status of relationship issues you examined last fall and note how well conscientious decisions aided in healing sore spots that resulted in more loving or compatible relationships. If the year has led to further breaches in understanding, you may be making plans to leave the personal or business relationships.

On October 14 the second Solar Eclipse of 2023 takes place in Libra and your solar sixth house of daily routine, health, nutrition, work environment, colleagues, organizational aptitude, and animal companions. When this eclipse hits, you could be surprised by what you discover regarding the efficiency of work practices, staff interaction, and the commitment to adhere to work timelines. You benefit most from listening to feedback, strengthening communications, and discussing critical goals. If challenges emerge, address them immediately to avoid misunderstandings or unnecessary delays.

The year's final eclipse is a Lunar Eclipse on October 28 in Taurus and your solar first house of action, self-interest, assertiveness, independence, and passion. The eclipse shares this house with Uranus in Taurus this year. This Lunar Eclipse falls on your Taurus Sun if you were born between April 25 and 27. You'll feel energized and eager to embrace new enterprises. Take advantage of personal leads you receive through trusted work contacts. Enjoy newfound optimism with the liberating choices you make while creating a successful, uplifting pathway.

Taurus | January

Overall Theme

If you started this year feeling like you had several loose ends to tie up, the three retrograde planets that are about to shift could be the cause. Mars in Gemini goes direct in your solar second house on the 12th and gives your cash supply a boost. Mercury in Capricorn moves forward on January 18 in your solar ninth house of long-distance enterprises, and erratic Uranus shakes loose in your solar first house on January 22.

Relationships

Family members gather on the 8th to discuss household plans and expenditures for 2023. People at a distance visit with you around the 17th, excited by the reunion and entertainment options you've scheduled. The New Moon in Aquarius on January 21 favors an upbeat talk with your boss, who shares important details about organizational goals and your role in the operation.

Success and Money

If you're shopping for bargains, grab them on the 3rd, when post-holiday clearances feature the furniture and household goods you've been waiting to purchase. Around the 30th you get good news about your increased assets in savings and retirement accounts. Salary increases and wise investments stabilize security.

Pitfalls and Potential Problems

Skip a social affair on the Full Moon in Cancer on January 6, when several guests cancel due to illness. You could be emotionally drained by your needy partner on the 16th, when viewpoints clash and conversations turn hostile. A financial report you receive on the 18th may contain several errors. Resolve the inaccuracies after the 22nd.

Rewarding Days

3, 8, 21, 30

Challenging Days

6, 16, 18, 20

Taurus | February

Overall Theme

You'll have a few relationship tight spots to work through this month due to lunar clashes. The Scorpio Moon on the 12th in your solar seventh house relates to challenging differences between you and your partner over money issues involving your agreed-upon budget. The New Moon in Pisces in your solar eleventh house on the 19th favors candid interaction on social initiatives with members of professional associations.

Relationships

Take advantage of a travel bargain and enjoy a mini vacation over the weekend of the 17th, a Valentine's Day gift for you and your loving partner. You'll be ready for a fun-filled break after irritating clashes earlier in the week leave you exhausted. Connect with siblings to set up a visit in March.

Success and Money

A meeting with your boss reveals a promising new assignment with increased responsibilities and compensation that will bear fruit in the next two months. Networking with coworkers helps you identify parties interested in the new initiative. Run staffing suggestions past hiring authorities especially after February 2.

Pitfalls and Potential Problems

You long for tranquility and can't wait until the Leo Full Moon on the 5th leaves your tension-filled solar fourth house, currently awash with irritating family squabbles. Initiate soothing talks with loved ones to lift their spirits. Encourage optimism and compliment peace seekers for their willingness to cooperate.

Rewarding Days

2, 17, 19, 24

Challenging Days

5, 7, 12, 16

Taurus | March

Overall Theme

Whenever Venus, your ruling planet, moves into Taurus, you spring to life and claim your power. That will happen this month starting on March 17, allowing you to exude your charm and impeccable good manners. Why not carve out quality time this month and focus on pampering your body with a massage, a new hairstyle, or a wardrobe upgrade? Use those money-saving coupons!

Relationships

The 2nd is an excellent day to invite siblings for a celebratory dinner to mark a milestone birthday or anniversary. The romantic vibes of the 11th create the perfect opportunity for a date night with your partner. Friends open their home to you and your family on the 19th for an enjoyable afternoon of fun, games, and feasting.

Success and Money

Finances look great this month. Your partner's salary increase sparks an interest in purchasing real estate. The two of you consider options. Research online to price homes in neighborhoods that interest you. You could find excellent buys in the jewelry or grooming industry around the 15th.

Pitfalls and Potential Problems

You feel peevish on the 5th and detect an aloof vibe at home base that chills a discussion of plans. The Full Moon in Virgo on March 7 creates too much tension for you and your partner to enjoy a productive week of crunching numbers, recreation, and shopping for homes or household goods.

Rewarding Days

2, 11, 15, 19

Challenging Days

5, 7, 26, 28

Taurus | April

Overall Theme

Venus lines up with Uranus in Taurus in your solar first house as the month begins, creating spontaneity in your love life or possibly introducing single Tauruses to a potential love interest. The Aries New Moon on the 20th is the year's first Solar Eclipse and conjuncts Jupiter in late Aries in your solar twelfth house, the perfect place to analyze details of pending plans.

Relationships

In-laws pay you a visit around the 9th and surprise you with tickets to a desirable entertainment venue and an invitation to an elegant dinner. Executives at your workplace review the quality of your work and your management style. Spend quality time with a child who seems fragile this month and could use a little extra TLC.

Success and Money

Validate purchasing power for big-ticket items through credit checks and a review of funding sources. Follow up with your boss to explore previous discussions of a promotion to a plum assignment that comes with a generous salary increase. The good news could greet you the week of the 23rd. Complete financial paperwork so you're ready to negotiate favorable terms for a planned purchase.

Pitfalls and Potential Problems

Be sure to avoid difficult coworkers on the 6th, when the Full Moon in Libra occurs in your solar sixth house of daily routines. Mercury goes retrograde in Taurus on the 21st, possibly leading to verbal mix-ups, garbled directions, and travel delays.

Rewarding Days

9, 12, 23, 25

Challenging Days

3, 6, 14, 21

Taurus | May

Overall Theme

Business travel highlights primary activity in your work world when new initiatives call for face time and diplomatic resolution of loose ends. The timeline for implementation is short yet complex. You want to quickly get major start-up tasks out of the way so you can enjoy a well-deserved vacation in June.

Relationships

Collaborate with family members at a distance to finalize upcoming vacation plans for agreeable dates and venues. Friends get together with you the second weekend of the month to celebrate career success and share exciting family news. The Lunar Eclipse of May 5 in Scorpio and your solar seventh house of personal and business partners has you looking for ways to improve your close partnerships.

Success and Money

After a few glitches and delays, a satisfying outcome results on the 22nd to seal an important deal you've been negotiating. The Taurus New Moon in your solar first house on the 19th truly represents a new beginning for major goals to materialize, which could include housing, earning power, and cordial relationships with family and friends.

Pitfalls and Potential Problems

Pluto turns retrograde on the 1st in Aquarius and your solar tenth house, coinciding with a need to look closely at critical documents related to a pending business deal. Put an extra pair of eyes to work assessing the need to request extra funds to cover space requirements. Don't make a spending decision until after the 11th, when you've had a chance to discuss details with your boss.

Rewarding Days

9, 13, 19, 22

Challenging Days

3, 5, 11, 31

Taurus | June

Overall Theme

Mars in Leo all month starts off on a hostile note when it tests the harmony with your partner on the 1st. Look for relief on the 6th, when Venus moves into Leo and puts a spark in your love life through the end of June. A little pampering goes a long way. Schedule a date night.

Relationships

Pack your bags on the 9th and make the most of vacation time you'll be spending with relatives, possibly in-laws, at a distance. Enjoy uplifting talks with family members while sightseeing or visiting spiritually significant points of interest. Treasure opportunities to bond with children by scheduling rewarding playtime. Participate in fun and games that include the whole family.

Success and Money

Friends provide a valuable tip on discount travel and entertainment venues that mesh with current travel plans and give you satisfying getaway options through the end of the year. Recent performance success results in a generous salary bonus that appears in your paycheck after mid-month, aided by Jupiter's recent entry into your sign.

Pitfalls and Potential Problems

Avoid surgery on the Full Moon in Sagittarius on June 3, with the prevailing unfavorable aspects. Saturn in Pisces makes a retrograde station on the 17th that could postpone plans with good friends. Feelings at home base may be sensitive on the 22nd. Tiptoe around someone in a funk. The energy could turn volatile with little warning.

Rewarding Days

5, 9, 11, 16

Challenging Days

1, 3, 22, 29

Taurus | July

Overall Theme

Why not host a lively 4th of July gathering at home base this year to avoid traveling on the Capricorn Full Moon on the 3rd? Neighbors, friends, and nearby relatives are sure to rave over your delicious and inclusive menu and thoughtful ideas for celebrating our nation's birthday. Watch the fireworks from the safety of your deck or patio.

Relationships

Sociability drives the energy this month. Friends invite you to a festive party on the weekend after the 4th. Accept graciously and bring your host's favorite bottle of wine or other treat. A sibling hosts a get-together on the 16th that has you raving over the food and festivities. You could meet some long-lost cousins at the event.

Success and Money

Giving credit to teammates at your workplace lifts morale, and spirits soar. A boss appreciates your inclusive gesture and works behind the scenes to give your reputation a boost to higher authorities. Toward the end of the month, you receive goods news of successful alliances and a lucrative contract for your organization.

Pitfalls and Potential Problems

You may have to forego cordial happy hour plans on the 21st when colleagues cancel late in the day. Venus goes retrograde in Leo on the 22nd, coinciding with a child's complaint of feeling ill, which leads you to postpone an outing. Things are better on the 23rd, when the child makes a quick recovery.

Rewarding Days

7, 11, 16, 31

Challenging Days

3, 5, 19, 21

Taurus | August

Overall Theme

If you've been wondering when to schedule vacation time this month with family or friends, you have several excellent options. A beach bash with good pals is perfect around the 4th for a nice change of scenery. A sibling and family join you around the 13th for a vacation to a favorite childhood haunt that captures fond memories.

Relationships

Maximize quality time with children around the 18th by treating them to a week of fun at water parks, amusement destinations that feature thrill rides and arcades, and historical sites that reveal interesting facts. Communication with your significant other around the 23rd reveals an element of confusion and a misunderstanding over plans for a romantic adventure.

Success and Money

Many a Taurus will be spending money on tuition this month while packing the car and helping students settle into college accommodations. A number of you may be starting an education program, with your eye on acquiring better qualifications that make you an attractive candidate for new job opportunities in your organization's career pipeline.

Pitfalls and Potential Problems

The end of the month is problematic for scheduling travel, when Mercury in Virgo goes retrograde on the 23rd and plans misfire. The week of the 28th starts off on a chaotic note when unpredictable Uranus in Taurus goes retrograde and triggers an unplanned work emergency instead of the start of a mini vacation.

Rewarding Days

4, 6, 13, 18

Challenging Days

3, 11, 23, 28

Taurus | September

Overall Theme

Venus goes direct in Leo on the 3rd, making your solar fourth house a warm, sociable place to congregate with family and entertain relatives or neighbors. Complete decorating projects you started this summer to get your home ready for holiday parties and festive entertaining. You have a great eye for color coordination.

Relationships

Bond with favorite cousins this month, especially on the 9th, when you might be collaborating on plans for a bridal shower or bachelor party. Make matters connected with your children and sports teams a priority on the 14th. Pursue romance with your partner on the 20th, when synchronicity creates vibrations of love.

Success and Money

A willingness to spearhead a plan to create a stronger homeowners' association puts you in the limelight. Suggest input for fundraising options. Neighbors volunteer to help or to coordinate ideas for adding desirable amenities to what the community currently offers. Accept an invitation to share ideas and discuss strategies.

Pitfalls and Potential Problems

Jupiter goes retrograde in Taurus on the 4th. Don't fall for a low price offered for desired goods on the 7th, when the product quality is poor. Mercury turns direct in Virgo on the 15th and highlights a change of heart regarding an invitation that was ignored. The Full Moon in Aries and your solar twelfth house on the 29th brings sensitive feelings to light. Encourage straightforward talk and offer to listen without judgment.

Rewarding Days

3, 9, 14, 20

Challenging Days

7, 12, 17, 29

Taurus | October

Overall Theme

Venus enters Virgo and your solar fifth house on the 8th and picks up the pace in your social life. Look forward to more camaraderie and fun with friends by booking tasty meals at your favorite eateries and adding day trips or short getaways to your calendar. Take advantage of networking opportunities that open up the possibility of exploring career moves.

Relationships

October is a banner month for acknowledging cordial relationships that influence your life. Medical professionals win points for their spot-on diagnoses, treatment, and approach to wellness. Financial experts provide savvy advice and help you turn a favorable win in your investment portfolio. Friends show thoughtfulness, loyalty, and love.

Success and Money

Your demonstration of personal performance excellence is acknowledged on the 3rd with a celebratory meal and cash bonus. The Solar Eclipse on October 14 in Libra and your solar sixth house of daily routine shines the spotlight on team collaboration and commitment to producing superior products. You are proud of the rapport you have with the team and appreciate the value it adds to your work environment.

Pitfalls and Potential Problems

Pluto in Capricorn turns direct on the 10th after being retrograde for several months. Take a breath and unload unwanted baggage before the final Lunar Eclipse of 2023 on October 28 in Taurus and your solar first house. Financial advice needs closer scrutiny on the 2nd, suggesting you check numbers carefully. Steer clear of temperamental authority figures on the 23rd.

Rewarding Days

3, 14, 21, 24

Challenging Days

2, 5, 18, 23

Taurus | November

Overall Theme

Time to send out those invitations to your elegant Thanksgiving dinner and start planning the multicourse menu that is sure to please every palate. Recharge your batteries so you're up for the extra work by taking a few days off to enjoy relaxing at a beautiful vacation destination around the 17th.

Relationships

You love to entertain at home. Looks like family members near and far will join you for the Thanksgiving holiday. Saturn in Pisces moves direct in your solar eleventh house on the 4th, just as you hear from an old friend who agrees to join you, too. Out-of-town visitors start arriving from the 20th to the 22nd. Accept and show gratitude to a sibling who offers to help with food preparation.

Success and Money

Single Tauruses may get engaged around the 8th or meet a potential partner with attractive qualities on that night. Fundraisers exceed expectations. Volunteer work you complete early on Thanksgiving morning helps community organizers provide a tasty feast to those in need.

Pitfalls and Potential Problems

The opposition of Mercury and Mars to your Sun through the 10th can be exhausting as you tackle a heavy workload and solve unexpected problems with your usual Taurus efficiency. The Gemini Full Moon on the 27th in your solar second house warns you against overspending on a child's gift. Compare prices.

Rewarding Days

2, 8, 17, 20

Challenging Days

1, 5, 13, 27

Taurus | December

Overall Theme

Your thrifty gene gets a workout early this month when exceptional online sales, with free gift-wrapping and delivery offers from vendors, allow you to complete holiday shopping by selecting perfect options for those on your gift list. If you have scheduled holiday travel plans to visit loved ones living at a distance, take advantage of these attractive terms.

Relationships

December's theme of love and togetherness is validated all month with transiting Venus in Scorpio in your solar seventh house through the 29th. You'll celebrate holiday-themed entertainment with children on the 5th, show goodwill toward favorite charities on the 14th, and attend a cheerful concert with your significant other around the 17th.

Success and Money

With Saturn in Pisces transiting your solar eleventh house now, you expanded your commitment to help favorite humanitarian causes and embraced the spirit of the season with increased support. Your efforts receive attention, allowing you to enjoy much-deserved rewards. By giving you a meaningful personal gift to express gratitude, your mate shows appreciation for your tender loving heart.

Pitfalls and Potential Problems

Planetary shifts dominate the landscape. Neptune in Pisces goes direct on December 6 in your solar eleventh house, highlighting spiritual associations. Mercury goes retrograde in Capricorn on December 13 in your solar ninth house, right after the December 12th Sagittarius New Moon. This transit is likely to delay travel plans. Jupiter in Taurus resumes direct motion in your solar first house on December 30.

Rewarding Days

5, 14, 17, 27

Challenging Days

3, 8, 12, 24

Taurus Action Table

These dates reflect the best—but not the only—times for success and ease in these activities, according to your Sun sign.

	JAN	FEB	MAR	APR	MAY	JUN	JUL	AUG	SEP	OCT	NOV	DEC
Move				12			31			21		14
Romance		2	11			11		18			8	
Seek counseling/ coaching					13		7		9			27
Ask for a raise	21			23								
Vacation		17			9			13	14		17	
Get a loan	3		15			16				3		

Gemini

The Twins
May 21 to June 21

Ⅱ

Element: Air

Quality: Mutable

Polarity: Yang/masculine

Planetary Ruler: Mercury

Meditation: I explore my inner worlds

Gemstone: Tourmaline

Power Stones: Ametrine, citrine, emerald, spectrolite, agate

Key Phrase: I think

Glyph: Pillars of duality, the Twins

Anatomy: Shoulders, arms, hands, lungs, nervous system

Colors: Bright colors, orange, yellow, magenta

Animals: Monkeys, talking birds, flying insects

Myths/Legends: Peter Pan, Castor and Pollux

House: Third

Opposite Sign: Sagittarius

Flower: Lily of the valley

Keyword: Versatility

The Gemini Personality

Strengths, Talents, and the Creative Spark

The classroom setting and diverse forms of education appeal to you. You collect certifications and new credentials routinely to build your substantial portfolio of qualifications. Many Geminis make excellent teachers for grade school through college students, mesmerizing them with little-known facts about the world. Your Sun sign rules the communication-oriented solar third house of cousins, siblings, and other relatives, neighbors, communities, seminars and workshops, transportation, media interests and communications vehicles (phones, computers, faxes, internet, social networks, TV), writing, and the mind, especially how it works and the impact it has on your mental state. This section of the chart describes your intellect and how you converse with others or form creative relationships. You probably have at least one sibling or a cousin with whom you have a close relationship and take into your confidence. That individual may be your favorite traveling companion, and the one you most frequently chat with via text or email. The third house is ruled by Mercury, and Gemini's symbol is the Twins. You are both an air sign and a mutable sign and fulfill your role as the conditioned analyst, one who questions relationships with people, objects, and ideas.

Deductive skills go a long way in helping you converse with people, analyze all types of problems, and share your conclusions. You have a great sense of humor and an abundance of information to share with others and enjoy the social scene to recharge your batteries. Your quick yet changeable mind misses little. You find ways to examine as many sides to a situation as possible, some of which you retain and much of which you discard after the reason for retention subsides. If the scenario is too exhausting, you bail. Boredom is a turnoff. You share your ruling planet, Mercury, with Virgo. Both of you are sticklers for using proper grammar, spelling, and punctuation, abilities that get you far in advertising, language, and writing fields.

Intimacy and Personal Relationships

When you want to talk politics or listen to an insightful debate, phone a Gemini. This sign loves to have their brain picked and will devote hours to sharing all the information their contacts need to make a good decision. Be sure to include witty Gemini individuals in social plans, as they provide entertaining conversation, an astute flair for playing games and winning them, ideas for spending leisure time enjoyably, and the ever-present display of sharp wit.

Even the shyest Gemini prefers a partner who engages in stimulating talk. You'll pick mates who can hold their own in the discussion zone and want someone who is willing to listen to frequent discourses on current events, community matters, entertainment, health care, and politics. You thrive on brain food, the nourishing kind that tests your intellect, asks you diverse questions, and gives you a chance to use your power by answering complex questions. Although you love the informative features of TV viewing, you seldom fall for a couch potato, preferring air-sign partners like Libra or Aquarius, who fall in love with your brain. A sense of excitement and willingness to travel attracts you to your opposite sign, Sagittarius, with whom you'll share exotic adventures. If you choose Aries as your love interest, the passionate fire sign will deliver on your mutual love of driving and action-oriented ventures.

Values and Resources

Work that gives you a leg up on current trends, innovation, and exciting breakthroughs in your field fits well with your versatile career path. That means you like to work with electronic equipment, applications, smart TVs and smartphones, leading-edge security systems, and gadgets that give you easy access to information streams. You treasure knowledge and from childhood find ways to acquire as much education as possible to compete in intellectual arenas. Modalities you choose to enhance education beyond college include advanced degrees such as MBAs or PhDs, certification programs, online courses, seminars, workshops, on-the-job-training, and cross-training that may include a detail to another location to master a new qualification. Many Geminis develop seminars and workshops based on books and articles they write to provide tools and know-how to attendees for use in business, government, real estate, and self-help psychology. Since you excel at teaching, you may conduct the workshops or train facilitators to present the courses. Your eloquence as a public speaker often brings requests to emcee awards programs or deliver keynote speeches.

Blind Spots and Blockages

In most circles you're known as the undisputed master of multitasking, as you juggle many assignments and meet numerous deadlines that occur in tight time frames. Most of the details are right in your head, and you hold them in your vision effortlessly. You get into trouble when you forget to keep your log current by marking pending due dates or noting the parties responsible for delivery. Sometimes you allow distractions to take you away from important tasks at the workplace or at home. This shortsightedness seems inconsistent with your normally organized method, resulting in unfinished tasks that you don't discover until you're facing critical deadlines. Intellectual pride prevents you from admitting that you just might have too much on your plate to handle everything efficiently. Another recurring blind spot occurs when your talk runs over the allotted time in a program or meeting. Aside from forgetting that others are waiting to deliver their information at the podium, which you have shortchanged, you have cut into response time and feedback on your presentation. Learn to adopt better time-keeping and listening skills.

Goals and Success

Diplomacy and tact, along with your amazing gift of gab, go a long way in giving you command of the communication sector of the zodiac. Whether it is a speaking or a writing task, you tackle every assignment with passion and polish your product until it shines. As a natural educator, you excel at developing and presenting courses and tailor them to fit the makeup of the participants. When you're running a meeting, you get it started on a high note with clever icebreakers that quickly engage participants and leave them wanting more. The effective body language and tonal qualities you use help listeners relax and retain meaningful context. The professionalism you demonstrate shows why you deeply internalize Mercury, the Messenger of the Gods, in your psyche.

Gemini Keywords for 2023
Language, learning, literature

The Year Ahead for Gemini

In 2023 two eclipses occur in fixed signs: Scorpio in the spring and Taurus at the end of October. A new eclipse sequence begins with a Solar Eclipse on April 20 in Aries, and another in the opposite sign of Libra in mid-October. Mars in Gemini ends a retrograde period in your solar first house on January 12, putting an end to erratic starts in implementing plans and improving your physical health. Mercury in Capricorn goes direct on January 18 in your solar eighth house, eliminating the round of delays in receiving mail, scheduling meetings, communicating clearly about finances, and revising your budget. Pluto in Capricorn is still meandering through this same house until March 23, when it transitions into Aquarius for several months.

Much to your relief, Uranus in Taurus and your solar twelfth house will turn direct on January 22, clearing a path for new learning opportunities in your career and a healthier outlook on life. Jupiter, the planet of expansion, has moved into Aries and your solar eleventh house of goals and groups, sending optimistic vibes your way for landing a plum assignment when the dust settles. Transiting Saturn in Aquarius finishes its two-and-a-half-year tour of duty in your solar ninth house, where you dealt with both finance-driven educational and travel restrictions. In early March, the planet of restriction moves into Pisces and your solar tenth house, where you'll broaden your field of expertise with new employment opportunities.

Jupiter

Although Pisces was the main driver of Jupiter's activity in 2022 in your demanding tenth house of career and ambition, you had an inkling of what life would be like when the planet of expansion occupied Aries and your solar eleventh house for a number of preview months. You achieved greater visibility, and some of you received awards, promotions, and personal recognition that played into your evolving plans. In 2023 Jupiter occupies Aries and races through your solar eleventh house of dreams, goals, wishes, friends, groups, associations, your employer's resources, and your quest for world-changing projects. Jupiter affects every degree of Gemini through May 16, when it moves into Taurus and your private solar twelfth house space, where you can lay out your plans, line up stakeholders, and identify the best way to fulfill your dreams. What credentials are you ready to use to make a meaningful investment in humanity? You have a chance to set the tone you desire in launching new enterprises. When you contact your networks, you'll widen your circle through professional memberships, neighborhood associations, clubs, peer groups, and volunteer services. When Jupiter begins its rapid trip through Taurus, it pauses for a few months by going retrograde on September 4 and turning direct on December 30. The planet of opportunity occupies your solar twelfth house for seven months in 2023, searching your brain for options that will boost your net worth, increase your salary, and add to your savings funds. Those of you born between May 22 and June 7 see the most action while Jupiter is in Taurus.

Saturn

As 2023 dawns, Saturn, the planet of restriction, continues its challenging journey in Aquarius and your solar ninth house of foreign cultures, higher education, in-laws, religion, long-distance travel, and writing. The added discipline you soaked up last year when faced with travel and educational cutbacks led you to explore new possibilities that may include a position as a research analyst that requires considerable communication and long-distance travel. Foreign connections yielded new offers that call for your superior writing or language skills, designed to improve health and economic security for world citizens. Those of you born between June 13 and 21 see the most action while Saturn wraps up its cycle in Aquarius. Authorities in charge saw how skillfully you added value to each undertaking.

Saturn moves into Pisces on March 7 in your solar tenth house of career, ambition, authority figures, government, maturity, and standards of excellence. Be prepared for emerging offers. While Saturn is in this house, you'll be pushed hard to adapt to changing work conditions: a new position possibly in a different field, a different leader who may be a stickler for discipline, or an opportunity to rewrite outmoded policies and structure a high-content, high-caring work environment that attracts motivated staff. During the remaining nine months of 2023, Saturn most affects those of you born between May 21 and 30. You'll welcome a chance to create a new venture, assess the talent of your team, refresh your psyche by taking a welcome vacation before starting a new position, and sharing goals with loved ones who support your vision.

Uranus

Uranus in Taurus has been in residence in your solar twelfth house of healing and seclusion since May 2018. Have you felt lively and liberated or hopelessly hog-tied by the chaotic planet's unexpected antics? Although Uranus is now making an unfriendly aspect with transiting Saturn in Aquarius, the delays in matters related to your solar ninth house will be far behind you soon. You will have one more Taurus eclipse here on October 28, which plays out through the spring of 2024. It could open your eyes to new possibilities that stimulate your spirit.

More than one job could manifest for you. This eclipse is compatible with the early degrees of Saturn in Pisces that manifest good career vibes. If you were born between June 5 and 16, the planet of wild rides and disruption has the greatest impact on your brilliant mind and complicated routines. The year starts out with Uranus in retrograde motion, going direct on January 22 in Taurus, shaking up the energy in your spiritually oriented solar twelfth house. You undoubtedly will experience a few unanticipated encounters or puzzling challenges that will influence your decision to scope out new work opportunities. The unpredictable planet will move into retrograde motion on August 28 and go direct on January 27, 2024. Find the humor in your upside-down world and write about it for an appreciative audience.

Neptune

When Neptune in Pisces stimulates action in 2023 in your solar tenth house of career, ambition, authority, and organizational matters, you'll reflect on what you've experienced with this hazy yet inspiring energy since April 2011. You recognize that dreamy Neptune has been getting in the way of your disciplined mind, and that willing or not, you have spent more time daydreaming than usual during this long transit. Focus on compassion this year, a Neptune trait that is essential to motivating the work team to perform at new heights. Be a good listener and the work plan you want to develop will fall into place more successfully than you anticipated. Saturn in Pisces shows up in this house in March to help you validate your feelings and reframe the way you express responsibility. Trust your instincts as you work with Saturn in Pisces to find a meaningful strategy for bringing important focus to projects. Work with management when introducing new procedures and you'll receive high praise for considering morale and the strength of the staff. Let Neptune help you get ahead by putting you in touch with your inner dreams as you use your astute mind for collaborative dealings. When using your psychic gifts, you get that strong gut feeling that you have discovered your true purpose. Geminis born between June 13 and 20 see the most activity from Neptune this year.

Pluto

Pluto in Capricorn first appeared in your solar eighth house of birth, sex, death, wills and estates, joint income and assets, loans, mortgages, rebirth, psychological depth, and mysteries in 2008. Pluto is winding up this long passage and directs you to address old issues you've held on to in this complex house, making sure you clear your subconscious and let go. You no longer have to fear the control freaks in your life, whose power is diminishing as you move toward release. Examine any baggage still affecting your life and let the Pluto-driven karma cleaners dispose of any remaining anxiety. You have conquered fears of intimacy, debt, stuffed feelings, or pent-up anger. Address any remaining aggravation. Pluto creates intensity in relationships that show up as power struggles, trust issues, and unpleasant confrontations. What's it like for you this year? Are you in a better place in your marriage or headed for divorce court? If circumstances result in the demise of painful issues, you can freely welcome the rebirth of your soul.

Pluto is slipping into the final degrees of its long transit through Capricorn, which finally wraps up in November 2024. Pluto forms an inconjunct aspect to your Sun this year if you're a Gemini born between June 18 and 22, the dates most affected by this transit. Pluto makes a brief entry into Aquarius starting on March 23. On May 1 it turns retrograde in the first degree of Aquarius and returns to Capricorn on June 11 to complete the remaining months of its transit, which seems to end but really doesn't until the cycle officially ends in November 2024. Geminis born between May 22 and 24 feel the impact of a brief, harmonious teaser when Pluto occupies Aquarius from March 23 through June 11. Decode the hints about future relocation options, shifting career aspirations, and foreign languages, ties, and travel during this Pluto-in-Aquarius teaser.

How Will This Year's Eclipses Affect You?

In 2023 a total of four eclipses occur: two Solar (New Moon) Eclipses and two Lunar (Full Moon) Eclipses, which create intense periods that start to manifest a few months before their actual occurrence. Two of the eclipse signs are changing this year. The first eclipse occurs in your solar eleventh house, the second in your solar sixth house, the third in your solar fifth house, and the final eclipse in your solar twelfth house. Eclipses unfold in cycles involving all twelve signs of the zodiac, and usually occur in pairs about two weeks apart. Don't fear eclipses—think of them as growth opportunities that allow you to release old and outworn patterns. They often stimulate unexpected surprises and windfalls. The closer an eclipse is to a planet or point in your birth chart, the greater the importance of the eclipse in your life. Those of you born with a planet at the same degree as an eclipse are likely to see a high level of activity in the house where the eclipse occurs.

The first Solar Eclipse of 2023 takes place on April 20 in Aries and your solar eleventh house of associations, friendships, goals, groups, hopes, and plans. Pressure mounts to join new professional organizations, hold an office in them, or develop initiatives critical to social needs. You'll be challenged to work on your goals, develop projects, keep promises about taking better care of yourself, and change your self-image if you have become too intense over checking all the boxes in your work world and letting downtime slide. Engage qualified consultants if you need help managing important areas of your life.

Two weeks later, on May 5, the first Lunar Eclipse of the year takes place in Scorpio and your solar sixth house of daily routines, fitness, health, nutrition, animal companions, and teamwork. The intensity of this eclipse could bring a heavier workload your way, when authority figures assign tasks that maximize your talent in communicating, editing, writing, problem-solving, teaching, training, and troubleshooting. Don't be surprised to find yourself moonlighting as a stand-up comic, tutor, writer, or sought-after emcee. When you have time to breathe, you would also benefit from scheduling medical and dental checkups.

On October 14 the second Solar Eclipse of 2023 takes place in Libra and your solar fifth house of children, their interests, sports, amusements, entertainment, recreation, romance, and risk-taking. If you have natal planets in this house, expect surprise revelations related to these themes. You'll gain insight into special people and have opportunities to strengthen bonds, travel with loved ones, and possibly build a meaningful connection with a new love interest that could lead to an engagement or marriage. Enjoy harmonious conversations that are free of tension and conflict.

The year's final eclipse is a Lunar Eclipse on October 28 in Taurus and your solar twelfth house of recovery, regrouping, healing, hospital visiting, metaphysics, psychic insight, secrets, and charities. Although you're tired of the unexpected jolts that interfere with your plans because of the presence of Uranus in Taurus here, you can be proud of what you accomplished in seclusion related to emerging projects and significant writing goals. If you write for a living, you've had a wealth of human-interest stories to explore. Continue to maintain cheerful optimism as you celebrate success and explore new paths along the way.

Gemini | January

Overall Theme

Planetary stations this month shift the flow of energy. Mars in Gemini goes direct in your solar first house on the 12th, calling attention to a stuck agenda that you're eager to move along. Keep anger in check. On January 18 Mercury goes direct in Capricorn and your solar eighth house, bringing a welcome release of funds. Complete a much-anticipated project proposal after the 22nd, when Uranus in Taurus goes direct.

Relationships

Family and relatives, including in-laws from distant locations, are the focus of attention through the 21st. Guests that are holdovers from holiday celebrations wind up their extended visits. Plan gatherings to accommodate the interests of children and adults. By the end of the month you'll be fully engaged with your boss handling pressing work demands and laying out a timeline for accomplishments.

Success and Money

Bonus money arrives just in time to help you pay off holiday expenses. The Aquarius New Moon on the 21st in your solar ninth house releases travel restrictions and puts you on the road again to lay the groundwork for implementing new company initiatives. Reserve cash from your performance award to fund upcoming purchases.

Pitfalls and Potential Problems

Don't be tempted on the 6th to spend money at sales before you repay credit card debt. Avoid an argument with a neighbor on the 9th, when lunar aspects throw good judgment off. Be a peacemaker on the 16th, when grouchy colleagues throw a Monday morning meeting off course.

Rewarding Days

1, 3, 21, 25

Challenging Days

6, 9, 16, 18

Gemini | February

Overall Theme

The Full Moon in Leo on February 5 in your solar third house steps up the volume of communication, but not without some confusing exchanges. Solve any misunderstandings as quickly as possible so you can plan upcoming meetings with clear information and support. Schedule Zoom calls to bring remote employees up to speed on major work undertakings. Set the bar high on performance expectations.

Relationships

Your social life picks up around the 15th, when you and your partner celebrate Valentine's Day with entertainment and an elegant meal. People at a distance visit the weekend of the 18th and spend time bonding with you and your family and taking in enjoyable local attractions. Friends or professional colleagues network at a power lunch on the 22nd.

Success and Money

Celebrate financial news on the 2nd, when funding comes through for a much-anticipated work project. The New Moon in Pisces on the 20th bodes well for salary and bonus adjustments scheduled for this year in your organization. Performance excellence makes you shine. New alliances promote your engaging language and presentation skills.

Pitfalls and Potential Problems

Internal tension creates confusing vibes at home base on the 8th. If there is anyone who is unwilling to discuss problems now, don't badger them verbally with sarcastic comments. Business travel may be canceled on the 12th due to overbooking of the flight. Curb a tendency to over-buy sweets on the 13th. Be kind to your blood sugar level.

Rewarding Days

2, 15, 18, 22

Challenging Days

3, 5, 8, 12

Gemini | March

Overall Theme

When the Aries New Moon shows up in your solar eleventh house on the 21st, this goal-oriented sector gets considerable attention based on availability of resources for new work projects. Your employer could give you the lead in attracting talent and finding the right vehicle to fund a new initiative. Brainstorm with colleagues to find serious contenders.

Relationships

Single Geminis attend work events or unique social affairs to meet new dating prospects on the 15th. Those of you who already have a partner enjoy love, tenderness, and a romantic dinner that day. Attend a medical lecture about breakthrough cures at a critically acclaimed facility on the 19th. You'll discover important facts helpful to ill family members.

Success and Money

Extra cash you discovered on the 2nd funds a welcome getaway on the 19th for you and your partner. Enjoy the appealing quality of togetherness. Jupiter in Aries in your solar eleventh house helps you expand contacts and attracts you to groups that are looking for creative leadership and life-changing concepts to launch a humanitarian cause.

Pitfalls and Potential Problems

Upset neighbors express concerns over rising taxes on the 5th. Suggest holding a meeting to let community members air their main objections. Don't let the Virgo Full Moon on the 7th interfere with your plans for pizza and a movie night at home base. Break the ice with moody family members to shift conversations toward upbeat topics.

Rewarding Days

2, 15, 19, 24

Challenging Days

3, 5, 7, 26

Gemini | April

Overall Theme

With a fiery Sun, Moon, Mercury, and Jupiter resonating harmoniously with your Gemini Sun, you should have a great time pulling April Fools' jokes on friends or have a few pranks played on you. Humor is in the air. Why not head to a favorite hangout to celebrate a lively Saturday with kindred spirits? Eat some spicy food and your favorite dessert.

Relationships

After a serious discussion of feelings, you and your partner enjoy a deep level of intimacy around the 12th. Bankers, financial advisors, and attorneys come through for you with sound advice and a lead for a favorable lending package that helps you consolidate debt and pay off an old loan. Encouraging words from your boss support an emerging learning opportunity.

Success and Money

The first Solar Eclipse of the year falls in your solar eleventh house on the 20th, conjoined to Jupiter in Aries, marking an opportune time to begin new collaborations, join prestigious groups, and invest your time in a life-changing initiative that electrifies the aspirations of human interests. Think big and lead.

Pitfalls and Potential Problems

On the April 6th Full Moon in Libra and your solar fifth house, you'll get nowhere with a child who exhibits stubborn behavior and pretends not to get the message. After the Solar Eclipse in Aries on the 20th, Mercury in Taurus turns retrograde in your solar twelfth house on the 21st, calling for a mental health break while you sort out the overload of new options.

Rewarding Days

12, 15, 17, 25

Challenging Days

3, 6, 14, 27

Gemini | May

Overall Theme

The energy of the May 5th Lunar Eclipse in Scorpio and your solar sixth house of health opposes Uranus in Taurus in your solar twelfth house of seclusion. Simultaneously, Mercury is retrograde in your solar twelfth house until May 14. Be prepared for disclosures of secrets and new revelations about health matters. Make plans to see a doctor or schedule tests for a loved one. A work team member may need your help.

Relationships

Legal experts and lenders continue to provide advice and assistance to your financial and estate transactions from the 9th through the 12th. You and your boss have genuine rapport on and off the job. Accept a social invitation to a party hosted by executives in your employing organization on the 13th. Strengthen a partnership bond while seeking solutions to a long-term health matter.

Success and Money

Jupiter advances into Taurus on the 16th and serves as a catalyst to accomplish several assignments calling for language skills, written material for new policies, and the analysis of resumes for anticipated new hires. Use the money you receive on the 22nd to start work on home projects.

Pitfalls and Potential Problems

Keep a clear head on the 1st when your outstanding logic aids in settling arguments between family members, especially those related to home improvements. Pluto in early Aquarius goes retrograde on the 1st in your solar ninth house, leading to a change of plans for a long-distance visit from relatives.

Rewarding Days

9, 13, 19, 22

Challenging Days

1, 5, 11, 31

Gemini | June

Overall Theme

The New Moon in Gemini shows up on the 18th along with an antici-pated bonus. Clear some space around the 27th for a few days of rest and recreation to hit the beach or amusement parks for some family fun. Confirm down payment details and the loan schedule for house-hold work that's about to begin.

Relationships

Work with your colleagues is on target for productivity. Everyone seems genuinely caught up in the team spirit. Leaders prove to be reliable sources of information and ask you to help with presentations to share details of an emerging organizational change. A vacation with your sweetie looks good during the last week of June.

Success and Money

Rapport is especially strong this month, starting with a report presented on the 2nd that reflects excellent revenue as a result of savvy teamwork. Your boss invites everyone to an event on the 11th to show apprecia-tion for a job well done. A promised bonus will aid in covering home remodeling costs.

Pitfalls and Potential Problems

Setback-oriented Saturn slips into retrograde motion on the 17th in Pisces and your solar tenth house and delays implementation of hiring plans for a new initiative. Family plans to travel will have to be modified for a few days. On the 30th Neptune in Pisces turns retrograde in this same house until December 6, creating confusion over finalization of business proposals.

Rewarding Days

2, 11, 18, 27

Challenging Days

4, 7, 22, 30

Gemini | July

Overall Theme

Lunar aspects may not be the best for travel over the 4th of July holiday. The Capricorn Full Moon on the 3rd extends a downer mood for a couple of days. Celebrate with fun and games at home and treat children and their friends to a tasty cookout. Attend a reunion hosted by a sibling on the 30th.

Relationships

Friends invite you to a gathering, possibly a pool party, on the 9th. Take a day trip with children on the 12th and explore a zoo or a nature trail. Ask them to discuss what fascinated them the most during the trip over a casual, relaxing dinner. Sports venues are an enthusiastic draw for the family on the July 17th New Moon in Cancer.

Success and Money

July proves to be a powerful money month for you, starting on the 7th, when your boss acknowledges your strong performance and hints that a promotion is in the works. A relative expresses gratitude for your kindness with an unexpected gift on the 17th, while a parent gives you a cash gift at month's end.

Pitfalls and Potential Problems

Transiting Venus in Leo in your solar third house sends mixed signals regarding support for a neighborhood gathering when the love planet turns retrograde on the 22nd. Participants may bail for lack of interest. Don't purchase luxury items or jewelry without researching their value carefully.

Rewarding Days

7, 12, 17, 30

Challenging Days

4, 5, 19, 22

Gemini | August

Overall Theme

The Moon turns full in Aquarius on the 1st, the first of two Full Moons this month. The second Full Moon occurs in Pisces on August 30. Lovely Venus aspects set a romantic tone on the 13th, when you feel the love spark and arrange a fancy dinner to honor the mood.

Relationships

Accept an invitation from a retired former colleague this month and reminisce about the positive value you experienced from the interaction you shared when you worked together. Bond with your family on the 18th by scheduling a game or movie night with input from all. Put a moratorium on cooking and call for takeout.

Success and Money

Your workplace continues to be a source of inspiration and a rewarding fit for the level of teamwork that allows you to meet pressing deadlines. When an old friend comes to town and asks to see you, cancel plans and enjoy the company. The networking information you receive can change your life if you act on it discreetly.

Pitfalls and Potential Problems

With Mercury in Virgo on a collision course with Saturn in Pisces on the 1st, a business trip is likely to be postponed due to new priorities. When Uranus in Taurus goes retrograde on the 28th in your solar twelfth house of solitude, expect displays of discord to disrupt your quiet time.

Rewarding Days

4, 13, 18, 27

Challenging Days

1, 10, 17, 28

Gemini | September

Overall Theme

Important planetary shifts take place this month. Get all the information you need to avoid making impulsive decisions. Venus in Leo goes direct in your solar third house on September 3, followed by Jupiter in Taurus turning retrograde in your solar twelfth house on the 4th until December 30. To your relief, Mercury turns direct on the 15th in Virgo and your solar fourth house of home.

Relationships

Romantic privacy is your fondest wish during the first week of September. Plan a secluded getaway with your partner. Bond with members of your immediate family on the 14th with a special dinner buffet and an entertainment menu that suits each person. Invite a friend with an adventurous palate to a sushi bar to sample new delicacies on the 27th.

Success and Money

Collaborate with your partner on the 23rd to discuss financial interests, and schedule an appointment with your attorney to revise your will and assess the strength of individual retirement accounts. Monitor the amount of tax you're withholding from your salary and increase accordingly based on current IRS tables. A mortgage payment adjustment is likely based on real estate tax increases.

Pitfalls and Potential Problems

Plans with a group of friends might fall apart on the 3rd, leaving you responsible for contacting travelers and notifying them of the change in status. The Full Moon in Aries on the 29th has you butting heads with a member of a professional group. By day's end you opt out of an agreement.

Rewarding Days

8, 14, 23, 27

Challenging Days

3, 7, 17, 29

Gemini | October

Overall Theme

If you aren't currently attached, Gemini, you'll have a number of opportunities to meet new people. An active love life could become the center of your universe for several months when the final Solar Eclipse of 2023 occurs in Libra and your solar fifth house on October 14. Mercury is on hand, too, to stimulate conversation and keep invitations flowing.

Relationships

The Moon and Venus hang out making harmonious music in the household in your solar fourth house on the 10th, helping to dispel lingering anger related to overspending that flared up on the 7th. You could be consulting with key executives to develop a critical path for organizational realignment. Accept the invitation to take the lead.

Success and Money

Attraction to another stirs your passion on the 4th and the 20th. When Mars moves into Scorpio on the 13th, you put your energy into important assignments by estimating the money and resources you'll need to finish a project's start-up phase. Successful mastery of a foreign language earns you a noteworthy certificate designating fluency.

Pitfalls and Potential Problems

When Pluto turns direct in Capricorn on October 10 in your solar eighth house, you anticipate withdrawing savings funds for a targeted purchase. Your partner disagrees, so watch for verbal fireworks on the 18th, when accusations about your personal self-interest hit the wall.

Rewarding Days
4, 10, 20, 24

Challenging Days
1, 7, 18, 23

Gemini | November

Overall Theme

Plan a holiday shopping trip with a sibling to get a jump start on purchasing gifts. Remember those less fortunate by writing a check for your favorite charity, especially those focusing on feeding families and providing goods to make the holiday season brighter and more memorable. Saturn turns direct in Pisces on the 4th in your solar tenth house of career, just in time for the company accountant to issue bonus checks.

Relationships

Set a place at your Thanksgiving table for unexpected guests, including longtime friends who visit from a foreign country. This group is about as diverse as you can find in origin and opinion. Guests marvel at the array of favorite dishes displayed on your holiday table. Give thanks for a feast that reflects a true meeting of hearts and minds.

Success and Money

Funds appear in your checking account after the 17th, along with a testimonial acknowledging your efficiency and professionalism in performance. Flowers arrive on your doorstep on the 22nd from contacts grateful for your presence in their lives. Surprise children with special gifts and mail packages early.

Pitfalls and Potential Problems

The Thanksgiving Moon in Aries has some testy aspects from the opposition of Venus in Libra and the Sagittarius Sun in hard aspect to Saturn in Pisces. Expect arguments over politics and health care systems to flare. Thaw out the chill in the air by breaking the tension with a few of your famous Gemini icebreakers.

Rewarding Days
4, 8, 17, 22

Challenging Days
11, 23, 24, 27

Gemini | December

Overall Theme

The holiday party season starts early for you with invitations on the 7th through 9th, right after Neptune goes direct in Pisces in your solar tenth house on the 6th. At least one gathering will involve your work team extending heartfelt thanks for the opportunity to unite in spirit all year. Contribute gifts for a community giving tree.

Relationships

Endearing children capture your heart this season, whether they are your offspring, your grandchildren, or those you meet through charitable institutions. Young ones bring out the playfulness in you and the desire to equip the youth in your circle with their favorite toys and amusements. Spend quality time with your significant other, too, and with visitors who celebrate the holidays ringing in the new year with you.

Success and Money

Jupiter now transits Taurus and your solar twelfth house, reminding you that your brilliant analytical gifts led to a prosperous year, with praise and monetary rewards for your leadership in the communication field. Authority figures continue to praise performance excellence. Invest in your future using bonus funds.

Pitfalls and Potential Problems

Planets shifting motion dominate the landscape this month. Neptune goes direct on the 6th in Pisces and your solar tenth house. Clarify confusing work directives immediately. Mercury moves into retrograde motion in Capricorn on the 13th, not an ideal day to begin long-distance travel. Expansive Jupiter goes direct in Taurus on the 30th, gearing up for vigorous action in 2024.

Rewarding Days
7, 14, 18, 22

Challenging Days
3, 8, 13, 26

Gemini Action Table

These dates reflect the best—but not the only—times for success and ease in these activities, according to your Sun sign.

	JAN	FEB	MAR	APR.	MAY	JUN	JUL	AUG	SEP	OCT	NOV	DEC
Move	21				9							7
Romance		15				27			23		17	
Seek counseling/coaching			24		19		12			10		
Ask for a raise	25			17		11		4				18
Vacation			19						14		22	
Get a loan		2		12			17	13		20		

![sunflower]

Cancer

The Crab
June 21 to July 22

Element: Water

Glyph: Crab's claws

Quality: Cardinal

Anatomy: Stomach, breasts

Polarity: Yin/feminine

Colors: Silver, pearl white

Planetary Ruler: The Moon

Animals: Crustaceans, cows, chickens

Meditation: I have faith in the promptings of my heart

Myths/Legends: Hercules and the Crab, Asherah, Hecate

Gemstone: Pearl

House: Fourth

Power Stones: Moonstone, Chrysocolla

Opposite Sign: Capricorn

Flower: Larkspur

Key Phrase: I feel

Keyword: Receptivity

The Cancer Personality

Strengths, Talents, and the Creative Spark

As the first of three water signs in the zodiac's lineup, Cancer, you have the intuitive Moon as the ruler of your solar fourth house of home and family. That includes people who live with you, your parents (especially your mother and sometimes your father), your base of operations, and your outstanding sixth sense. You're the chief nurturer in the household, and often among friends, neighbors, and relatives as well, and are never too busy to comfort, protect, and soothe those you love. With your remarkable memory, you never forget a birthday, sending cards and making phone calls or preparing feasts for those you cherish. One of your treasured domains in the household is your kitchen, where you whip up tasty quick meals or elaborate spreads for all the hungry people who dine at your table. You seldom ask for assistance but will collaborate with another who has excellent culinary skills and understands your entertainment style. Cancer, you rarely refuse help with the dishes after you have packaged take-home treats for guests and stored the remaining leftovers. Did I mention that you cook more food than you need to feed the crowd, preferring not to run short at a meal? Guests have been known to request doggie bags filled with favorite dishes.

Your brain has a tremendous capacity for absorbing copious amounts of information, which others frequently tap to build a complete picture of an organization, a project, or anticipated personnel hires. Bosses appreciate your thoroughness and select you for leadership or management roles based on your astute grasp of the psychology and team dynamics of the workplace. The scope of your knowledge allows you to excel in more than one career field, showing your versatility and carrying these experiences into your next venture. The depth of your intuitive nature lies behind many executive decisions and captures the sensitivity that goes into making astute staff assignments.

Intimacy and Personal Relationships

Most Cancers have strong ties to family members, including parents, grandparents, children, siblings, cousins, aunts, and uncles. You enjoy nurturing children and showering them with love and affection. People who know you sometimes feel you are overly protective of your own offspring, when you should actually allow them to experience life, deal with lessons, and grow. Romance is never out of range for you when seeking a partner. You know a thing or two about finding your soul mate. You're likely to avoid blind dates and cringe at the thought of an arranged marriage, which probably won't last if your heart's not in it. As a cardinal sign you want much more control in searching for the ideal love, yet sometimes your emotions get in the way and you fall hard and fast for the lucky person who captures your sensitive soul. You prefer to feel safe before declaring your love for your dream person. A partner will just have to get used to the amount of affection you like to bestow on them when you hug and kiss them at every opportunity.

Suitable partners for Cancer are the other water signs, Scorpio and Pisces, along with the earth signs, Taurus, Virgo, and Capricorn. You seem to have a magnetic attraction with your opposite sign of Capricorn. Unless you have considerable fire sign planets in your chart, you would be better off avoiding relationships with Aries, Leo, and Sagittarius, or you could wind up sacrificing your needs to accommodate another. Run in the opposite direction if you encounter a partner who is too cold to nurture your sensitive spirit and has an aversion to whispering sweet nothings in your ear. You'll feel promptly rejected.

Values and Resources

The strong ties of relationships resonate with the security you seek to stay in balance. That includes family and people you can treat like family. These people and workplace associates you respect and trust are the real treasures in your life. Home is your favorite base of operations, whether for work, play, or hosting a large group for a meal or celebration. Your party-giving skills are well known in your circle, and you have an uncanny memory for recalling the favorite dishes of guests and making sure their preferences appear on the menu. A state-of-the-art kitchen is a must-have feature for your lovely home. Your memory serves you well in the business world, with your superb financial instincts and talent for making money. Those who know you comment on your astute observation skills that miss nothing while receiving a hearty boost from your uncanny intuition. Cancers often hold more than one interesting job and usually seek a fallback position.

Blind Spots and Blockages

When your talent is not adequately used in the workplace, you are likely to engage in a pattern of job-hopping. You work best in a career that offers you opportunities to use your leadership skills and gives you autonomy to manage your position without feeling smothered. At times your emotional Moon gets the better of you and you lie low when subordinates shirk duties and ignore deadlines. Instead of taking corrective action, you let things slide and often pick up the slack by doing the work yourself. It's your responsibility to see that employees develop desirable work habits that allow them to grow professionally. Choose wisely in selecting the best romantic alliance. Cancer, for example, may be a better friend than lover. A less demonstrative love partner may consider you overly possessive and never understand the depth of your emotional nature. Learn to control your moods and to recognize when they have gone out of control due to a hurtful exchange or criticism.

Goals and Success

Assess your talents and your personal preferences on how to live, where to work, and who to love. Are you living in the ideal state or do you feel a lack of fulfillment? You possess abundant talent, which makes it hard to choose the employment path of your dreams. The entrepreneurial side of you longs to break out of the mold of secure government or organizational stability, yet many of you stay there indefinitely, choosing a predictable paycheck. In your heart you know that self-employment is the route to take to free your creative spirit in the fields of independent contracting, consulting, training, writing, and food service management. With courage and sass, for example, you can be the owner of the trendy new restaurant that takes the neighborhood by storm. If you take the time to define your goals, your can-do attitude will lead you to success. Get moving!

Cancer Keywords for 2023
Security, sentiment, subconscious

The Year Ahead for Cancer

In 2023 you begin a new phase with eclipses in the cardinal energies of Aries and Libra that occupy your solar tenth and fourth houses. Uranus in Taurus continues to shake things up in your solar eleventh house, in retrograde motion until January 22. In mid-May Uranus will be joined by Jupiter in Taurus through the end of the year. Look to this house for signs of high activity related to your hopes, wishes, associations, and goals, a wonderful position for expanding your visibility and increasing your financial holdings to fund special projects. The solar seventh house of personal and business connections continues to host transiting Pluto in Capricorn, reminding you of the need to eliminate blocks to freedom that keep you stuck in undesirable patterns. It doesn't help that Mercury is retrograde here in Capricorn at the beginning of the year and adds confusion to pending decisions that will come to pass after this planet goes direct on January 18. Pluto will make a teaser appearance in Aquarius in your solar eighth house for a few months starting on March 24. Expect new insights regarding legal matters connected with wills and estates.

All of the 2023 Mercury retrograde periods occur in earth signs, adding emphasis to ground you in taking stable action. Saturn occupies your solar eighth house of joint income, partnership assets, and debt in the late degrees of Aquarius as it completes this cycle and moves on to occupy Pisces starting on March 7 in your solar ninth house of higher education, spirituality, and travel. While in Aquarius, the planet of limitations reminds you to clear away any lingering conditions that restrict the use of your funds or a means to save money. Already in full mystical mood in your solar ninth house is Neptune in Pisces, stimulating your higher mind and inspiring creativity and psychic intuition.

Jupiter

The hearty planet of prosperity starts out the year in Aries and your solar tenth house of career, ambition, management authority, and the status quo. Your outstanding work performance led to greater visibility and much-deserved rewards that included bonuses, promotions, and raises along with esteem-building personal recognition from the hierarchy in your organization. You can't beat having Jupiter in this house if you're looking for a new job or anticipating a career change. Jupiter in Aries affects every Cancer degree through May 16, when it moves into Taurus and occupies your solar eleventh house of goals, dreams, wishes, friends, groups, professional associates, your employer's solvency, and your stakes in the humanitarian side of your world. Get ready to lay out your plans and be counted when employers come searching for highly skilled performers who fit right in to the evolving work scene that a new work culture demands. Clean up any remnants of tasks from your current organization so you can be free to network and widen your circle of contacts affiliated with professional memberships, associations, and peer groups. During Jupiter's rapid trip through Taurus, it takes a time-out by going retrograde on September 4 and turns direct on December 30. This opportunity-driven planet occupies your solar eleventh house for seven months this year, finding a way to boost your salary, replenish your savings, and increase your net worth. Those of you born between June 21 and July 9 will see the most action from this year's Jupiter in Taurus transit.

Saturn

Once again the planet that signifies discipline and restriction appears in Aquarius and your solar eighth house of joint income, partnerships assets, money owed by you and a partner (which may include mortgages, credit cards, student loans, or personal debt), investments, estates, retirement funds, birth, death, rebirth, regeneration, sex, karma, taxes, and psychological depth. After being on duty here since December 2020 and teaching you a thing or two about managing your financial affairs, this taskmaster planet is ready to explore the mystical territory of your solar ninth house when Saturn moves into Pisces on March 7. While still in Aquarius, Saturn has the greatest impact on Cancers born between July 14 and 22, allowing you to settle money conflicts, old debt, estates, and any holdings that affected you and a partner who are in the process of a divorce or a dissolution of a business. Selling off assets is a good move to pare down debt as long as you spell out details in agreements, parties concur, and you don't hang on to old sentiments that prevent you from disposing of holdings equitably.

When demanding Saturn enters Pisces, a sign compatible with your own, you could be absorbed in dealings connected to ninth-house matters: foreign cultures and languages, higher education (including advanced degrees), in-laws, medical and legal professionals, the world of writing and publishing, and long-distance travel. During the remaining months of 2023, Saturn in Pisces affects those of you born between June 21 and 30. Become an expert in an emerging field that speaks to the health, welfare, and daily habits of the workforce. Go for a new degree or certificate of discipline that enhances your career value or elevates personal accomplishment. Have fun when Saturn joins Neptune in Pisces in this solar ninth house. Visualize your dreams coming true and listen carefully to your inner voice.

Uranus

Your solar eleventh house of goals, plans, dreams, wishes, associations, friends, groups, and organizations has been subject to a number of disruptions and demands on your time with the passage of Uranus in Taurus here since May 2018. The year started out with Uranus in retrograde motion and going direct on January 22, which most likely sent a few challenges your way or created delays in finalizing financial requests for start-up transactions. With two eclipses in Taurus last year and another occurring in late fall of 2023, your solar eleventh house has been very active, full of surprises related to group and professional activity, and an interrupter of plans you may have initiated regarding projects, conventions, conferences, and fundraising. You appreciate security, but Uranus, even in a sign compatible to yours, is not going to let you have it. Establishing strong communication links and increasing membership in organizations is part of your current work cycle. You may be appointed to lead a professional group, run for a local office, or identify humanitarian goals that better serve your community. Those of you born between July 7 and 17 experience the most interaction from this year's Uranus transits.

Neptune

Slow-moving Neptune continues its long transit through Pisces and your solar ninth house that began in April 2011. Alignments this year create favorable conditions for unusual creative projects, education, and travel. You'll pick the perfect location to visit if it has a body of water located nearby that emanates soothing vibes and enhances your psychic talent, kicking your intuition up a notch. With Saturn transiting this same house in Pisces simultaneously, you'll make room for increased responsibilities that include your children, family, and work colleagues situated a long distance from where you live. Certain Cancers will possibly arrange more than one visit to check up on family matters or provide solutions to problematic work projects. Studying a new language or internalizing cultural norms is likely for those of you with military or medical credentials who may be on temporary assignments. The experience you gained may have accelerated the flow of creative writing you enjoy and led to publication of books, articles, and scripts compatible with sign activity this year.

Pluto

The only outer planet transiting the sign of Capricorn right now is Pluto, which occupies your solar seventh house of business and personal partners, roommates, advisors, collaborators, consultants, legal and medical professionals, and the public, including frenemies. Pluto gives your subconscious a total workout. This transformative planet, which aids you in unearthing stuck parts of your psyche, first showed up in your partnership house in 2008 and hopefully has aided you in identifying those who try to control your mind or important facets of your life. Self-examination will help you identify who or what is interfering with the freedom you desire as you move toward a new set of guidelines for dealing with relationship issues. Perhaps you have solved some of the partnership matters over the last fifteen years, but if some of them prevail, you can count on the karma-cleaning side of Pluto to identify the gap. If you are ignoring the obvious, it's possible that you'll experience one big wake-up call in the next two years. Pluto opposes your Sun with challenges while in Capricorn if your birthday falls between July 19 and 22 or you have late-degree Cancer planets in your birth chart. Pluto makes a brief entry into Aquarius starting on March 23. On May 1 it turns retrograde in the first degree of Aquarius and returns to Capricorn on June 11 to complete the remaining months of its transit, which doesn't really end until the full cycle wraps up in November 2024.

How Will This Year's Eclipses Affect You?

In 2023 a total of four eclipses occur: two Solar (New Moon) Eclipses and two Lunar (Full Moon) Eclipses, which create intense periods that start to manifest a few months before their actual occurrence. Two of the eclipse signs are changing this year. The first eclipse lands in your solar tenth house, the second in your solar fifth house, the third in your solar fourth house, and the final eclipse in your solar eleventh house. Eclipses unfold in cycles involving all twelve signs of the zodiac, and usually occur in pairs about two weeks apart. Don't fear eclipses—think of them as growth opportunities that allow you to release old and outworn patterns. They often stimulate unexpected surprises and windfalls. The closer an eclipse is to a planet or point in your birth chart, the greater the importance of the eclipse in your life. Those of you born with a planet at the same degree as an eclipse are likely to see a high level of activity in the house where the eclipse occurs.

The first Solar Eclipse of 2023 takes place on April 20 in Aries and your solar tenth house of career, ambition, authority, recognition for achievements, organizational matters, and the status quo. You could be tested when an eclipse lands in this house, reminding you to adhere to commitments or forge new ones. Accountability and responsibility come into play, making what you do the driving force behind promotions, rewards, and an elevated status in the work world. Refine critical goals that lead to greater productivity and adapt new work norms that fit with the evolving work culture for greater success. Hire a coach if you need help managing career change.

Two weeks later, on May 5, the first Lunar Eclipse of the year takes place in Scorpio and your solar fifth house of children, amusements, romance, social life, sports, and speculation. People related to this house could rise in importance in your life and command a great deal of time and energy as you strengthen bonds, find solutions for problems, and enjoy downtime. Scorpio is compatible with your sign. Be on the lookout for manifesting wins and happy surprises. Schedule a full calendar of fun and relaxation.

On October 14 the second Solar Eclipse of 2023 takes place in Libra and your solar fourth house of home, foundation, family, and current conditions related to structure and temperament surrounding home base. If you have natal planets in this house, expect revelations related to these themes as you gain insight into those you live with and those with whom you share bonds. Strengthen communications, share adventures and quality time, and cultivate the love principle. Complete work on pending home projects. Increase happiness through enjoyable, harmonious conversations that are free of tension and conflict.

The year's final eclipse is a Lunar Eclipse on October 28 in Taurus and your solar eleventh house of friends, groups, associates, goals, plans, and dreams. Although you may be exhausted from the unanticipated disruptions that interfere with your plans because of the presence of Uranus in Taurus in this house, the new connections coming into your life will lead to significant achievements that benefit humanity. During this cycle you're able to weed out the unfulfilling membership links that waste your time and leave you exhausted. Search for worthy causes and find a group that wants to improve living conditions and motivate others to live a meaningful life. Celebrate success that reflects unity through cooperation for future generations.

Cancer | January

Overall Theme
Career prospects look good for you through May 16 while Jupiter in Aries resides in your solar tenth house of ambition and organization, bringing your quality performance to the attention of higher authorities. Connect with younger children and treat them to preferred entertainment venues that favor family bonding time.

Relationships
You could start the new year off on a celebratory note by hosting friends on the 1st at a festive dinner while each of you recalls happy holiday moments and shares a committed goal with guests. Accept invitations from close associates on the 29th to enjoy a show and a classy meal at a favorite entertainment spot.

Success and Money
Enjoy outings with special people like partners or children using holiday gift certificates for a night of fun. Spend cash gifts on household goods during January sales on the 21st when you find outstanding bargains. Check retirement and savings account balances for surprising increases resulting from astute money management. A Mercury station to move direct on the 18th in Capricorn and your solar seventh house allows you to pick up the pace in partnership dealings. Execute plans in early February.

Pitfalls and Potential Problems
Mars goes direct on the 12th, energizing your approach to setting goals you abandoned in October. Postpone travel until after Uranus in Taurus turns direct on the 22nd. Be cautious when the Cancer Full Moon on the 6th stirs up touchy feelings in the household, including your own.

Rewarding Days
1, 3, 21, 29

Challenging Days
6, 9, 14, 20

Cancer | February

Overall Theme

In one of the rare cycles this year, no planets are currently in retrograde motion. Use this calm period to book a spa date to pamper yourself, especially around the 2nd. Cultivate important relationships and review plans and goals to improve the dynamics, show sensitivity toward others, and build rapport. Locate resources you need to accomplish work.

Relationships

Jupiter and Mars are on friendly terms and highlight communication rapport among groups and friends. February dates that favor romance are the 10th and 17th. Celebrate Valentine's Day with your loved one in a romantic, irresistible setting. Introduce singles to other eligible friends at a social event.

Success and Money

Your most productive cycle this month occurs from the 10th to the 17th, when you, your partner, and family members collaborate on upcoming plans for pleasure or for improving your living quarters. Take a poll to see which projects get a high five and set aside funds to work on the highest priority. Around the 22nd, you and your boss agree on career objectives and develop strategic goals.

Pitfalls and Potential Problems

Avoid a tug of war over spending on the Leo Full Moon of the 5th. Haggling won't get you very far in negotiating a lower price. A sibling could be argumentative on the 7th, a day when you feel under par and unwilling to take on the challenge. Disappointment could occur if you have to cancel an outing with a child on the 12th.

Rewarding Days

2, 10, 17, 22

Challenging Days

5, 7, 12, 25

Cancer | March

Overall Theme
When Venus moves into Taurus on the 17th, socializing with friends accelerates. You'll fill your calendar with dates if single or with lunches, dinners, or entertainment venues with close associates. Add a little pizzazz to your style by purchasing new clothing and accessories at sales. Get a *wow* haircut, too.

Relationships
Be on the lookout for romantic vibes at your workplace while Venus and Jupiter connect in your solar tenth house and a new arrival flashes a flirtatious eye your way. The 11th might be good for a first date. If you're already taken, the 19th works well for intimacy for you and your partner—light the candles and buy a bottle of expensive wine.

Success and Money
The New Moon in Aries on the 21st triggers talk of career-related changes when you and your boss discuss advancement prospects. Finances favor both you and your partner, putting you in line to earn higher salaries. If an interesting promotion opportunity pops up, apply before Mercury goes retrograde in the latter half of April.

Pitfalls and Potential Problems
Table a Virgo Full Moon confrontation on March 7 with a sibling. You'll need a referee to settle a nagging issue that involves the two of you. Review and revise project details before the 16th to bring a productive close to the workweek with colleagues. Mars is at odds with Mercury on that date.

Rewarding Days
2, 11, 19, 21

Challenging Days
5, 7, 14, 16

Cancer | April

Overall Theme

The Full Moon in Libra on April 6 highlights your solar fourth house, bringing attention to domestic affairs like spring cleaning, planting flowers, and washing windows. You'll have little time to work on these chores until after the 12th while you grapple with unexpected financial issues, tense household situations, and the loss of personal items that may have been tossed in the trash during a closet purge.

Relationships

Around the 17th, pleasure travel is in the cards that may include your partner and close in-laws as you gather at a favorite resort to enjoy beaches, good food, and fine entertainment. Friends invite you to dinner on the weekend of the 21st, and you'll feel pampered by the quality setting and elegant meal.

Success and Money

The Aries New Moon on the 20th is the year's first Solar Eclipse and conjoins Jupiter in late Aries in your solar tenth house as details emerge related to a pending promotion. Your partner may be sharing news of a raise. You learn the start date for the promotion you earned during the week of the 23rd. Remember to change the amount of your tax withholding.

Pitfalls and Potential Problems

Check details of written material and proofread carefully before signing and releasing contracts or proposals to affected parties. Mercury goes retrograde in Taurus on the 21st, possibly leading to mixed messages, incomplete travel directions, missing mail, and the cancellation of plans.

Rewarding Days

12, 17, 21, 25

Challenging Days

1, 6, 14, 27

Cancer | May

Overall Theme

The quality and timeliness of communication improves. Collaboration and cooperative agreements with others dominate the landscape this month. New professional initiatives call for business travel and tactful negotiation of problematic facets of the work. Challenge yourself to accomplish in a week what normally takes a month.

Relationships

Enjoy a vacation with your love partner after the Lunar Eclipse on the 5th occurs in Scorpio and your solar fifth house of leisure time and getaways. In-laws lobby for a visit over the next two months. Mercury turns direct in Taurus on the 14th, clearing a path for compatible group activity. A get-together with friends around the 18th features both entertainment and romantic components that raise your spirits.

Success and Money

The Taurus New Moon in your solar eleventh house on the 19th leads to adjusting goals as a result of recent work with long-distance colleagues. Resourceful solutions lead to greater profitability for the organization's bottom line. Seal a deal involving a loan or important financial transaction around the 28th.

Pitfalls and Potential Problems

Pluto turns retrograde on the 1st in Aquarius and your solar eighth house, coinciding with a need to look closely at financial paperwork related to a pending personal loan. Say no to a child's request to purchase computer equipment on the 5th or you'll probably pay a higher price than necessary. Neutralize home-based tension on the 3rd and 31st.

Rewarding Days

9, 14, 19, 28

Challenging Days

3, 5, 25, 31

Cancer | June

Overall Theme

For the entire month, Mars dashes through Leo and your solar second house, tempting you to spend money on attractive goods and gifts. On the 5th, Venus joins Mars in Leo and favors romance while increasing the chance of splurging on amusements, dining, and treats for your sweetheart. On the 11th you are vulnerable to engaging in unplanned spending. Hide your wallet.

Relationships

Have fun during the weekend of the 2nd as you enjoy outdoor recreation with children or a favorite date. Sentimental Cancers feel the connection with romantic partners on the 5th. If you have vacation time planned, clear your calendar for the week of the 11th and pack in sightseeing, swimming, and boating with favorite companions. Relatives at a distance may join you.

Success and Money

Money seems to buy you some temporary happiness as you scope out travel and lodging deals that are hard to beat. Good thing you put money from earned bonuses aside so you can take advantage of these opportunities. Jupiter's transit of your solar eleventh house in Taurus attracts influential connections and strengthens your career marketability.

Pitfalls and Potential Problems

Surgery dates to avoid this month are the 3rd (Full Moon in Sagittarius), the 17th (when Saturn turns retrograde in Pisces), and the 30th (when Neptune stations to move retrograde in Pisces). Check the environment for extreme sensitivity to criticism on the 4th, when a minor incident could get out of control.

Rewarding Days

2, 5, 11, 19

Challenging Days

4, 17, 22, 30

Cancer | July

Overall Theme
If your Cancer birthday falls near the New Moon of July 17, the year can be exceptionally symbolic for you. Study your solar return chart and set an agenda that lets you focus on home life, learn more about your ancestors, and track your roots, possibly through a visit to their country of origin. Write about your revealing discoveries.

Relationships
What a sociable month you'll experience! Relatives at a distance invite you to visit and by month's end return the visit by staying at your home. Old friends make contact and invite you to a midweek reunion dinner around the 11th, where you and other guests fondly relive old memories. Graciously accept and buy the wine.

Success and Money
Your significant other, much deserving of performance recognition, brings home a much bigger paycheck. The two of you discuss household projects you're ready to fund with the extra cash. You discover errors on work-related financial statements. After bringing the matter to your boss's attention, you acquire new accounting duties and substantial praise for your discovery.

Pitfalls and Potential Problems
The internal weather in your home could be emotionally intense for a couple of days over the 4th of July holiday. External weather conditions produce storms resulting in the cancellation of planned celebrations. On the 22nd Venus goes retrograde in Leo, coinciding with a trip to purchase expensive jewelry, which you quickly postpone to avoid a mistake.

Rewarding Days
7, 11, 16, 31

Challenging Days
3, 5, 10, 22

Cancer | August

Overall Theme

With two Full Moons in two different signs this month, you could be entertaining more than one choice for enjoying vacation time. Consider seashore options after the Aquarius Full Moon on the 1st, although the 4th looks better if this is a family trip where you can line up entertainment that pleases everyone. The second Full Moon falls in Pisces and your solar ninth house of long-distance travel on the 30th.

Relationships

Enjoy quality time with household family members and those living at a distance who may be joining you for a unique vacation. Host relatives for a week of fun that lets the inner child of those attending run loose and gives them a fascinating experience they won't soon forget. Communication and bonding with your significant other on the 29th spells romance.

Success and Money

Make arrangements to pay bills and school tuitions around the 13th, then clear away work demands and finalize travel plans. Keep a checklist as chores pile up related to vacation accommodations and school purchases. Siblings or cousins join you for a late summer weekend of fun at a favorite place on the 18th.

Pitfalls and Potential Problems

When Mercury in Virgo goes retrograde on the 23rd, any loose ends related to plans may unravel. By the time you correct them, you'll have to keep a sharp eye on Uranus in Taurus on the 28th, when the unpredictable planet turns retrograde and could interrupt plans for a lively but short getaway.

Rewarding Days

4, 13, 18, 29

Challenging Days

1, 10 , 23, 28

Cancer | September

Overall Theme
The New Moon in Virgo on the 14th falls in your solar third house, highlighting activity related to going back to school, new routines, and beginning a class you've wanted to take for a long time. Venus goes direct in Leo on the 3rd in your solar second house, making it possible to shop for luxury items such as a new vehicle, home, or jewelry item.

Relationships
Bonding time revolves around renewing relationships with people from your past, such as friends or members of professional groups. It's time to pay annual dues and commit to new responsibilities for humanitarian projects. Expect frequent interactions with relatives and cousins this month, especially on the 16th, when you may be invited to a special party event. Pursue romance with your partner on the 23rd.

Success and Money
A willingness to get to know new neighbors and familiarize them with the high points of your neighborhood shines a positive light on the local environment. Make suggestions for becoming familiar with community amenities. Host neighbors for coffee and cake.

Pitfalls and Potential Problems
Jupiter goes retrograde in Taurus on the 4th, delaying the start to a Monday morning meeting. Mercury turns direct in Virgo on the 15th, creating a flurry of activity to wrap up the workweek productively despite last-minute edits to financial reports. The Aries Full Moon in your solar tenth house on the 29th could bring criticism your way, stirring your sensitive feelings.

Rewarding Days
3, 14, 16, 23

Challenging Days
4, 12, 17, 29

Cancer | October

Overall Theme

Home life begins on an upbeat note when the Solar Eclipse in Libra on the 14th occurs in your solar fourth house of family, home, and base of operations. Sentiments of gratitude well up in your heart when new attitudes lead to greater rapport with household members. Add day trips or short getaways to your calendar. Take advantage of networking opportunities that open up the potential for exploring career moves.

Relationships

Camaraderie reigns supreme this month in several relationships, starting with family. Then you and your love partner plan a short getaway around the 21st, strengthening romantic bonds and showing appreciation for cherished understanding. Maintain cordial relationships with those at a distance and schedule a Zoom call with loved ones on the 24th to affirm your love.

Success and Money

A run of good luck begins when Venus enters Virgo and your solar third house on the 8th. You're among the honorees at an awards event that celebrates your performance with a generous cash bonus. Organizational higher-ups laud your work and team spirit. Tune in to an upcoming promotion opening. Throw your hat in the ring when it materializes.

Pitfalls and Potential Problems

After a lengthy retrograde period, Pluto in Capricorn turns direct on the 10th in your solar seventh house, releasing pent-up angst over relationship issues. The final Lunar Eclipse of 2023 occurs on October 28 in Taurus and your unusually active solar eleventh house. Scrutinize pending business deals and clear implementation with authorities.

Rewarding Days

8, 14, 21, 24

Challenging Days

1, 7, 16, 28

Cancer | November

Overall Theme
Purchase holiday decorations so your home is ready for the Thanksgiving week entertaining you're hosting. You bought the high-capacity double ovens thinking of the savvy feast you'll cook up for guests in a couple of weeks. Be sure your checklist covers all anticipated purchases. Saturn moves direct in Pisces and your solar ninth house on November 4, a favorable time to schedule travel.

Relationships
Give the foodies in your life a gourmet treat with a Thanksgiving dinner that covers all the diverse palates that gather in your home from the 19th to the 25th. Include neighbors, relatives from local and long-distance turfs, work colleagues, and friends. Delegate dessert making to an adept relative who loves to bake pies. Poll guests for favorite holiday memories.

Success and Money
Sale bargains exceed expectations on the 7th while you shop for early holiday gifts, finding perfect choices. Enjoy a festive date night with your partner on the 17th using an anniversary gift card for a magnificent shared meal at an upscale restaurant. Recruit helpers when you volunteer to cook for a community pre-holiday meal on the 19th.

Pitfalls and Potential Problems
Mercury and Mars in Scorpio and your solar fifth house opposite Uranus in Taurus in your solar eleventh house leads to the discovery of a difficult romantic liaison before November 11. If this problem involves a child, step in and resolve the issue quickly. Relax on the November 27th Gemini Full Moon and get some much-deserved extra sleep.

Rewarding Days
4, 7, 17, 22

Challenging Days
3, 11, 13, 27

Cancer | December

Overall Theme

The planets demonstrate high activity in two of your most popular solar houses this year, the ninth and the eleventh. Although you won't be traveling far, relatives at a distance will visit you over the holidays after Neptune in Pisces moves direct on December 6 in your solar ninth house.

Relationships

Transiting Venus in Scorpio moves passionately through your solar fifth house of romance for most of the month, influencing your desire to splurge on a special gift for your true love. Celebrate the holiday spirit at parties and gatherings extending goodwill toward those in your circle. Special friends meet on the 22nd to share gifts and cash donations with favorite charities. Treat children to a play or holiday concert on December 14.

Success and Money

Spiritual insight deepens when you agree to donate a substantial amount of money targeted for gifts to an altruistic concern. The spirit of the season increases your love for humanity. You might win a lottery prize on the Sagittarius New Moon of December 12. Buy that ticket! Another's generosity touches your grateful heart.

Pitfalls and Potential Problems

Maintain awareness on the 13th when Mercury goes retrograde in Capricorn, potentially affecting morning flights and transportation plans. Keep your eye on your wallet and especially your credit cards. Carelessness could delay travel and shopping plans. Jupiter in Taurus resumes direct motion in your solar eleventh house on December 30 and inspires you to commit passionately to pending goals for 2024.

Rewarding Days

6, 12, 14, 22

Challenging Days

3, 8, 13, 26

Cancer Action Table

These dates reflect the best—but not the only—times for success and ease in these activities, according to your Sun sign.

	JAN	FEB	MAR	APR	MAY	JUN	JUL	AUG	SEP	OCT	NOV	DEC
Move			11		14					24		6
Romance		17		12		5	31	29	23		17	
Seek counseling/ coaching	29		19			11		4		21		22
Ask for a raise		22							14			
Vacation				17			7				7	
Get a loan	21				28							

Leo

The Lion
July 22 to August 23

♌

Element: Fire	Glyph: Lion's tail
Quality: Fixed	Anatomy: Heart, upper back
Polarity: Yang/masculine	Colors: Gold, scarlet
Planetary Ruler: The Sun	Animals: Lions, large cats
Meditation: I trust in the strength of my soul	Myths/Legends: Apollo, Isis, Helios
Gemstone: Ruby	House: Fifth
Power Stones: Topaz, sardonyx	Opposite Sign: Aquarius
	Flowers: Marigold, sunflower
Key Phrase: I will	Keyword: Magnetic

The Leo Personality

Strengths, Talents, and the Creative Spark

The Sun rules your sign and the adventure-oriented solar fifth house of games, social life, children, lovers, dating experiences, sports, exercise, romance, speculation, freelancing, and entrepreneurial undertakings. You have quite a flair for creativity, and what you express often highlights the qualities most affiliated with Leo, giving you the determination to go after what you want until you achieve it. Add bravery to that list, too, because courage becomes you, and you have had abundant chances in your lifetime to prove it. Personal qualities include pride of accomplishment, entertaining and socializing finesse, adoration of love interests, and all things romantic. Planets that appear in the fifth house describe the complexity of emotions and the range of creative and recreational interests you have. A number of you are sports fans, whether playing, coaching, or spectating, while others prefer entertainment, showmanship, and leadership. Yours is the second fixed sign and the second fire sign of the zodiac.

I'm happy to know two types of Leos: the exuberant Lions that get the most publicity and the more reserved Cats that are equally powerful but go for the limelight at a different pace. Don't second-guess them, because they really own their power. Your Sun sign affiliation with royalty often means you wear or decorate with magenta, rich purple tones, and majestic blues. Crown motifs and swag jewelry sometimes adorn your lapel, cuff links, or home decorating scheme. With your flair for individuality and ownership of a magnetic personality, you are no doubt eager to demonstrate your can-do attitude this year to get the ball rolling in a new enterprise.

Intimacy and Personal Relationships

With drama and panache, you usually bring good cheer to your many friends and fans. Your gift of generosity attracts many associates and colleagues charmed by your display of enthusiasm. When someone rejects you or bashes your ego, you retreat, licking your wounds, pretending it doesn't matter, and finding new interests. If a parent, you are enthusiastic and get involved in your children's activities, especially their education and participation in sports. You want to be their friend and will schedule fun events such as visits to amusement parks, sports events, attending their team games, and burger feasts, just so you can pick their brains to see how they are acing their schoolwork and other commitments. Leos are cool about playing the field until unmistakable chemistry from across the dance floor gets you hooked. Then you deeply tune in to romance and have a flair for winning the heart of the person you find worthy of becoming your soul mate. You'll talk nonstop about their attractive attributes. Aries, Sagittarius, and your opposite sign, Aquarius, often make suitable lovers. Geminis and Libras fit the bill as worthy communicators. Other Leos might be good, too, as long as you don't fight each other for control of your den.

Values and Resources

In the professional arena, you treasure autonomy and a chance to take the lead in managing assignments. You feel secure knowing that you developed a workable plan, a doable timeline, and a strategy that gives you solid results. When your daily environment looks neat, well organized, and decorated with a royal flair, you excel at working with others to create an inspiring vibe that motivates them to turn out polished products and winning solutions. You value loyalty and truth in others and offer it to friends and colleagues, planting seeds of optimism in major undertakings and unexpected challenges. When you make a promise, you keep your word. This trait assures you of long-standing friendships, some dating back to your childhood, which often floods your consciousness with cherished memories. Children mean the world to you, too. You pamper them, entertain them, and guide them to succeed by using their talents to participate in a variety of life-enriching activities. You'll work tirelessly to create a warm and loving home where family gathers in comfort and elegance to bond in meaningful traditions and share in activities that manifest spiritual growth and prosperity.

Blind Spots and Blockages

You have the courage to stand up for your convictions when placed in an adversarial position. At times your strong opinions and beliefs get in your way when you refuse to compromise and shut down a discussion prematurely that is worth listening to and could lead to a more desirable outcome. Part of the problem is that you don't like criticism, and when it comes your way, you have a run-in with your adversary. On a positive note, once you let the frustration out with a heated exchange, you forgive quickly unless the unsavory behavior continues. Holding a grudge can escalate into health setbacks. Your sign rules the back, blood, circulatory system, heart, spine, and metabolism; illness often results when your emotions are blocked or when you don't know how to release your anger. Pride is often the source of that inner tension. People who are hurtful bruise your ego, and you deeply feel the pain. Letting go beats the side effects of taking medicine that throws your equilibrium off-balance. Engage in prevention measures and breathe deeply. An important part of ensuring career fulfillment lies in making sure you are appropriately compensated. When that is not the case, you suffer from rejection and may turn to drinking, overeating, or becoming a resentful workaholic.

Goals and Success

The perfect career makes the most of your leadership assets and becomes your quest to find the right match. You don't have to be the big boss in the organization, but you do want opportunities to showcase your talent by taking charge of projects assigned to you. Situations that give you a chance to use creative, entrepreneurial strategies that receive acknowledgment from higher-ups are your objective, especially if appropriate bonuses compensate you for your unique efforts. Lack of recognition is a turnoff and could send you packing for a more appreciative venue that values your strengths. Leos have a flair for the performing arts, teaching students, coaching teams, or running their own businesses. You love an audience, a winning season, and a chance to show your passion in all you do. These specialties put you at center stage, behind the microphone, giving motivating talks, providing guidance to those you counsel, or calling the shots as the owner of a successful business. Cultivate full understanding that it takes the whole team to accomplish desired goals. Be sure to delegate authority and share the limelight with those who took accountability for delivering an outstanding outcome.

Leo Keywords for 2023
Personal power, potential, prosperity

The Year Ahead for Leo

Jupiter starts off the year in Aries and your solar ninth house of higher education, publishing, and long-distance travel and could mean that your business trips escalate as you cover new territory to develop solid plans and visit professional contacts. You might even travel for pleasure, which is a special treat for you and loved ones after enduring a few stifling years of social distancing and putting vacations on hold. Your solar ninth house will also be the site of the first Solar Eclipse of 2023 in Aries, which could stimulate your interest in furthering your education, relocating to another geographic area, or reuniting with friends and relatives at a distance. Since August 2022, Mars in Gemini has occupied your solar eleventh house of groups, friendships, goals, and professional organizations. It will turn direct on January 12, leading you to resolve issues related to membership priorities and strengthen networking ties. The Messenger planet, Mercury, moves direct in your solar sixth house of daily activity on January 18, facilitating the implementation of work plans that have been on the shelf since last month. Outer planet Uranus is in Taurus and your solar tenth house of career and ambition, where it makes a station to move direct on January 22 as you come to grips with recent shakeups and look for ways to restore equilibrium to your employing organization.

Saturn in Aquarius is quickly moving through your solar seventh house to conclude its two-and-a-half-year trek through your partnership sector, where you have sifted through any restrictions that affected full participation or enjoyment of relationships. Neptune in Pisces continues to move through your solar eighth house of partnership money and debt, opening your eyes wide at times and clouding them over when confusing monetary entanglements surface this year, challenging you to ask questions and resolve discrepancies. Finally, transiting Pluto in Capricorn occupies your solar sixth house in the remaining years of its long transit, suggesting that you examine ongoing patterns in your daily routine to determine which ones could use a makeover to give you energy and a more stimulating life in 2023.

Jupiter

In 2023 Jupiter starts out in Aries and your solar ninth house, renewing your passion for long-distance travel, foreign cultures, advanced degrees, and spirituality. All members of your sign benefit from this compatible transit, which generates refreshing adventures that stimulate your spirit and send you packing for a new experience. Start planning for your future, because Jupiter in Aries leaves on May 16 and begins a rapid trip through Taurus and your solar tenth house, where it shines in your career house. You'll have opportunities to demonstrate the leadership skills you honed while redirecting your focus to decision-making, managing teams, and setting strategic goals to improve the strength of your employing organization and satisfy the hierarchy that directs the mission. While trekking through Taurus, Jupiter is going to pause for a few months by turning retrograde on September 4 and turning direct on December 30. What a fantastic opportunity to have Jupiter occupying the last seven months of 2023 in your solar tenth house! Astute behavior can lead to a promotion, raise in pay, performance award, or professional recognition from the chain of command. Those of you born between July 24 and August 9 see the most action while Jupiter is in Taurus. Work on your career aspirations and other cherished goals to help your dreams come true.

Saturn

The planet that has been making a standoff in your solar seventh house of business and romantic partnerships still lingers there as 2023 begins. Saturn in Aquarius has been on duty since December 2020, adding tension to long-standing liaisons and giving you a reason to pay attention to messages and communication from those who play a vital role in your life. You have a few more months to settle differences and strengthen bonds. If you don't succeed, you could be looking at a parting of ways or a nullified business relationship. Those of you born between August 15 and 23 see the most action while Saturn remains in Aquarius. Weigh facets of key relationships carefully. Are they healthy or toxic? What have you done to address identified problem areas? On March 7, Saturn will be moving into Pisces for the next two and a half years in your solar eighth house of partnership assets, savings, debt, loans, estates, and wills. These matters are often involved in dissolving unions or in setting up a new union, paying child support, or initiating a business collaboration or partnership arrangement. What will it be for you? While Saturn is in Pisces, Leos born between July 23 and August 1 will notice the strongest impact from this transit. Use the time to review your budget, open a savings account, add to retirement funds, and pay down debt. Seed savings accounts with any bonuses or raises you receive.

Uranus

The new year begins with Uranus in Taurus in retrograde motion and going direct on January 22, when it shakes up the energy in your solar tenth house of career, authority figures, ambition, state of the organization, family, and the status quo. You have seen the disruptive effects of Uranus in your work environment since the unpredictable planet entered this sign back in May 2018. In addition to any COVID-19 constraints, you've come to expect chaotic action, blowups, out-of-the blue arguments, layoffs, firings, acquisitions, mergers, and inconvenient do-overs of plans and processes that used to keep the work flowing. If you were promised a new position or expected to leave your current place of employment, you probably ran into a delay or two that modified the start date, eliminated the desired position, or led you in a new direction, totally out of the blue. On the other hand, you may have received an unexpected reward for the extra work you put in to keep the organization afloat. Some of you won on a lottery ticket or netted a large profit on the sale of a property. This year those of you born between August 7 and 18 see the most activity with this surprise-generating planet.

Neptune

This watery, mystical planet started putting moves on your solar eighth house all the way back in April 2011, which has been the home for transiting Neptune in Pisces ever since. Your solar eighth house represents the financial holdings of you and your partner, including your debt load, mortgages, credit cards, insurance, wills, and estates. Neptune identifies with compassion, healing, secrets, and psychological health and has been known to throw a few curveballs laced with confusion and doubt your way when you're in the middle of solving decisions related to partners. Anyone who's been there knows that emotional encounters can be very intense and draining and can lead to unpleasant side effects if you don't resolve them. Think affairs, racking up credit card debt, going on eating binges, and engaging in excessive daydreaming, for example. Plan on having a heart-to-heart talk with your intimate or business partner to address your fears and develop solutions. Leos born between August 15 and 21 see the most activity from Neptune this year. Enjoy your dreams and have fun interpreting their meanings.

Pluto

Roll back the calendar and highlight January 2008, the year when Pluto, the planet affiliated with psychological depth, arrived in your solar sixth house of daily routines, work habits and conditions, health, animal companions, interaction with teammates, management style, and nutrition. Have you noticed any issues associated with these themes that have created blocks for you? The last thing you need is a buildup of stress that affects performance and erodes the quality of cooperative relationships, attitude about your work, and level of self-care. The angle of transiting Pluto in Capricorn to your Leo Sun in its waning degrees this year is creating the inconjunct aspect, a flagrant stress giver, especially if your birthday falls between August 20 and 22. Take an inventory of your work and health habits and determine the level of satisfaction you feel. Get real about fears and ask for help if you're ready to let go of them but feel trapped. If you got used to stuck patterns in the status quo or rationalized that external forces have kept you from fulfilling work goals, do a reality check. You know that you hold the keys to a richer life. Pluto will make a brief entry into Aquarius starting on March 23. It turns retrograde on May 1 in the first degree of Aquarius and returns to Capricorn on June 11 to complete the remaining months of its cycle, which officially ends in November 2024. Leos born on July 23 or 24 will feel a bit of a ping when Pluto moves into Aquarius in late March and occupies your solar seventh house of romantic and business partners, dropping a few hints about how the transformational planet will operate in your relationship arena. Be proactive about dealing with intimacy issues, sharing information with partners, and using personal power to interact harmoniously with close contacts. Use the tools of meditation, contemplation, and prayer to clear those blocks to a happy, healthy life.

How Will This Year's Eclipses Affect You?

In 2023 a total of four eclipses occur: two Solar (New Moon) Eclipses and two Lunar (Full Moon) Eclipses, which create intense periods that start to manifest a few months before their actual occurrence. Two of the eclipse signs are changing this year. The first eclipse occurs in your solar ninth house, the second in your solar fourth house, the third in your solar third house, and the final eclipse is in your solar tenth house. Eclipses unfold in cycles involving all twelve signs of the zodiac, and usually occur in pairs about two weeks apart. Don't fear eclipses—think of them as growth opportunities that allow you to release old and outworn patterns. They often stimulate unexpected surprises and windfalls. The closer an eclipse is to a planet or point in your birth chart, the greater the importance of the eclipse in your life. Those of you born with a planet at the same degree as an eclipse are likely to see a high level of activity in the house where the eclipse occurs.

The first Solar Eclipse of 2023 takes place on April 20 in Aries and your solar ninth house of the higher mind, higher education, foreign countries and cultures, in-laws, philosophy, religion, publishing, and long-distance travel. You could be juggling plans related to your work schedule and possibly a relocation that could not be implemented last year. If enrollment in a degree program was curtailed due to lingering pandemic effects on funding, you could resume your goal in the fall. Take some quality downtime to reflect on next steps. Work on your resume if you are contemplating a job change. Consult a mentor if you need a referral.

Two weeks later, on May 5, the first Lunar Eclipse of the year takes place in Scorpio and your solar fourth house of home, foundation, family (especially parents), occupants of your home, the physical structure of and conditions in your home, and features of your home, including the kitchen, dining quarters, and family room. Look at any planets that occupy this house in your birth chart for clues about the nature of conflict that may have surfaced during the past year. Review the status of family relationships for signs of improved compatibility. Take action to minimize tension if it has escalated. Harmony first!

On October 14 the second Solar Eclipse of 2023 takes place in Libra and your solar third house of communication, education, electronics, local travel, neighbors, siblings, and transportation. You have experienced numerous changes in communication practices that affect your work and home routines, including equipment upgrades or new purchases. Your morning commute may have changed to allow riding public transportation, or you may purchase a new vehicle. Shop wisely to benefit from attractive offers. Meet emerging challenges by addressing them quickly to avoid misunderstandings or unnecessary delays.

The year's final eclipse is a Lunar Eclipse on October 28 in Taurus and your solar tenth house of job growth, career aspirations, authority, performance recognition, and organizational changes in direction. This eclipse shares this house with Jupiter in Taurus for most of the year and with Uranus in Taurus all year while it challenges your Leo Sun if you were born between July 28 and 30. Enjoy a boost of confidence and feel energized to move in new directions, eager to take on innovative projects. Follow through on networking provided by trusted advisors. Embrace a desirable new option and generate plans that bring out the finest assets of your polished leadership style.

Leo | January

Overall Theme

With three retrograde planets about to make a shift, you're restless and ready to explore evolving plans with key contacts. Mars in Gemini goes direct in your solar eleventh house on the 12th, when the first special interest meeting of the year gets underway. On the 18th, Mercury in Capricorn moves forward in your solar sixth house of work routines, while unpredictable Uranus in Taurus surprises staff in your solar tenth house on January 22.

Relationships

Members of a professional organization gather on the 3rd to discuss funding and anticipated expenses for a high-priority initiative that rolls out in 2023. You celebrate a romantic dinner with your love partner on the January 21st New Moon while Venus in Aquarius hovers close by to create more intimacy with harmonious Mars in Gemini.

Success and Money

You learn about favorable moves up the career ladder on the 29th when your manager discloses details of an organizational shift that brings changes in duties, position titles, and salary level. Keep adding extra income to savings and retirement accounts.

Pitfalls and Potential Problems

If you're feeling under the weather on the Full Moon in Cancer of January 6, the universe is telling you to chill and get more rest instead of dragging yourself to attend a post-holiday party. Family disagreements surface on the 16th when you discover that information you acted on related to current events was a fairy tale. Get to the bottom of rumors by the 22nd.

Rewarding Days

3, 8, 21, 29

Challenging Days

4, 6, 16, 18

Leo | February

Overall Theme

If you were born between August 8 and 10, the Leo Full Moon of February 5 is conjunct your Sun in your solar first house. Minimize tension by visiting a museum hosting a well-publicized art piece, enjoy an early dinner, and see an entertaining movie featuring comedy relief. After the 10th, several days favor socializing and business rapport through the 22nd.

Relationships

Have dinner with a favorite neighbor who invites your family members to join them on the 10th. Call a sibling who could use some advice and meet for a private lunch on the weekend. You and your love partner schedule a late Valentine's Day celebration around the 18th, enjoying romantic downtime by expressing love and gratitude for your relationship.

Success and Money

The Pisces New Moon on the 20th highlights your solar eighth house of financial matters. You could learn that you overpaid on escrow or interest and have an unexpected refund coming to you. Business travel around the 22nd, possibly with your boss, identifies the need to expand operations at satellite offices. Discuss options to aid productivity.

Pitfalls and Potential Problems

Avoid shopping impulsively on the 2nd, when prices are inflated and bargains are few. Stay calm when you discover a huge error on the 16th in a work document that was ready for release. Engage with staff to divide the proofreading so you can reconcile errors and present corrected material to the proper authority.

Rewarding Days

10, 17, 18, 22

Challenging Days

2, 12, 16, 25

Leo | March

Overall Theme

The Aries New Moon in your solar ninth house on March 21 gives you ample opportunity to stretch your boundaries and demonstrate personal power. You'll be on the hunt for recognition and adventure when you network with professional contacts at a distance. The spring equinox, when the Sun enters Aries, stimulates extra energy and passion for favorite people and pet projects.

Relationships

Family connections grow closer the first half of the month when scheduled get-togethers celebrate Pisces birthdays, anniversaries, and educational milestones. Mark the 11th as a good time to gather, as Venus, Mars, and Jupiter complement your plans. Save the 15th for playtime with your children and the 19th for a romantic date night for you and your significant other.

Success and Money

Having a strong business ethic pays off for you this month when authorities at your workplace note outstanding accomplishments. Keeping costs down and work quality up reflects your conscientious management style and put you in line for a generous raise this spring. Finances look impressive this month.

Pitfalls and Potential Problems

Don't push your partner to support buying an expensive household item on the Virgo Full Moon of the 7th. You'll land a better deal and feel more prosperous if you wait until the 15th. Mars dukes it out with Mercury on the 17th, creating relationship tension in your solar seventh house and stifling plans to shop for vacation bargains.

Rewarding Days

11, 15, 19, 21

Challenging Days

7, 14, 17, 26

Leo | April

Overall Theme

Venus lines up with Uranus in Taurus in your solar tenth house of career and ambition as the month begins. Matters connected to diverse relationships will fill up your time, some of it pleasant and other facets challenging. The Aries New Moon on the 20th showcases the year's first Solar Eclipse and conjuncts Jupiter in late Aries in your solar ninth house, validating participation in travel plans.

Relationships

You and your partner finally get to travel on the 15th and share a few days of welcome rest and relaxation. A work-related social gathering takes place the weekend of the 21st that includes dancing, entertainment, and an elegant meal. Friends may announce their engagement or marriage and invite you to a celebratory party on the 23rd.

Success and Money

The raise you've been waiting for comes through around the 17th. Decide how you want to allocate the increase in funds. Consider putting a portion in your cash reserves and the rest into your retirement account. Follow up on a job lead that has promotion potential during the week of the 23rd. Seek advice from your mentor or career advisor.

Pitfalls and Potential Problems

The April 6th Full Moon in Libra and your solar third house of communication cautions you against making announcements prematurely or squabbling with neighbors. Mercury goes retrograde in Taurus on the 21st, possibly leading to an unexpected outcome to plans or the cancellation of a trip.

Rewarding Days
15, 17, 20, 23

Challenging Days
3, 6, 8, 14

Leo | May

Overall Theme

The month highlights the role of coworkers in accomplishing assignments, meeting deadlines, and collaborating with your boss to incorporate new initiatives that make better sense during this time of organizational transition. Expect to be pulled in two directions, but know that you can handle the changes once you learn additional details.

Relationships

The Lunar Eclipse of May 5 lands in Scorpio and your solar fourth house of home and family. Share new information with those at home base. Meet with friends after the middle of the month to make decisions regarding travel plans.

Success and Money

Spend time on financial matters around the 13th by considering how investments that pay generous dividends may better suit your savings plans. The Taurus New Moon in your solar tenth house on the 19th coincides with a new assignment that could result in a physical move to a different location. Your timing is spot-on for making a desirable purchase on the 28th that saves you several hundred dollars.

Pitfalls and Potential Problems

Pluto turns retrograde on the 1st in Aquarius and your solar seventh house, emphasizing the need to closely examine personal and business relationships. Look at areas related to intimacy, shared responsibility, and cooperation for possible blocks. Don't put older relatives on the spot until you have a chance to research a pending decision and obtain answers to questions.

Rewarding Days

9, 13, 19, 28

Challenging Days

3, 5, 11, 31

Leo | June

Overall Theme

You're on an energy overload with Mars in Leo all month charging your batteries and supporting your desire to clear away numerous assignments that allow you to proceed with vacation plans. Venus in Leo joins Mars in your solar first house on the 5th, favoring romance for you and your partner. With action from fixed signs on all the angles of your solar chart, make love, not war, with close connections.

Relationships

Enjoy bonding time with your family on the 2nd to determine what vacation attractions they're anticipating. Then pack your bags on the 18th, start your getaway, and make it a trip you'll all remember. By detaching from your intense work routine, your family benefits from special attention and enjoys the rewards of spontaneity, fun, and dedicated playtime.

Success and Money

A bonus/raise arrives in your paycheck after the middle of the month and makes it possible to enjoy an unplanned treat with family and friends. Your work team is grateful for the way you took charge of a problem and showed them the way to realize a more efficient operation.

Pitfalls and Potential Problems

The June 3rd Sagittarius Full Moon in your solar fifth house puts a damper on social plans. Saturn goes retrograde in Pisces on the 17th in your solar eighth house and represents a delay in finalizing a large loan or purchase. On June 30 Neptune goes retrograde in Pisces and your solar eighth house, suggesting you recheck loan details.

Rewarding Days

2, 5, 11, 15

Challenging Days

1, 3, 17, 30

Leo | July

Overall Theme

You're gifted with outstanding hosting talent, always knowing how to make guests feel welcome and pampered. Why not invite your nearest and dearest friends and relatives for a 4th of July bash? The July 3rd Capricorn Full Moon could set a patriotic tone for your celebration.

Relationships

Conflicts with partners or roommates emerge on the 5th. The issues call for immediate attention and seem related to Neptune-driven financial errors made close to the 1st of the month. Although you receive an invitation from a sibling for an event planned late this month, unforeseen circumstances prevent you from accepting.

Success and Money

You could finally sign loan or mortgage papers around the 7th, when favorable aspects occur. An after-hours work-related gathering takes place around the 12th and appears to be a success, inspiring your boss to put these events on the calendar quarterly. Performance commendations abound in the final days of the month, ensuring your growth potential in your organization.

Pitfalls and Potential Problems

Unexpected events affect planned activities toward the end of the month starting on July 21st. When Venus goes retrograde in Leo on the 22nd, an adjustment to weekend plans is necessary to accommodate the sudden arrival of relatives who were confused over the dates set for a visit. Some of you learn of a family member's illness.

Rewarding Days

7, 12, 17, 30

Challenging Days

1, 5, 10, 22

Leo | August

Overall Theme

For the majority of Leos, this is your month to shine and celebrate your magnanimous spirit. Five planets in earth signs dominate the landscape, and two of them, Mercury and Mars, are transiting your solar second house. Mercury in Virgo turns retrograde on the 23rd, while Uranus turns retrograde on the 28th in Taurus and your solar tenth house.

Relationships

Plan a short outing with your partner and children on August 18 to add a little levity to a checklist-driven month. Treat family to a trip to a water park or a beach location. Shop for school supplies and electronic equipment before the 23rd. Include romance with your partner.

Success and Money

Financial dealings progress smoothly for you on the 4th and 18th, which are advantageous dates if you are seeking a loan or consulting with your financial advisor. Pay your child's tuition bill before the 23rd and sign loan papers by the 18th.

Pitfalls and Potential Problems

Two Full Moons occur this month, the first one on the 1st in Aquarius and your solar seventh house of close partnerships and the second one on August 30 in Pisces and your solar eighth house, signaling a need to proceed cautiously in monetary dealings. Be cautious in accounting activity with Mercury in Virgo retrograde in your solar second house of income. Uranus in Taurus starts the workweek off on an unpredictable note on the 28th but gets some relief from good aspects from Pluto in your solar sixth house.

Rewarding Days

4, 13, 18, 28

Challenging Days

1, 10, 17, 23

Leo | September

Overall Theme

You may feel you can talk to anyone about your love life when Venus goes direct in Leo on the 3rd in your solar first house. Your outlook on life emanates warmth and a benevolent feeling. Pick a sociable place to congregate with family and entertain relatives or neighbors.

Relationships

Share a lunch with a colleague on the 5th. Visit with siblings and cousins this month, especially on the 16th, when you might attend a sports event to see a relative's child participate. Host a casual pizza party after the game. Schedule a movie date with your partner on the 20th.

Success and Money

A return to your workplace after the holiday puts you in close contact with your boss and an opportunity to work out major differences over how to handle a sensitive personnel matter. You'll be in the limelight to take the lead in suggesting key training for employees who need to broaden their skills.

Pitfalls and Potential Problems

After Jupiter goes retrograde in Taurus on the 4th, you learn that operating policies are subject to revision to be in compliance with new regulations. Start working on a plan for accomplishing the task—it will come together more thoroughly once Mercury turns direct in Virgo on the 15th and you delegate assignments. The Full Moon in Aries and your solar ninth house on the 29th features a well-attended Zoom meeting that brings employees in remote locations up to speed.

Rewarding Days

5, 8, 16, 20

Challenging Days

7, 17, 19, 29

Leo | October

Overall Theme

The temptation to spend accelerates when Venus in Virgo enters your solar second house on the 8th and you comparison shop for planned purchases. Reunite with members of professional groups on October 4. Suggest a happy hour at a favorite bistro afterward to celebrate the success of a productive meeting.

Relationships

Committee members help make October a memorable month by acknowledging the diversity of group talent and promoting these specialties at networking events. Follow through with leads for a promotion or career transition. The Solar Eclipse in Libra on the 14th highlights cordial relationships with neighbors. Treat your partner to a one-day getaway around the 24th and share a meal at your favorite dining spot.

Success and Money

During the week of the 22nd, consult financial experts for a thoughtful dose of savvy advice that increases returns in your retirement portfolio. Use money you saved from a recent raise to seed your holiday gift spending. Show your appreciation for the rapport you have with siblings and invite them to Sunday brunch.

Pitfalls and Potential Problems

Pluto in Capricorn is the only planet turning direct this month, on the 10th in your solar sixth house. Examine your work environment to determine conditions where you feel stuck and release old patterns by changing behavior and attitude. The final Lunar Eclipse of 2023 on October 28 in Taurus falls in your solar tenth house of work. Steer clear of a cranky partner on the 23rd.

Rewarding Days

4, 11, 14, 24

Challenging Days

1, 16, 18, 23

Leo | November

Overall Theme

Provide service to a charitable organization to coordinate a food bank or a pre-holiday dinner around the time of the Scorpio New Moon on the 13th. Show your elegant hand and generous heart in selecting special items for the menu that guests will rave over for years to come. Purchase a takeaway gift for each participant.

Relationships

Although you love to entertain at home, it's possible that this year you'll travel to see distant relatives to celebrate Thanksgiving. Exude cordiality while volunteering to help with the cooking or drink preparation. Successful collaboration with colleagues wraps on the 17th, freeing you to start your Thanksgiving holiday early.

Success and Money

Saturn in Pisces moves direct in your solar eighth house on the 4th just before you hear good news about investments. Money matters favor purchasing power on the 7th, when you and your partner shop for new holiday decorations and gifts. You'll solve problems with your usual Leo competence on the 16th.

Pitfalls and Potential Problems

Mercury and Mars connect in your solar fourth house of home through the 10th, opposing transiting Uranus in Taurus in your solar tenth house of work. The energy can put you on overload as you cope with unexpected news related to work projects and scramble to resolve issues. The Gemini Full Moon on the 27th in your solar eleventh house favors a travel date to return home on the 24th or 28th.

Rewarding Days

4, 7, 17, 22

Challenging Days

10, 11, 25, 27

Leo | December

Overall Theme

Time for holiday planning! Even with postage rates up, you'll find excellent free delivery offers waiting for you if you act no later than the 5th to make your purchases. For those of you scheduling travel to visit loved ones, confirm plans by the 12th and finish shopping for those living at a distance. Neptune in Pisces goes direct on the 6th in your solar eighth house, highlighting spiritual insight and increasing intuitive vision.

Relationships

Invite siblings, cousins, and other close relatives to join you in preholiday festivities when your home sparkles with holiday cheer and embraces the spirit of togetherness the week of December 3. Transiting Venus in Scorpio in your solar fourth house through the 29th exudes love while you enjoy the treasures of the holidays, starting with family.

Success and Money

With Saturn in Pisces transiting your solar eighth house now, you bank bonus funds to cover the cost of new furniture that arrives early in 2024. Contribute to a favorite charity around the 18th that encompasses the season's spirit and warms your heart. You magnificently pay it forward. Celebrate the holiday season with workmates on the 22nd at a favorite restaurant.

Pitfalls and Potential Problems

Mercury goes retrograde in Capricorn on the 13th in your solar sixth house and could delay travel plans or the completion of a work project due to the absence of key personnel. Jupiter in Taurus helps when it goes direct in your solar tenth house of profession on December 30.

Rewarding Days

6, 18, 22, 30

Challenging Days

3, 13, 16, 24

Leo Action Table

These dates reflect the best—but not the only—times for success and ease in these activities, according to your Sun sign.

	JAN	FEB	MAR	APR	MAY	JUN	JUL	AUG	SEP	OCT	NOV	DEC
Move		22								14		
Romance	21		15		13	5	7		16			
Seek counseling/ coaching		10			9			18			17	
Ask for a raise	29			15			12		8			30
Vacation			21					28			22	
Get a loan				17		11				24		6

Virgo

The Virgin
August 23 to September 22

♍

Element: Earth

Quality: Mutable

Polarity: Yin/feminine

Planetary Ruler: Mercury

Meditation: I can allow time for myself

Gemstone: Sapphire

Power Stones: Peridot, amazonite, rhodochrosite

Key Phrase: I analyze

Glyph: Greek symbol for containment

Anatomy: Abdomen, gallbladder, intestines

Colors: Taupe, gray, navy blue

Animals: Domesticated animals

Myths/Legends: Demeter, Astraea, Hygeia

House: Sixth

Opposite Sign: Pisces

Flower: Pansy

Keyword: Discriminating

The Virgo Personality

Strengths, Talents, and the Creative Spark

Lucky you, Virgo, to have mind-driven Mercury ruling your sign and drawing you to employment in communication-oriented careers, fact-finding, editing, the health field, massage and bodywork, patient advocacy, problem-solving, or administrative roles. Your solar sixth house of work hums with potential, giving you dominion over your daily work environment and the latitude to interface with colleagues or supervise them, organize work flow, and specialize in kitchen and food management, including outfitting your cooking center with supplies and equipment. Certain Virgos have a keen interest in veterinary medicine or work with training or grooming small animals. You have an eye for detail and scrutinize pieces of information until you have the big picture and put it all together. Born with a knack for finding the quickest way to do just about anything, you excel at planning. If you find something that looks like it needs to be organized, you make it a priority to drop everything to tackle the chore, tossing out what you believe is unusable clutter.

As you move into your thirties, many of you overcome shyness and develop the confidence to speak up to make your views known. With Virgo ruling the bowels and intestines, digestion problems bother some of you, while others display signs of hypochondria or overdo the dosages of vitamins and supplements. Manage your gut to avoid developing ulcers, eating disorders, or colitis. Some of you are known to be germophobes. Others cling to the other end of the spectrum, displaying extreme messiness. Few know better than you that if you organize your life and personal space, you'll find the closest thing to nirvana. Your claim to fame might be in how well you've mastered your work scene and how much pleasure you derive from the accolades you receive.

Intimacy and Personal Relationships

Monogamy appeals to you. You're not one to play the field and dislike trying out compatibility with multiple potential mates. A single relationship is your jam, even if you don't formally commit to it until several years have passed. You're picky, but when the right person comes along, you're ready to acknowledge your passion and show your sensual side. Sentimentality is at the heart of your love and affection toward others. Date nights are special to you. You could find your love match with one of the water signs, Cancer or Scorpio, or be drawn to your opposite sign, Pisces, the third member of the water trio in the zodiac. Earth signs Taurus or Capricorn bring stability and happiness, as would a mate who has Virgo on the Ascendant in their birth chart. Mutable signs Gemini and Sagittarius could make you feel unsettled by displaying too much spontaneity. Some of you marry later in life and have only a few children whom you dote on and support in their success. You're likely to push them toward developing a solid work ethic and could encourage them to start earning money at a young age. Help young ones build self-confidence by praising accomplishments, and watch the tendency to go overboard in criticizing efforts.

Values and Resources

Yours is a sign that moves through processes and does it well. Attractive, spacious homes appeal to you especially if they have room for your reading material, artifacts, animal beds, and music collection. A sizable garden plot is a must, with plenty of trees, an area conducive to entertaining lots of guests, and space for a hammock. Your practical nature attracts you to do-it-yourself projects to upgrade your home for a reasonable price. You're willing to put up with long periods of clutter while working on the desired outcome, but you will have to clean as you go to avoid feeling suffocated and losing access to valuables. Why not pay for a cleaning service periodically to get out from under the drudgery of sanitizing the house when you're bucking a schedule that is on overload? Although a number of people come in and out of your life periodically to help you learn relationship lessons, you especially enjoy the company of people who are close friends and feel like family. Sometimes you develop close friendships with coworkers and colleagues who bond with you and join you in entertainment, dining, and enjoyable social outings. As long as you aren't a direct supervisor, these individuals may prove to be valuable connections you count on and cherish.

Blind Spots and Blockages

Too much editing or analyzing will clog up your timetable for meeting deadlines. You can easily get lost in details and sometimes show intense reactions over trivial matters. Be careful not to criticize severely the very colleagues you work with who have the skills to help you deliver your product with efficiency and quality. Jumping to conclusions prematurely is a habit to curb. Doing so allows you to be more objective in dealing with others. Some of you refuse to take a stand when you know the truth about certain circumstances and throw others to the wolves because you don't speak up or leave out key facts when you describe the incidents. Learn to admit there are unfounded accusations and give others the benefit of the doubt. Be generous toward others who have paid for lunches or outings for you by pulling out your wallet once in a while, and treat them to a round of drinks or a movie.

Goals and Success

Find a way to balance your love of work with the tendency to become a workaholic. Stay away from job environments that generate complaints from you as the norm. The gastric buildup could wreck your health and your internal discomfort could leave you focusing too much on your "stomach" problems. You thrive on harmonious relationships and often apply for positions where you know the work environment favors calmness. You have a fond appreciation for the way employee talent is held in high esteem and the team works together to meet goals. As we move toward stabilizing work norms, you'll hear more about changing careers and picking a specialty that you've always wanted to try but lacked the confidence to pursue. The food industry is going through revolutionary changes. Chefs or excellent cooks often have planets in the sixth house of their birth chart, your sign's natural domain. Look for opportunities to create recipes, publish articles that discuss cooking and presenting food, open a bakery, intern at a restaurant, or enroll in culinary school to learn the creative art of food preparation. Someday, if that is your goal, you could be the Top Toque at a fine dining establishment.

Virgo Keywords for 2023
Efficiency, enterprise, execution

The Year Ahead for Virgo

In 2023 you have no outer planets in your sign, Virgo, although several planets are making an aspect to your Sun, depending on when your birthday falls. Jupiter in Aries and your solar eighth house makes a stressful quincunx aspect to your Sun through May 16. Then Jupiter moves into Taurus and your solar ninth house, making a compatible trine aspect with your Sun through the end of the year. Saturn challenges your work environment in Aquarius until it moves into Pisces on March 7, and Uranus shows a compatible face to your Sun while in Taurus all year.

Neptune opposes your Sun if you were born in later degrees of Virgo, and Pluto completes a harmonious cycle for those of you born toward the end of Virgo. Mars in Gemini is the first planet to go direct in 2023 in your solar tenth house of authority on January 12, giving the go-ahead to plans that were put on hold related to employment, projects, and promotions in your organization. Mercury in Capricorn goes direct on January 18 in your solar fifth house, encouraging you to make vacation plans and increase social activity. Pluto in Capricorn is still plodding through this same solar fifth house of romance until March 23, when it transitions into Aquarius for several months.

Uranus in Taurus, transiting your solar ninth house, will turn direct on January 22, clearing a path for resumption of business travel, interaction with in-laws, and enrollment in advanced education programs. Jupiter, the planet of good fortune, is moving through Aries and your solar eighth house of joint assets and debts for the first part of the year, showing promising signs that financial health will get a boost. Transiting Saturn in Aquarius finishes its two-and-a-half-year tour of duty in your solar sixth house, where you juggle duties from more than one job and scramble to hire skilled employees to fill vacant positions. On March 7, the planet of restriction moves into Pisces and your solar seventh house, where you'll assess the strength of both personal and business partnerships.

Jupiter

While Jupiter in Aries dashes through your solar eighth house of joint funds, debts, assets, investments, estates, wills, sex, birth, death, and mortgages, you'll come up with a solid financial plan. Jupiter affects every degree of Virgo through May 16, when it moves into Taurus and your solar ninth house, allowing you to make decisions related to long-distance moving, a job transfer, and how you can best fulfill higher education goals. Market your resume to potential employers. If an assignment over the last year was related to the pandemic, you may be writing reports to finalize projects that still have an effect on the public or private sectors, medical breakthroughs, or food services. You have a chance to shine in launching a new enterprise or starting a business. When Jupiter begins its rapid trip through Taurus, it pauses for a few months by going retrograde on September 4 and turning direct on December 30. The planet of opportunity occupies your solar ninth house for seven months in 2023, helping you look for ways to connect with in-laws, offices, publishers, and educators in distant locations. Find options for building your nest egg. Virgos born between August 24 and September 9 see the most action this year while Jupiter is in Taurus.

Saturn

At the start of 2023, Saturn, the planet of restriction, continues its challenging journey through Aquarius and your solar sixth house of your daily environment, work and coworkers, fitness, health, nutrition, and animal companions. The added discipline you soaked up last year when faced with budget and staffing cutbacks led you to explore new possibilities that may include a new position, the start of your own business, or completion of a certificate program to expand skills in evolving markets. Communication plays a big role in your employment future. Those of you born between September 15 and 22 see the most action while Saturn wraps up its cycle in Aquarius.

Saturn moves into Pisces on March 7 in your solar seventh house of personal and business partners, collaborators, advisers, consultants, medical and legal professionals, and the public. The choice of whether to stay or go is in your hands. Adapt to changing relationship conditions. If you have a business partner, you may be pressed to execute policies, practices, and operating procedures. You could share space with someone who is a stickler for discipline and doesn't like change. If you're the one who is hard-nosed, personalities clash. During the remaining nine months of 2023, Saturn most affects those of you born between August 24 and September 1. Welcome a chance to enjoy the benefits of a harmonious relationship with your partner or business partner. You'll feel a lot more objective if you take a decent vacation break before you start work on revamping your business. Share goals with your partner and agree on the scope of your vision. You'll have the company of transiting Neptune in Pisces in this solar seventh house giving you the intuitive insight to assess the strength of your relationship and the intuition to implement your dreams.

Uranus

The year starts out with Uranus in retrograde motion and going direct on January 22 in Taurus, shaking up the energy in your philosophically oriented solar ninth house of the higher mind, education, foreign countries and cultures, in-laws, philosophy, religion, publishing, and long-distance travel. You have probably noticed that activity in this house has been hampered by delays or setbacks. That's because the chaotic planet Uranus has been here since May 2018. Although the planet of surprises is in a sign compatible with yours, the Uranian energy conflicts with your laid-back demeanor. Have you felt the erratic energy resulting from the unpredictable planet's explosive antics? One more Taurus eclipse lands in your solar ninth house on October 28, with effects that could be relevant through the spring of 2024, opening your eyes to new possibilities. A long-distance job search could manifest multiple offers or increase business travel. If you were born between September 7 and 18, Uranus has the greatest impact on your analytical mind and complex routines. Get ready to experience unanticipated challenges that will influence your decision to consider alternative work opportunities. Let go of the intensity in your serious gene and let in a ray of sunshine to reverse the setbacks of recent years. You have the resilience to do it.

Neptune

Your solar seventh house of personal and business partners, which includes advisors, cooperators, consultants, dreamers, lovers, psychics, the public, and legal or medical professionals, is the site of considerable activity in 2023 when Neptune in Pisces reinforces the role it has been playing since April 2011. Reflect on what you've experienced with this hazy yet inspiring energy that opposes your practical view of life and insists on distracting you from the orderly, organized life you prefer. Neptune tempts you to daydream rather than take a pragmatic view of the issues that complicate partnerships. Saturn in Pisces shows up in this same solar seventh house in March to aid in validating your feelings and reworking the way you handle responsibility. Trust your instincts as you work with Saturn in Pisces to find a dynamic strategy for bringing important focus to relationship concerns. Use more humor and Neptune compassion in your exchanges with others, traits that are essential to motivating partners to find their cooperative spirit. Talk over differences openly. After a few years of COVID-related frustration, unsuitable partners may have surfaced, affecting emotional and physical attitudes. Assess the facts if you are a single Virgo. Be a good listener. What you desire may fall into place, allowing you to develop a successful lasting connection. Neptune aids in validating feelings by putting you in touch with your inner vision, using your astute mind for collaborative dealings. Use your psychic gifts; your strong gut feeling rarely steers you wrong. Virgos born between September 15 and 22 see the most activity from the opposition of Neptune in Pisces to your Sun this year.

Pluto

Pluto in Capricorn first appeared in your solar fifth house of children, fun, games, romance, social life, vacations, speculation, and sports in 2008. As Pluto winds up this long passage, the slow-moving planet directs you to address old issues you've held on to in this complicated house. Clear up discrepancies in how your subconscious evaluates relationships connected to this house. If you have identified control freaks, say goodbye and make choices while pursuing personal freedom. Examine any baggage still affecting your life, and invite the Pluto-driven karma cleaners to dispose of remaining anxiety. Bond with children, walk down the aisle, and make time for leisure activities instead of hiding behind a timetable. Release fears of intimacy, stuffed feelings, or lingering anger. If Pluto has identified relationship power struggles, assess them and have a serious talk with key people. Further confrontations mean you are hugging your blind spot. Let go and live. Release painful issues and master the hurdle. Pluto's journey through Capricorn finally wraps up in late 2024. The transformer makes an easy trine aspect to your Sun this year if your birthday falls between September 20 and 23, the most affected dates. Pluto makes a brief entry into Aquarius starting on March 23. It turns retrograde on May 1 in the first degree of Aquarius and returns to Capricorn on June 11 to complete the remaining months of this cycle, which officially ends in November 2024. Workplace messages may lead you to question job satisfaction and shift career aspirations during this Pluto in Aquarius teaser.

How Will This Year's Eclipses Affect You?

In 2023 a total of four eclipses occur: two Solar (New Moon) Eclipses and two Lunar (Full Moon) Eclipses, which create intense periods that start to manifest a few months before their actual occurrence. Two of the eclipse signs are changing this year. The first eclipse occurs in your solar eighth house, the second in your solar third house, the third in your solar second house, and the final eclipse in your solar ninth house. Eclipses unfold in cycles involving all twelve signs of the zodiac, and usually occur in pairs about two weeks apart. Don't fear eclipses—think of them as growth opportunities that allow you to release old and outworn patterns. They often stimulate unexpected surprises and windfalls. The

closer an eclipse is to a planet or point in your birth chart, the greater the importance of the eclipse in your life. Those of you born with a planet at the same degree as an eclipse are likely to see a high level of activity in the house where the eclipse occurs.

The first Solar Eclipse of 2023 takes place on April 20 in Aries and your solar eighth house of joint funds, debts, assets, investments, estates, wills, sex, birth, death, and mortgages. You'll be challenged to work on your financial goals, develop savings and retirement plans, reduce debt, and purchase or dispose of real estate. Engage qualified consultants if you need help managing important areas of your life.

Two weeks later, on May 5, the first Lunar Eclipse of the year takes place in Scorpio and your solar third house of communication, education, local travel, neighbors, siblings, your mind, and transportation. The intensity of this eclipse could unleash considerable mental chatter and decisions related to contracts, safety, and the welfare of family and neighbors. Assignments involve tasks that maximize your talent in organizing procedures, communicating, teaching, editing, and troubleshooting problems. Apply for a part-time job or take on independent writing assignments if you plan to supplement income.

On October 14 the second Solar Eclipse of 2023 takes place in Libra and your solar second house of assets, money, personal income, planned purchases, self-development, and what you value. You'll gain insight into purchasing power, how others view your work, evolving career interests, and the views of financial specialists. Have frank conversations with experts that are free of tension and conflict.

The year's final eclipse is a Lunar Eclipse on October 28 in Taurus and your solar ninth house of the higher mind, higher education, foreigners and foreign countries and cultures, in-laws, publishing, and long-distance travel. Although you are tired of the unexpected jolts that interfere with your plans because of the presence of Uranus in Taurus in this house, be proud of what you accomplished to communicate, provide training, and solve problems for those located at a distance. Consider work details to build experience for those unable to relocate for work. Share experiences with others to help them cope with recent changes in their lives and point them in the direction of valuable expertise. Maintain optimism as you celebrate current achievements and explore new directions.

Virgo | January

Overall Theme
Several planets shift direction this month. Mars in Gemini is the first to go direct in your solar tenth house of work on the 12th, calling attention to administrative plans that are ready to implement. On January 18 Mercury goes direct in Capricorn and your solar fifth house, encouraging you to bond with children and schedule enjoyable entertainment for them. A much-anticipated trip is a go after the 22nd, when Uranus in Taurus turns direct in your solar ninth house.

Relationships
Fill your calendar with social events as relatives, including parents and in-laws from distant locations, wrap up holiday celebrations through January 3. Then whisk visitors to the airport to catch return flights home. Enjoy gatherings that capture the interests of all guests. By the end of the week you'll be fully absorbed with pressing tasks as your boss spells out the critical agenda for completing projects in the first quarter of 2023.

Success and Money
The Aquarius New Moon in your solar sixth house on the 21st puts a smile on your face as you meet new employees hired to accomplish the added goals and escalating workload you'll be managing. Pay off holiday bills with your bonus award.

Pitfalls and Potential Problems
Don't be tempted to spend money on friends on the January 6th Full Moon in Cancer before you check cash flow. Avoid a dispute with an auto repair representative on the 14th if you feel the bill has been inflated. Use good judgment and ask for a detailed explanation of charges.

Rewarding Days
2, 3, 21, 24

Challenging Days
6, 14, 18, 20

Virgo | February

Overall Theme

You'll be able to sleep in when the February 5th Full Moon in Leo lands in your solar twelfth house and gives you an opportunity to stay in bed all day, if that is what it takes to recharge your sluggish batteries. Venus in Pisces occupies your solar seventh house for most of the month, showcasing the love and warmth between you and your partner.

Relationships

Friendships perk up your social life on the 2nd when you and a favorite pal share lunch and the latest family news. Celebrate Valentine's Day on the 17th when your sweetheart's schedule opens up and you share a romantic meal that includes hand-holding in the moonlight. Work colleagues gather for a power lunch on the 18th.

Success and Money

Celebrate positive news on the 10th with the announcement that you've been promoted to manage a high-visibility work project. Make an enthusiastic acceptance speech and acknowledge the value of teamwork. The New Moon in Pisces on the 20th brings a loving vibration to your solar seventh house of partnerships. Time to canoodle.

Pitfalls and Potential Problems

Tension with a neighbor creates hard feelings over groundskeeping responsibilities and frosts the already prickly relationship you share on the 12th. Don't take the bait if your neighbor makes a few snide remarks. Treacherous weather may be the cause of canceled business travel on the 5th. A sensitive child responds to withheld privileges by sulking.

Rewarding Days

2, 10, 17, 18

Challenging Days

7, 12, 16, 25

Virgo | March

Overall Theme

The Aries New Moon on the 21st shows up with a few surprises in your solar eighth house this month, among them the likelihood of a tax refund you weren't expecting or a generous interest payment. Venus in this same house in Aries activates your loving feeling toward your mate or awakens your interest in meeting someone new if you are single.

Relationships

Accept a party invitation from a friend on the 2nd, when you could meet a potential dating partner. Family cohesiveness blossoms on the 15th while you gather to play board games, share a casual meal, and discuss schedules to determine availability for travel in the next quarter. Your partner schedules a much-appreciated romantic meal on the 19th.

Success and Money

The extra cash you discovered on the March 21st New Moon in Aries covers the cost of a mini vacation for you and your family. Enjoy the opportunity for bonding together. Jupiter transiting your solar eighth house is full of surprises such as a win from a scratch-off ticket, putting a dent in paying down debt and providing relief from anxiety over job insecurity.

Pitfalls and Potential Problems

Eat foods that give you energy and avoid sugar on the March 7th Virgo Full Moon. It's possible that your body has felt sluggish in light of a particularly intense cycle that interfered with your sleep pattern and stimulated a craving for sweets. Don't show your nit-picking side to your boss on March 26.

Rewarding Days

2, 15, 19, 21

Challenging Days

5, 7, 26, 28

Virgo | April

Overall Theme

The fiery Sun, Mercury, and Jupiter show up in Aries and your solar eighth house on April 1. Make sure you don't play an April Fools' joke that suggests you filed for bankruptcy, or people could spread the untrue rumor all over the media outlets. With humor filling the air, head to the local comedy club to tickle your funny bone and share a savory dish with friends.

Relationships

Children have your attention around the 12th when you attend sports events, chaperone a class trip, or treat them to a favorite amusement. Coworkers accept a dinner invitation from you that includes their partners and express gratitude for your thoughtful inclusion of mates. You and your lover enjoy quality alone time on the 17th.

Success and Money

Lucky you to have the very first Solar Eclipse of the year falling in your solar eighth house on the 20th, joining prosperity-driven Jupiter in Aries and highlighting an opportune time to begin new financial cycles, pay off debt, reap benefits from partnership ventures, and increase the amount of money you put into savings and retirement funds. Dream big.

Pitfalls and Potential Problems

At the April 6th Full Moon in Libra, you may get lost in too many offers for purchases of luxury goods that you are merely shopping for but are not ready to buy. Table decisions for now. Mercury in Taurus turns retrograde in your solar ninth house on the 21st, calling for a careful look at planned long-distance travel.

Rewarding Days

12, 15, 17, 20

Challenging Days

6, 8, 14, 21

Virgo | May

Overall Theme

The energy of the May 5th Lunar Eclipse in Scorpio in your solar third house of communication opposes Uranus in Taurus in your solar ninth house of travel. If you didn't get the message, be sure to postpone trips until mid-month. Mercury in Taurus stations to move direct in your solar ninth house on May 14. Revise your itinerary to accommodate a team member at a remote work site on the 18th.

Relationships

You receive good news about a child's academic or athletic performance around the 9th. Show your offspring how proud you are and schedule a celebratory outing on the 13th with your partner, including classmates if possible. See a doctor on the 18th to address a health matter, and follow up with recommended tests on the 22nd.

Success and Money

Activity in your solar ninth house increases when Jupiter in Taurus arrives on the 16th and you explore assignments related to publishing, program audits for out-of-the-area work projects, and current business practices. Local outreach scores potential interest from parties wanting to join your organization.

Pitfalls and Potential Problems

Take care to put a stop to any petty arguments expressed during a Monday morning meeting. Offer to share the floor with hotheads when the passion cools and logic returns to the discussion. This could be a sign of what might happen when Pluto in early Aquarius goes retrograde on the 1st in your solar sixth house.

Rewarding Days

9, 13, 18, 22

Challenging Days

1, 5, 11, 25

Virgo | June

Overall Theme

A contract for remodeling entertainment space and adding another bathroom awaits your signature on the June 3rd Full Moon in Sagittarius. Weigh in on how well the specs match your needs and use of this multipurpose space before signing. Begin the work before Saturn goes retrograde in Pisces on the 17th.

Relationships

Be sure you and your partner schedule time for rest and recreation during the week of the 11th. Enjoy the outdoors and explore new territories. After the middle of the month, accept an invitation from a company executive to attend a party that includes an opportunity to bond with the organization's management team and size up the level of rapport they share.

Success and Money

At the New Moon in Gemini on the 18th, you have a discussion with your boss about a new position that is yours if you apply for it. Look for the job announcement and prepare your resume. The added salary increase reflects your solid expertise and meticulous performance. A generous bonus award helps cover home makeover costs.

Pitfalls and Potential Problems

Expect to put out a few fires at your worksite on the 7th when tempers flare over a delay in meeting a critical deadline. On the 30th Neptune in Pisces turns retrograde in your solar seventh house until the 6th, creating confusion over partnership agreements. The situation calls for a private discussion to sort through details. Modify plans to keep the peace.

Rewarding Days
2, 11, 18, 27

Challenging Days
4, 7, 22, 30

Virgo | July

Overall Theme
Although the Capricorn Full Moon on the 3rd makes a harmonious aspect to your Virgo Sun, lunar aspects are not up to par for travel over the 4th of July holiday. Host a backyard bash instead, inviting friends and neighbors over for a tasty cookout, and serve a patriotic-themed cake to mark the nation's birthday.

Relationships
The best day to enjoy a festive time out with your significant other is the 7th, when the Moon in Pisces shines in your partnership house and you bond through loving communication. Planetary aspects favor vacation travel from July 11 to the 16th. Devote the 12th to enjoyable children's activities, and let them select the dining venue. Accept a friend's invitation for fun and games on the July 17th New Moon in Cancer.

Success and Money
Uranus has been bombarding you with financial surprises this year from relatives, a higher return on investments, and your boss's appreciation for your performance in managing a difficult organizational transition. July uncovers another source of financial power when you land the promotion you desire and the acknowledgment lifts your spirits.

Pitfalls and Potential Problems
Transiting Venus in Leo in your solar twelfth house sends love signals to your mate, who encourages you to set aside time for music and romance. You no sooner schedule a mini vacation for two when the love planet turns retrograde on the 22nd, delaying your trip until the 31st due to workload demands.

Rewarding Days
7, 11, 17, 31

Challenging Days
3, 5, 22, 27

Virgo | August

Overall Theme

There are two Full Moons this month. The first Full Moon occurs on the 1st in Aquarius and your solar eighth house of shared finances. The second Full Moon occurs on August 30 in Pisces and your solar seventh house, putting the spotlight on a close relationship matter.

Relationships

You and your partner are ready for a Friday night rendezvous on the 4th and meet up with old friends at a favorite dining-dancing spot to reminisce and show off your moves. Members of a professional group hold a brunch gathering on the 13th to welcome new officers at a meet and greet. Serve takeout at a movie night family gathering on the 27th.

Success and Money

Entertainment bargains and vacation discounts help your money go far this month. Friends scoop up tickets to a musical production that is high on your must-see list, inviting you and your partner to attend. A networking event pays off, putting you in touch with an administrator of a humanitarian enterprise that you generously support.

Pitfalls and Potential Problems

Watch the opposition aspect between Mercury in Virgo and Saturn in Pisces on the 1st, when friction affects the rapport of a business or personal partnership. Mercury turns retrograde in Virgo on the 23rd, affecting decision dates on priorities. When Uranus in Taurus goes retrograde on the 28th in your solar ninth house of travel, expect a schedule disruption and a shift in plans.

Rewarding Days

4, 13, 18, 27

Challenging Days

1, 3, 23, 28

Virgo | September

Overall Theme

Pay attention to multiple planetary shifts this month. Pause before making important decisions. First, Venus in Leo goes direct in your solar twelfth house of solitude on September 3, followed by Jupiter in Taurus turning retrograde in your solar ninth house of long-distance travel on the 4th until December 30. Business as usual resumes when Mercury goes direct on the 15th in Virgo and your solar first house.

Relationships

Attend an awards ceremony on the 9th to honor a professional colleague's achievements. Make complimentary remarks regarding the honoree's performance. The Virgo New Moon on the 14th offers quality time to gather with family to celebrate Virgo birthdays, perhaps yours. A sibling invites you to sample an exotic menu that wakes up your palate on the 27th.

Success and Money

Jupiter in Taurus and your solar ninth house in favorable aspect to your Virgo planets all month favors travel discounts on a dream vacation, pursuit of advanced education, and better relationships with relatives at a distance. Refinancing at a lower rate gives you more purchasing power after the 14th.

Pitfalls and Potential Problems

A meeting with a lender after the Labor Day holiday is disappointing when you learn the offered loan rate is less favorable to your plans. By day's end, you're shopping for a better deal. A neighborhood meeting on the 19th falls short of member count to vote on a community proposal. Avoid closing on a loan on the September 29th Full Moon in Aries.

Rewarding Days

9, 16, 18, 27

Challenging Days

4, 17, 19, 29

Virgo | October

Overall Theme

Unattached Virgos receive abundant attention from potential partners this month when Venus hangs out in your solar first house. The flirtation begins on the 8th. Married Virgos enjoy romantic discussions and share mutual recreational pursuits on the 24th.

Relationships

The final Solar Eclipse of 2023 occurs in Libra and your solar second house on October 14. You and your mate feel at one with emotional and practical decisions. Scholastic and sports achievements by your children have you beaming and thrilled to reward achievement with attendance at favorite entertainment venues.

Success and Money

An executive rewards you with a coveted assignment on the 4th and urges autonomy in selecting a team and a workable timeline. You enjoy being in charge and discover that key staff have the outstanding qualifications that spell success. When Mars moves into Scorpio on the 12th, you put your energy into finalizing plans and estimating expenses for completing the work.

Pitfalls and Potential Problems

When Pluto turns direct in Capricorn on October 10 in your solar fifth house, you'll feel relief to be letting go of a burdensome relationship problem that had you vacillating over solutions for several months. Friends are argumentative on the 7th, a day that you set aside for a fall outing. Watch out for nasty exchanges and bail if necessary.

Rewarding Days

4, 14, 21, 24

Challenging Days

1, 7, 18, 23

Virgo | November

Overall Theme

You're in a problem-solving mood on the 1st when the Moon is in Gemini. Look over the workload that begs for action. After deciding what is most critical, tackle some of it and delegate the rest to capable staff. Schedule holiday shopping with a friend on the 2nd, and create a mailing list for gifts intended for out-of-town recipients.

Relationships

Children arrive home after the 17th to gather for a Thanksgiving feast. Set a place at your table for guests who are workmates and live too far away from family to travel home. Ask guests to share their favorite customs and enjoy the beautiful way the group comes together. Display an array of tasty dishes and give thanks for a feast that reflects a loving feeling.

Success and Money

Saturn turns direct in Pisces on the 4th in your partnership house just in time for delivery of your holiday bonus. Provide those in need with food and supplies to make the holiday season merrier around the 17th. Write a check to your favorite charity to buy meals for Thanksgiving dinners.

Pitfalls and Potential Problems

Take note of the Thanksgiving Moon in Aries in your solar eighth house, which encounters harsh aspects from the opposition of Venus in Libra. The Sagittarius Sun also receives hard aspects from Saturn in Pisces in your solar seventh house. Avoid discussion of sensitive subjects at the Thanksgiving table, or arguments will put a chill in the festive air.

Rewarding Days

2, 8, 17, 20

Challenging Days

1, 11, 23, 27

Virgo | December

Overall Theme

Your social life is solid from December 7 to the 22nd. Right after Neptune goes direct in Pisces on the 6th in your solar seventh house, expect holiday invitations to fill your mailbox. Party season seems nonstop, with special events filling your calendar.

Relationships

Holiday recitals or plays scheduled for the 14th involve your children or grandchildren. Be sure to cheer them on to applaud their participation. Remember the needs of children living in charitable institutions. Host a lunchtime gathering for your work colleagues on the 18th to express gratitude for efficiency and loyalty all year. Make reservations to ring in the new year with your significant other, too, as you celebrate the holiday spirit at the dawn of 2024.

Success and Money

Jupiter now transits Taurus and your solar ninth house, reminding you of the lucrative contract that recently came your way, allowing your flair for organizing to shine. Peaks of prosperity came through at various intervals this year that rewarded your communication expertise. Your analytical savvy broke new ground in your challenging work environment.

Pitfalls and Potential Problems

Planets are busy this month shifting direction and making a dominant statement. Besides Neptune's shift into direct motion on the 6th, Mercury goes retrograde in Capricorn in your solar fifth house on the 13th, suggesting you stay close to home in lieu of traveling. Jupiter goes direct in Taurus on the 30th in your solar ninth house, laying the groundwork for long-distance business travel in the enterprising new year.

Rewarding Days

7, 14, 18, 22

Challenging Days

3, 8, 13, 26

Virgo Action Table

These dates reflect the best—but not the only—times for success and ease in these activities, according to your Sun sign.

	JAN	FEB	MAR	APR	MAY	JUN	JUL	AUG	SEP	OCT	NOV	DEC
Move	2				18			27				22
Romance		2	19	12		11				24		
Seek counseling/ coaching							17		18		20	
Ask for a raise	3			23				13		4		
Vacation		17			9		31				17	
Get a loan			21			27			16			7

Libra

The Scales
September 23 to October 23

♎

Element: Air

Glyph: Scales of justice, setting sun

Quality: Cardinal

Anatomy: Kidneys, lower back, appendix

Polarity: Yang/masculine

Colors: Blue, pink

Planetary Ruler: Venus

Animals: Brightly plumed birds

Meditation: I balance conflicting desires

Myths/Legends: Venus, Cinderella, Hera

Gemstone: Opal

House: Seventh

Power Stones: Tourmaline, kunzite, blue lace agate

Opposite Sign: Aries

Flower: Rose

Key Phrase: I balance

Keyword: Harmony

The Libra Personality

Strengths, Talents, and the Creative Spark

Good manners are at the center of your considerable collection of social skills. The significance of your partnership-oriented air Sun sign is that it rules the solar seventh house of romantic, business, and professional relationships, as well as roommates, the public in general, advisors, counselors, diplomats, professionals, and your shadow self. Venus rules your sign, and many of you find yourselves occupied in careers where you exude charm and tact in your communication style, provide service to clients and customers, and show flair for social organization. Most of you are big internet communicators or social networkers, and if you aren't, you probably talk a lot and spend copious amounts of time on the telephone. Most of you like routines that keep you on track and prefer a predictable work schedule. Libras often show creativity through arts, crafts, and decorating, or they compete in sports or take up dancing. Indecisiveness or procrastination may get in the way of your plans. If you have a healthy earth presence in the planetary lineup of your birth chart, you won't have this distraction.

So much is on your plate this year: money, home, relationships, work, and play. You're wondering if you'll get it all done after having to cope with several years of delays. Libra is the second air sign in the zodiac, with love goddess Venus ruling your sign. Your astrological symbol is the scales, and your mission is to bring them into balance. You favor vibrant colors in your home in the blue shades often with a mix of green, including aqua, azure, teal, bright greens, rosy pinks, mauve, and lime. Libra rules the kidneys, pancreas, lower back, and urethra.

Intimacy and Personal Relationships

Born in the sign of relationships, you place great value on them, experiencing several energizing ones during your lifetime. Most of you feel incomplete without a partner. If a relationship doesn't work out, you will remarry or bond with another in a short period of time. You're a joiner, too, and search for a love connection in the group, or adamantly insist that your partner come along for the planned events if you are already involved. Your network is vast and you look for ways to stay in touch with all your contacts. The signs that work for you are air signs Gemini and Aquarius, plus the magnetism of your opposite sign, Aries, and the passionate spark of the fire signs Leo and Sagittarius. Unless you have a strong connection with water or earth signs, Cancer and Capricorn could make life difficult. Most of you are traditionalists and want daily bonding time with family, along with frequent connections with older relatives. Whether you invite them for a formal dinner or a sumptuous backyard picnic, you enjoy the company of loyal friends and take pride in entertaining them at special events.

Values and Resources

Harmony, cooperation, and positive approaches to problem-solving appeal to your peace-loving nature. You can keep the momentum going as long as you address issues when they come up. Mediation appeals to a significant number of Libras, who either incorporate the talent into everyday life or seek out these services when troubleshooting. Time-saving tech devices, including smartphones and apps, appeal to you. One of your best assets comes to life when you learn to listen to what others have to say; many of you will have rewarding careers in the fields of consulting, coaching, teaching, and psychology. You are at your best when in learning mode and feel good about absorbing new information, which you internalize to bring out your best qualities. As a member of the sign that rules the solar seventh house of partnerships, be sure to nurture close relationships. With your strong sense of ESP, you can usually tell when something unsettling is in the air, and your body language will tip off your partner even if you think you're hiding your feelings. Be open, ask questions, and put concerns on the table to maximize the quality of your cherished connection.

Blind Spots and Blockages

Libras are sensitive about their flaws and will tune out messages that seem too critical. Some among you "forget" to listen, especially if you don't like the message. Creative avoidance, indecisiveness, and procrastination are downfalls, yet may be minimized with the presence of a practical Moon or strong Mercury in your birth chart. Be sure to solve problems to avoid getting stuck in anger, which is an unforgettable outburst if your buttons are pushed too hard. You don't care for tense situations and chaos, so be sure to exercise to relax more and work out the stress. Accountability is an issue you sometimes lack, and you get yourself in hot water by manipulating facts or omitting critical ones. Those affected will be mad at you. You take great pride in courting your friends and associates and staying in touch with them frequently. Some of you have trouble hiding your dislike for others, showing partiality for some and tarnishing your gift of tactfulness. Some of you may be oblivious to how your actions slight or hurt others when you appear to undervalue another's self-worth by excluding important facts from discussions and leaving them with the wrong impression. Remember that you're here to find balance and will enjoy greater success in demonstrating that quality by how well you treat others.

Goals and Success

Count on your excellent communication skills to create collaborative environments at the workplace, at home, or in your social circles. Cultivate the ability to recognize and reward excellent performance, and be sure to acknowledge all participants on the team. Encourage competition among players and suggest strengthening negotiation skills so that staff members have the tools to work out issues if they arise. Look for ways to restore harmony when differences of opinion create tension and lead to a stalemate. Many Libras show a penchant for creativity in arts, crafts, and decorating. Other Libras find appeal in competing in sports, coaching, or politics. Those Libras who like adventure, with an emphasis on expanding their social life or pampering clients who enjoy these experiences, become travel agents, booking agents for entertainment or wedding venues, and enthusiastic participants in the hospitality industry. Your warm and gracious demeanor and people skills, along with diplomacy, make you valuable to leaders in these industries. Persuasive communication skills, which you possess in abundance, make you an excellent candidate for sales in the industries that most appeal to you. Boost self-confidence by acknowledging your preferences and finding the perfect outlet to use them in your daily life. Let quality be the driver of your contributions to your work and personal life in 2023.

Libra Keywords for 2023
Agreement, alliance, appraisal

The Year Ahead for Libra

A Solar Eclipse in your sign, Libra, makes its debut in October, giving you increased visibility and an opportunity to put your diplomatic skills to work and use them to strengthen relationships, which are going to be an important part of your life in the new year. In April there will be a Solar Eclipse in your opposite sign of Aries, the sign on the cusp of your solar seventh house of personal and business partners. Since August of 2022, Mars in Gemini has occupied your solar ninth house of higher education, spirituality, and travel, where it turned retrograde on October 30 of that year, delaying plans for long-distance business trips, reunions with relatives, and enrollment in advanced coursework. Mars moves direct on January 12 this year, facilitating plans to resume business and personal travel or start a personal development program or work detail. The infamous Messenger of the Gods, Mercury, has been retrograde in Capricorn since December 2022 in your solar fourth house and moves direct on January 18, helping you and family members communicate more clearly and openly about current expectations for sharing household duties and coordinating schedules to accommodate responsibilities. Pluto in late Capricorn is also in your solar fourth house, urging you to call a truce with estranged family members and get rid of festering anger. On January 18, Uranus in Taurus makes a station to move direct in your solar eighth house of joint income, resources, and debt, where it has been retrograde since August 2022.

Jupiter

When the planet of expansion and wealth comes calling in Aries and your solar seventh house, you and your romantic and business partners enjoy healthy collaboration and lucrative financial agreements. Those of you headed for the altar may be planning weddings, honeymoons, and the purchase of the perfect residence to put down blissful new roots. In 2023 Jupiter occupies Aries and races through your solar seventh house of intimate and professional relationships and affects every degree of Libra while it visits this house through May 16, the date when it heads for Taurus and your solar eighth house. Perhaps you are celebrating a milestone anniversary when Jupiter transits your seventh house. Why not plan a party or an intimate getaway as a show of love? You could also be attracting publicity for a major accomplishment with cooperators that puts you in the public eye. If you're getting back in the groove after an employment gap, you may prefer independent consulting in your career field. Those of you who like to take chances on new ventures may start your own business. When Jupiter begins its rapid trip through Taurus, it pauses for a few months by going retrograde on September 4 and turning direct on December 30. You could arrange for a home appraisal, if contemplating a residential purchase, or see a lender to obtain a favorable mortgage loan. Those of you born between September 23 and October 10 benefit the most while Jupiter occupies Taurus.

Saturn

At the dawn of 2023, Saturn, the planet of restraint and responsibility, makes progress in its journey through Aquarius and your solar fifth house of entertainment, risk-taking, romance, sports, social life, vacations, and children and their interests. Distancing requirements may have kept you from a budding romantic interest or from taking time for much-deserved travel to a favorite getaway destination. You learned a lot about self-discipline as you restructured important daily routines, yet those in charge of your work life saw how well you adapted to changes and kept momentum going to complete assignments. Those of you born between October 15 and 23 will see the most action as Saturn wraps up its cycle in Aquarius on March 7.

When Saturn moves into Pisces and your solar sixth house on March 7, you experience a high degree of activity in your daily routine, including your work environment, involvement with coworkers, health, nutrition, and animal companions. In Pisces, Saturn may be a little less fussy about details but will surely urge you to take a closer look at operational conditions, skills matches, hiring practices, and compatibility among work team members. While Saturn is in this house, you'll be pushed hard to adapt to changing work conditions, such as a new position possibly in a different field or a different leader who may be hard-nosed about discipline. During the remaining nine months of 2023, Saturn most affects those of you born between September 23 and October 1. You'll welcome a chance be more creative in your work, assess employee talent, take time off to refresh your psyche, and share goals with loyal employees who support your style.

Uranus

With Uranus in Taurus in residence in your solar eighth house of joint income and debts since May 2018, you may be dealing with unexpected bills or mail delays or perhaps a mix-up with your tax returns. The year starts out with Uranus in retrograde motion, going direct on January 22 in Taurus and shaking up the energy in your money-oriented solar eighth house. Be prepared to experience a few unanticipated encounters or unplanned challenges that will influence your decision to review the strength of your budget and financial status. You will have one more

Taurus eclipse in your solar eighth house on October 28, which could play out through the spring of 2024. It could create new revelations or strengthen monetary goals with partners. With Uranus, anything goes, so stay open to new possibilities. The eclipse is compatible with the early degrees of Saturn in Pisces, which manifest good financial vibes. If you were born between September 28 and 30, this eclipse has the greatest impact on your life and complicates routines. Those of you born between October 8 and 15 see the most action this year from Uranus in your quest to reduce stress and find the perfect solution to your money goals.

Neptune

When Neptune in Pisces stimulates action in 2023 in your solar sixth house of daily routines, health, and work collaboration, you'll reflect on what you've experienced with this dream-inspiring energy since April 2011. You'll see that impression-oriented Neptune has been getting in the way of your disciplined mind, which has led to excessive daydreaming or extensive focus on less important matters during this long transit. Focus on understanding the plight of others in your work circle this year, a Neptune gift that motivates your work team to perform more assertively after a few years of frustration due to delays that prevented accomplishment of planned goals. Be a good listener while you watch work plans fall successfully into place. Saturn in Pisces shows up in this solar sixth house on March 7 to help you reframe the way you manage responsibility and make changes to behavior that slows down success. Work with Saturn in Pisces to implement a viable strategy for concluding key elements of work projects. Remember to use humor to break the ice when conditions feel tense as colleagues become acclimated to new procedures that you'll introduce while Saturn insists on perfecting products. Be sensitive to the needs and morale of staff when assigning staff and setting timelines. Pass out compliments and be sure management knows about top performers. Let Neptune help you manifest your fondest vision for reaching your goals. When your gut rumbles, use your psychic gifts to lead you toward your life purpose. Libras born between October 15 and 22 see the most activity from Neptune this year. Recharge your metaphysical spirit.

Pluto

The planet of transformation came calling in Capricorn and your solar fourth house of home, family, base of operations, foundation, and the end of matters back in 2008. Pluto's goal is to complete this long passage while it directs you to address old issues you've held on to in this critical house, making sure you release your subconscious thoughts and let go. Never fear the control freaks in your life whose power diminishes your courage as you move toward release. If you still have baggage that keeps you hanging on, let the karma cleaners unload the remaining anxiety. Rid your home of piles of clutter, items you never use, clothing you haven't worn in years, and fear that you'll purge something you still need. Release anger and trust issues that remain in the home, acknowledging any remaining angst. Pluto creates intensity in family relationships that shows up as power struggles and troublesome confrontations. What's your home "temperature" like? Have you made peace with difficult members? It's time to experience a rebirth of your soul.

Pluto is slipping into the final degrees of this long transit through your solar fourth house. Pluto forms a square aspect to your Sun this year if you're a Libra born between October 19 and 23, the dates most affected by this transit. Pluto makes a brief entry into Aquarius starting on March 23. It turns retrograde on May 1 in the first degree of Aquarius and returns to Capricorn on June 11 to complete the remaining months of its transit, which lingers until the cycle officially ends in November 2024. Focus on what you would like to change in your household in 2023, decide on staying in or selling your home, and facilitate healing any fragile family relationships. Libras born on September 23 or 24 feel the impact of a brief, harmonious teaser when Pluto occupies Aquarius from March 23 through June 11. Consider matters involving children and travel during this interlude.

How Will This Year's Eclipses Affect You?

In 2023 a total of four eclipses occur: two Solar (New Moon) Eclipses and two Lunar (Full Moon) Eclipses, which create intense periods that start to manifest a few months before their actual occurrence. Two of the eclipse signs are changing this year. The first eclipse occurs in your solar seventh house, the second in your solar second house, the third in your solar first house, and the final eclipse in your solar eighth house. Eclipses unfold in cycles involving all twelve signs of the zodiac, and usually occur in pairs about two weeks apart. Don't fear eclipses—think of them as growth opportunities that allow you to release old and outworn patterns. They often stimulate unexpected surprises and windfalls. The closer an eclipse is to a planet or point in your birth chart, the greater the importance of the eclipse in your life. Those of you born with a planet at the same degree as an eclipse are likely to see a high level of activity in the house where the eclipse occurs.

The first Solar Eclipse of 2023 takes place on April 20 in Aries and your solar seventh house of personal and business partners, including spouses. You may feel the pressure to address romantic issues or to expand professional contacts. You'll be challenged to work on goals with your significant other and take care of any differences the two of you have that keep you from enjoying loving bliss. Engage qualified consultants if you need help managing important areas of your life.

Two weeks later, on May 5, the first Lunar Eclipse of the year takes place in Scorpio and your solar second house of income, assets, resources, and self-development. The intensity of this eclipse may result in a complicated workload due to staffing cutbacks or new technology that takes time to implement. If making a job change is a priority, this eclipse may easily push you in a new direction. Be sure the attractive position makes use of your excellent communication and problem-solving skills. Negotiate for a nice salary boost. Sign up for job-enhancing classes or certification programs.

On October 14 the second Solar Eclipse of 2023 takes place in Libra and your solar first house of appearance, assertiveness, character, enterprise, personality, self-image, and self-development. If you have planets in this house in your birth chart, expect revealing insights related to these themes. You'll understand more about mentors, teachers, and collaborators who facilitate opportunities to strengthen your position in the world, stimulate innovative ideas, and attract you to travel that has been difficult to accomplish in the last few years. Show your charm by engaging in harmonious conversations that are informational and witty.

The year's final eclipse is a Lunar Eclipse on October 28 in Taurus and your solar eighth house of joint income, assets, debt, karma, psychological matters, estates, wills, and financial management. Although you are tired from these unexpected upsets that interfered with your plans because of the presence of Uranus in Taurus in this house, new goals and projects gave your reputation a boost. Interactions under trying circumstances shed light on how others coped and give you a brilliant perspective to deal with human capital and what will make work performance more productive for all concerned. Bring your cheerful optimism to those you encounter as you explore emerging paths to success.

Libra | January

Overall Theme

Greet the new year by welcoming the shifting planetary energy that means you can finalize your educational plans, set new goals, and enjoy connecting with family and friends again. Mars in Gemini goes direct in your solar ninth house on the 12th, making visits with relatives a reality. On January 18 Mercury moves direct in Capricorn and your solar fourth house, reworking the timeline for home renovations. Money you're expecting hits your checkbook after the 22nd, when Uranus in Taurus turns direct.

Relationships

Join relatives from out of town at a post-holiday gathering on the 3rd. Have a great time with friends at a trendy restaurant for Sunday brunch on the 8th. The Aquarius New Moon on the 21st allows you to share a meaningful entertainment event with your children that makes a lasting impression and inspires a show of gratitude from them.

Success and Money

Enjoy a prosperous start to the new year after mid-January, when bonus money, gifts, and dividends increase your spending power. You pay the feeling forward by sharing the bounty with treats for family and neighbors. Although your work schedule intensifies, you'll enjoy harmonious working relationships with colleagues.

Pitfalls and Potential Problems

Avoid negotiating a contract on the Cancer Full Moon of January 6, as parties could be argumentative and unwilling to compromise. Money will not go far on the 16th when an attractive sales pitch turns out to be a bust. Walk away from a costly proposition.

Rewarding Days

3, 8, 21, 25

Challenging Days

6, 7, 9, 16

Libra | February

Overall Theme

This month accentuates the quality of your personal and business relationships. The February 5th Full Moon in Leo in your solar eleventh house highlights any communication issues that confront you related to friends or group involvement in organizational projects. Make plans to discuss differences of opinion in professional dealings and clarify objectives in the presence of all involved parties.

Relationships

A work-related social gathering sparks your interest around the 2nd and gives you and your colleagues a boost in team spirit morale. You and your romantic partner celebrate Valentine's Day around the 10th, preferring an intimate evening and elegant meal. Encourage the family to gather for fun and surprises on the 17th, reflecting the loving bonds you share.

Success and Money

The announcement of setting higher salary levels gives you a reason to celebrate the possibility of a raise or promotion on the 2nd. The New Moon in Pisces and your solar sixth house on the 20th continues the optimistic financial theme and gives you a reason to showcase your commitment to demonstrating performance excellence. Perfect speaking and presentation skills.

Pitfalls and Potential Problems

Neither February 12 nor the 25th works well for financial transactions for different reasons. Say no to splurging on a wish list item that will prove disappointing on the 12th. Don't apply for a loan on the 25th before checking with at least two more companies that are likely to offer more favorable terms. Schedule a health checkup on the 17th.

Rewarding Days

2, 10, 17, 20

Challenging Days

5, 12, 16, 25

Libra | March

Overall Theme

When the Aries New Moon shows up in your solar seventh house on the 21st, your partnership sector gets the spotlight, calling attention to exciting new projects, plans, and pending agreements that are in the works. A marriage is a strong possibility for single Libras. If collaborative ventures are driving work assignments these days, enjoy a successful period to show your best stuff.

Relationships

Accept a lunch invitation from your boss on the 2nd and expect to talk business and future career prospects with the organization. Attend a meeting in your local community on the 15th and offer tactful suggestions to resolve persistent neighborhood issues. Enjoy alone time with your significant other on the 22nd, beginning with a romantic dinner and ending with a declaration of love.

Success and Money

Nothing sends a better message about how well your talent fits the work environment than a vote of support from your management team. Expect positive feedback and praise from your boss during the period from March 2 to the 11th. Don't be surprised when extra cash comes your way, with Jupiter in Aries in your solar seventh house.

Pitfalls and Potential Problems

Home base could use a break from a burst of tension on the 16th, when family members show annoyance over setting new household responsibilities. Cool off with ice cream treats. Cancel travel plans on the 26th, when key individuals are unable to accommodate plans due to illness.

Rewarding Days
2, 11, 15, 22

Challenging Days
7, 14, 16, 26

Libra | April

Overall Theme

Your solar seventh house soars with activity on April 1 when a fiery Sun, Moon, Mercury, and Jupiter relate strongly to your Libra Sun, setting the tone for playing unique April Fools' jokes on contacts. With three Aries planets opposing your Sun, expect paybacks and pranks from other spirited souls.

Relationships

Heart-to-heart talks are in order on the 12th, when family members gather around the table for a take-out meal and a chance to talk about upcoming needs and commitments of time for spring events. On the 15th, children ask for advice, permission, and a budget for accepting coveted social invitations. Output from your work team exceeds expectations and supports adjusting the timeline for goal accomplishment.

Success and Money

The first Solar Eclipse of the year falls in your solar seventh house on the 20th conjunct Jupiter in Aries, highlighting both intimate and business relationships. Declare your love and loyalty to your partner. Begin new professional alliances by consulting with trendsetters in your field of employment.

Pitfalls and Potential Problems

With the April 6th Full Moon in your sign, you could use extra rest to recharge your batteries. Partners throw up roadblocks to your plans, so table nighttime activity. Mercury in Taurus turns retrograde in your solar eighth house on the 21st, calling for the review of a loan proposal while you examine alternative proposals.

Rewarding Days

12, 15, 17, 20

Challenging Days

1, 6, 8, 21

Libra | May

Overall Theme
Money talk dominates the conversation this month. The May 5th Lunar Eclipse in Scorpio in your solar second house of income and resources opposes Uranus in Taurus in your solar eighth house of joint income and debt. Mercury in Taurus is retrograde in your solar eighth house until May 14, urging you to recheck estimates, terms, and loan documents. Be prepared to deal with unexpected disclosures.

Relationships
Family members claim your time with spontaneous get-togethers, a friendly card game, and a taco takeout around the 9th. Professional and work relationships dominate the rest of the month, beginning with a team meeting on the 13th to lay out emerging goals and assignments. After the 23rd, authority figures provide status details on pending projects, leaving you grateful for the outstanding rapport you share with your boss.

Success and Money
Jupiter advances into Taurus on the 16th and makes debt reduction a priority in your solar eighth house. Use the money you receive from a raise to seed a targeted savings fund. Legal experts offer advice on your estate management plan around the 18th.

Pitfalls and Potential Problems
Keep a clear head on the 1st, when your brain is on overload from managing too many colliding deadlines. Rest to recoup energy. Pluto in early Aquarius goes retrograde on the 1st in your solar fifth house, adding drama that involves close family ties. Use logic to settle disputes among children on the 11th.

Rewarding Days
9, 13, 18, 23

Challenging Days
1, 5, 11, 31

Libra | June

Overall Theme

You get good news this month regarding available funds for scheduling a much-deserved summer vacation. The New Moon in Gemini shows up on the 18th in your solar ninth house of long-distance travel, emphasizing career contacts in remote locations. Themes related to advancing your education, checking out schools for college-bound children, and spirituality dominate.

Relationships

Bankers and finance managers work with you to broaden your perspective of a pending transaction and reassure you that the proposal meets your needs. Teammates show their cooperative spirit and ingenuity in meeting challenging deadlines. You may travel with a colleague who is in line for a transfer to another location to provide orientation and training.

Success and Money

Lenders have agreements ready for your signature on the 15th. A much-anticipated family vacation looks good after June 17. You earn a bonus that comes in handy to fund your recreational pursuits. Your supervisor invites the team to celebrate early completion of a critical project around June 11.

Pitfalls and Potential Problems

Unplanned auto expenses eat into cash and lead to the cancellation of weekend plans on the 3rd. Your solar sixth house is the site of major activity now. First, Saturn in Pisces shifts into retrograde motion on the 17th, delaying plans to hire extra staff to prepare competitive proposals for bidding on a new initiative. On the 30th, Neptune in Pisces turns retrograde until December 6, leaving critical business plans up in the air.

Rewarding Days

2, 11, 15, 18

Challenging Days

1, 3, 7, 22

Libra | July

Overall Theme

Work and family relationships compete for your time this month. Lunar aspects conflict with your Sun over the July 4th holiday, when the Full Moon in Capricorn on the 3rd puts a damper on travel for late-born Libras. Host a gathering at home and invite the neighbors for a lip-smacking cookout. Top off the meal with a slice of patriotic-themed dessert cake.

Relationships

Join workmates for a Friday night bash on the 7th that offers tantalizing food, fantastic music, and a chance to unwind to get an upbeat start to the weekend. Bring one of your noteworthy desserts to the midday festivities your boss hosts on the 17th to mark the start of a long-term work project. Enjoy a park outing with children on the 30th by exploring thrill-seeking rides or getting soaked at a water park.

Success and Money

Money gravitates your way in July after organizational assignments land abundant praise from the management team. Employees you supervise chime in to give you a vote of support for your attitude and leadership style. Performance power soars, giving your career a boost with a high-profile assignment.

Pitfalls and Potential Problems

When transiting Venus in Leo in your solar eleventh house turns retrograde on the 22nd, you learn that a preferred community initiative is severely underfunded. Put in time to revisit key players to stimulate support and turn the tide in a favorable direction by early September.

Rewarding Days

7, 11, 17, 30

Challenging Days

3, 5, 10, 22

Libra | August

Overall Theme

Lunar activity gets your full attention this month when two Full Moons occur. The first one, on the 1st in Aquarius and your solar fifth house, puts a damper on your love life. The second Full Moon occurs in Pisces on August 30, with opposing Mercury in Virgo adding fuel to commitment disputes.

Relationships

After an especially demanding workweek, you and key colleagues unwind for a relaxing dinner on the 4th and agree not to talk shop. Your boss treats the work group to a waterside outing on the 13th to show appreciation for the grit and commitment that went into meeting major goals ahead of schedule. Surprise your partner with a night off from cooking on the 15th. Order in to bond and catch up on news.

Success and Money

Bask in the signs of appreciation you receive when your boss continues to applaud the caliber and success of your work, especially during the week of the 13th. Networking tips that come through professional groups score very talented candidates for the vacancies you plan to fill for ongoing projects.

Pitfalls and Potential Problems

A romantic relationship starts unraveling on the 1st due to incompatible priorities among partners. On August 1, Mercury in Virgo clashes with Saturn in Pisces. When Uranus in Taurus goes retrograde on the 28th in your solar eighth house of investments, savings, and loans, expect money disagreements between you and your partner.

Rewarding Days
4, 13, 18, 27

Challenging Days
1, 3, 10, 28

♎ Libra | September ♎

Overall Theme

Watch the location of planetary shifts taking place this month. If any of the planets occupy the first, fourth, seventh, or tenth house in your birth chart, be cautious of making sudden decisions. Venus in Leo goes direct in your solar eleventh house on September 3, followed by Jupiter in Taurus turning retrograde on the 4th in your solar eighth house until December 30. Mercury turns direct on the 15th in Virgo and your solar twelfth house, offering you a peaceful night's sleep after a hectic week solving financial problems.

Relationships

September 4 through the 8th favors romantic interludes with your partner. Take off for a private retreat and enjoy the renewal of intimacy. Family gatherings prove successful on the 20th, when your hosting includes food, fun, and entertainment that caters to everyone's tastes. Treat the late-working crew to a catered dinner on the 24th to reward their commitment to meeting your deadlines.

Success and Money

Pleasant surprises await you as you review financial statements and find a considerable increase in dividends on the 3rd. Collaborate with your boss on the 8th to prepare last quarter goals and review the staff budget. Cut travel expenses if you are close to the margin.

Pitfalls and Potential Problems

Planned activity with your significant other falls apart on the 4th when unexpected relatives come to town, leaving you to make arrangements to entertain and feed them. The Full Moon in Aries on the 29th could stimulate an argument with your partner over a pending purchase agreement.

Rewarding Days

3, 8, 20, 24

Challenging Days

4, 7, 12, 29

Libra | October

Overall Theme

Two eclipses this month call attention to Venus themes. The final Solar Eclipse of 2023 occurs in Libra and your solar first house on October 14. You're oozing sex appeal and have many opportunities to meet new people if you're unattached. The final Lunar Eclipse of the year occurs in Taurus and your solar eighth house of intimacy on October 28, activating loving vibes.

Relationships

The Moon in Gemini manifests great conversation via engaging aspects from harmonious Venus and Mars on the 4th in your solar ninth house, creating the perfect romantic vibe for a short getaway. Share quality time with family members on the 20th, starting the weekend off on a positive note with a shopping trip and a savory meal.

Success and Money

You can't get your mind off the new romantic prospect in your life and feel that synchronicity was present when you accepted social invitations after the October 14th Solar Eclipse. When Mars moves into Scorpio on the 12th, obtain estimates for a bathroom remodeling project. Write a deposit check if the vendor can complete the project in a month.

Pitfalls and Potential Problems

When Pluto turns direct in Capricorn on October 10 in your solar fourth house, you call a meeting with family members to discuss upcoming holiday festivities and learn what's on their wish lists so you can shop for gifts. If some members aren't available, wait until the 20th.

Rewarding Days

4, 10, 20, 24

Challenging Days

1, 7, 18, 23

Libra | November

Overall Theme
Meet with the executive team at work early in the month to regroup and review the timeline to keep a current project on track. Send a check to a favorite charity by the 7th so that those less fortunate have money for meals and a brighter holiday season. Saturn turns direct in Pisces on the 4th in your solar sixth house, adding a beat of confidence to your daily environment.

Relationships
Welcome your partner's relatives to your Thanksgiving table after a three-year hiatus. Enjoy the tantalizing array of favorite holiday foods that please every palate. Pipe in seasonal music. Pass the after-dinner drinks and watch a holiday movie that has universal appeal. Offer thanks for a successful gathering of kindred spirits.

Success and Money
The New Moon in Scorpio on the 13th gives your income a boost that lasts well into 2024 with a generous salary increase. Take a bow for successfully paying down debt and building a nice cash reserve in your savings account. Shop with children on the 24th, letting them select holiday gifts for others.

Pitfalls and Potential Problems
On the 23rd, tune in to the Thanksgiving Moon in Aries, which makes an opposition aspect with Venus in Libra. Simultaneously, the Sagittarius Sun makes testy moves on Saturn in Pisces. Socially sensitive topics are bound to crop up involving political and health care arguments. Warm the chill in the air with a slice of your luscious pumpkin pie and hot cocoa.

Rewarding Days
4, 7, 17, 21

Challenging Days
11, 22, 23, 27

Libra | December

Overall Theme

You start off December on a happy, healthy note when compatible Mars in Sagittarius gives you a boost by encouraging daily exercise that gets you pumped for the hectic pace of the holiday party season. Neptune goes direct on the 6th in Pisces and your solar sixth house, enabling you to clarify misconceptions that have affected work management.

Relationships

Family and children warm your heart this season when you gather to celebrate the holidays and enjoy their company on the 7th or 14th. Celebrate with workmates on the 18th at a pre-holiday gathering. Suggest that attendees bring a toy for a charity to gift to those who will appreciate the generosity and care. Spend quality time with your partner and welcome visitors who celebrate the December holidays with you.

Success and Money

Jupiter in Taurus blesses your solar eighth house, reminding you that your conscientious work ethic has rewarded you with a prosperous year, along with the recognition and monetary rewards you earned for your outstanding performance. Put extra cash into savings.

Pitfalls and Potential Problems

Three planets shift motion this month. Less confusion in communication occurs when Neptune in Pisces goes direct on the 6th. Mercury goes retrograde in Capricorn on the 13th, a day that could result in travel or mail mix-ups. After slowing down plans for investing in real estate, expansive Jupiter goes direct in Taurus on the 30th, getting ready for months of influence in 2024.

Rewarding Days

7, 14, 18, 30

Challenging Days

3, 13, 16, 26

Libra Action Table

These dates reflect the best—but not the only—times for success and ease in these activities, according to your Sun sign.

	JAN	FEB	MAR	APR	MAY	JUN	JUL	AUG	SEP	OCT	NOV	DEC
Move		17				18			23			
Romance	21		22	15			11				21	
Seek counseling/coaching		2				11		18		10		18
Ask for a raise					23		17				13	
Vacation	3			17				27		4		
Get a loan			11		18				3			22

Scorpio

The Scorpion
October 23 to November 22

♏

Element: Water

Quality: Fixed

Polarity: Yin/feminine

Planetary Ruler: Pluto (Mars)

Meditation: I let go of the need to control

Gemstone: Topaz

Power Stones: Obsidian, garnet

Key Phrase: I create

Glyph: Scorpion's tail

Anatomy: Reproductive system

Colors: Burgundy, black

Animals: Reptiles, scorpions, birds of prey

Myths/Legends: The Phoenix, Hades and Persephone, Shiva

House: Eighth

Opposite Sign: Taurus

Flower: Chrysanthemum

Keyword: Intensity

The Scorpio Personality

Strengths, Talents, and the Creative Spark

You are a force to be reckoned with, Scorpio, as a member of the eighth sign of the zodiac, a fixed water member of the psychologically oriented solar eighth house of money you owe, deep space, sex, birth, death, rebirth, estate matters, goods of the dead, debts of all types, crimes, joint assets or investments as well as liabilities, mysteries, the subconscious, and complex human needs. Pluto rules your sign, with Mars as coruler, planetary proof that you take obligations seriously. At some point in your life you may have found yourself in circumstances where you underwent drastic changes or transformed what existed and no longer worked, often shedding excess baggage or false illusions. Mysteries were made for you to solve. Scorpios crave some downtime and go inward to attune inner energies. Your sign has dominion over the private parts of the body, and your colors are dark reds, maroon, magenta, oxblood, wine, dark browns, and black.

Regeneration is at the core of your belief system, and you work hard to get back on track after setbacks or encountering situations that call for new thinking skills. With Pluto, the Lord of the Underworld, as your ruler, you value secrecy and are drawn to professions where protecting the privacy of others is critical. You like cracking the code, figuring out what makes others tick, finding the bodies that are buried, and doing a top-notch job of researching facts to validate theories, hunches, feelings, and evidence for criminal, medical, and research cases. A host of career opportunities are yours for the choosing. Work diligently to find them and satisfy your passionate spirit.

Intimacy and Personal Relationships

Those who know you call you secretive because you hesitate to reveal much of what you're thinking. On an intimate level, you are very serious about love and seldom take relationships lightly. You put prospects through a test to make sure they possess the qualities you desire. If they ask too many questions too soon, you'll probably bail; you like to do the "grilling." Trust issues and a fear of abandonment often lie behind the pace you're willing to travel in a budding relationship. Once some of the barriers disappear, you talk freely and confide intimately in your partner, often picking a mate for life. Individuals in your circle find you easy to confide in and often bare their souls, which results in you being the keeper of secrets on both a personal and a professional level, a beautiful asset in your life and career. You stay in touch with old friends for decades. You're a sign that makes a compatible connection to your opposite sign, Taurus, another sensual sign that is tactile and cuddly. Virgos can be fun and keep you on the go. Cancer displays emotion and kindness, and Pisces resonates with your compassionate side. Family means the world to you and gives you part of your purpose for living when you communicate openly, entertain their friends, and offer them a safe haven. You get involved to solve problems and often work on behalf of a charity to raise funds or donate time.

Values and Resources

Financial security means a lot to you, Scorpio, so you look for work that provides a steady paycheck, such as in government, an investment field, or police work. You do your homework in looking at pay and benefits before applying for a job and actually look forward to the interview process. You shine in fields where extraction plays a key role in carrying out eighth-house activities, like a CPA balancing the books. A lab environment gives you a sense of accomplishment as you get to the bottom of criminal activities, analyzing clues critical to solving crimes such as assault, rape, robbery, and murder. Many Scorpios find their passion in fields that cater to addiction management, marriage, self-help psychology, and psychotherapy practices. As one who has had your share of painful life lessons, you may find a good fit as a city police officer on the beat, riot control specialist, judge, attorney, coroner, clerk of the court, or forensic scientist. Among the many clients I've had the pleasure of working with are Scorpios in varying careers in the medical professions, ranging from dentistry to research science and surgery. Certain Scorpios prefer high-stakes games such as gambling, and select a risk-taking career as an astronaut, member of the military, stunt double, or race car driver. You are very loyal to caregivers who have aided you and your family in the past. Likewise, you are true to your friends and relatives who think the world of you and show love and affection in good times and bad.

Blind Spots and Blockages

With a fixed sign as your inner driver, you don't easily let go of attitudes, behaviors, or feelings that sometimes keep you from enjoying life. Obsessive behavior is one of your sore spots, and no one should press you to do something you dislike. You do believe that all meaningful change comes from within, and you prefer to make changes in your own time and space. Pluto is in charge of baggage handling, and when you finally let go of an issue, the purge is going to affect anyone in the path. You're known for shocking individuals with your sudden revelations or declarations. The Scorpio tongue can sting when others suddenly find out that you're a scorekeeper and have been holding a grudge for years. Don't take everything others say at face value without questioning the source or you'll wind up with an ulcer. The worst thing you can do is take action impulsively on something you hear from a not very reliable party. Once you check the facts, you'll be wiping the egg off your face and thinking twice about acting rashly with no proof. Things aren't always what they seem to be. Find soothing ways to work on the stress you bottle up inside you by engaging in meditation, tai chi, yoga, or brisk walks.

Goals and Success

How fortunate you are to have deep insight, the ability to travel between the worlds, and the gift of intuition strongly associated with your water element. What an aid this sixth sense is to helping you do spot-on research, get to the bottom of questionable facts, and coordinate the facts you need to present a case for appropriate action. Set your sights on assignments that give you information into what motivates others. You aren't judging—your role is to understand it and provide solutions to help others cope. With your complex psyche, very little would shock you. You're used to meeting the bad and the beautiful. This year could be one where others share their biggest fears and deepest, darkest secrets with you. One of your goals is to engage in work that gives you passion and keeps your energy high and mentally challenged. Since you're a natural strategist, this might be the ideal year to get involved with politics and vie for a place on the campaign of a leading contender for office. In the aftermath of a couple of especially challenging years, you could be ready to rise up from the ashes like the Phoenix, one of your avatars, by rewarding yourself with an intriguing new career. Since you benefit tremendously from private time to recharge your batteries and heal from within, why not enjoy spiritual satisfaction by finding the perfect fit for your talents?

Scorpio Keywords for 2023
Satisfaction, spiritual rebirth, support

The Year Ahead for Scorpio

Uranus is retrograde in Taurus as the year begins. You have had a lot to think about regarding relationships, and your thoughts are compounded by the recent presence of the last Lunar Eclipse in Taurus shaking up this house in November 2022, whose presence stays relevant until May 5. You won't see the last of these eclipses in Taurus until October 2023, and your sign will host the first Lunar Eclipse of 2023 in your solar first house. A new eclipse sequence begins on April 20 in Aries, with one in its opposite sign of Libra in mid-October. Fasten your seat belts and ride out the impact. Mars in Gemini ends a retrograde period in your solar eighth house on January 12, putting an end to erratic financial fluctuations and helping you implement plans for reducing your debt load and identifying ways to save money. Mercury in Capricorn goes direct on January 18 in your solar third house, restoring balance to communication matters including mail service and meeting schedules. Pluto in Capricorn continues to wander through this house until March 23, when it transitions into Aquarius for several months and then cycles back to complete the Capricorn transit.

Jupiter, the planet of expansion, has moved into Aries and your solar sixth house of daily routines, health, workmates, and conditions, sending positive vibes your way as you consider hiring more employees to cover the increase in project work. Transiting Saturn in Aquarius finishes its two-and-a-half-year tour of duty in your solar fourth house of home and family, where you have been dealing with situations related to your household maintenance and relationship dynamics in the home. On March 7, the planet of restraints moves into your solar fifth house in Pisces, where it influences your choices for recreation, romance, and interacting with children.

Jupiter

Although Pisces was the main player in Jupiter's activity in 2022 in your solar fifth house, adding a little spice to adventure, dating, children's interests, and vacations, you had a preview of what life would look like when the planet of expansion occupied Aries and your solar sixth house of health, work, and daily environment for a long teaser stretch that whetted your appetite for more recognition in 2023. Jupiter is in Aries as the year begins. The sixth house is often the hub of activity where you explore the demands of the workload, assess goals, assign staff to do the work, and examine the strengths of employee performance. You can improve your health, too, by changing eating habits, adding targeted exercise, managing weight, scheduling doctor visits and routine tests, and adding playtime to your busy week to unwind and free your mind of pressing worries. When Jupiter begins its rapid trip through Taurus and your solar seventh house of close personal and professional relationships on May 16, it pauses for a few months by going retrograde on September 4 and turning direct on December 30. The planet of opportunity occupies your solar seventh house for seven months in 2023. Some members of this sign may be planning a wedding or forming a lucrative professional partnership. Scorpios born between October and November 9 see the most action while Jupiter is in Taurus.

Saturn

By hanging out since December 2020 in your solar fourth house of home, foundation, family, parents, domestic undertakings, relatives residing with you, household projects, real estate matters, and issues that have run their course in your domestic environment, Saturn in Aquarius suggests that discipline has contributed to the changes you desire. Your resolutions led to desirable adaptations in home conditions that make it possible to hand the baton over to compatible Pisces on March 7, when this demanding taskmaster moves into your solar fifth house of children, creativity, entertainment, entrepreneurial ventures, romance, socializing, and vacations. Scorpio, you aren't fond of change, yet you made adjustments in the past year that made sense for your key solar fourth house. While Saturn winds down in Aquarius this year, those of you born between November 14 and 22 will see the most action to modify your domestic goals and wrap up loose ends. Once Saturn moves into Pisces on March 7, Scorpios born between October 23 and November 1 will examine relationships and make decisions about children, participation in sports, and leisure time during the remaining months of 2023. In search of greater satisfaction, risk-takers may decide to open a business or change careers.

Uranus

In 2023 Uranus starts out in retrograde motion and goes direct on January 22 in Taurus, shaking up the energy in your solar seventh house of personal and business partners, consultants, advisors, public enemies, and those connected to the law and medical professions. When a planet like the great disrupter crashes through your solar seventh house, you can count on erratic encounters with partners, the emergence of quirky personalities, disruptive routines and perplexing challenges with them, and sudden mood swings. This pattern has been around you since May 2018. Plans you hoped to finalize may have led to long delays that affected personal or professional matters. If you thought you were going to get engaged or married in 2023, the actual date may have been postponed. Uranus transits trigger unexpected circumstances, changes in attitude, and disruptions to the flow of your schedule, and sometimes bring unanticipated windfalls, such as an engagement ring, a bonus, or a job promotion. You won't want to feel powerless if there is any facet of your love life that is on the fence. You prefer to have control of your domain. Uranus transits change conditions in your outer world, but the real change is the internal shift that affects the inner you. You could shock those who know you well by your sudden responses. This year those of you born between November 6 and 17 experience the most activity from Uranus in the house of relationships.

Neptune

Back in 2011, Neptune arrived in your solar fifth house of children, fun, games, romance, social life, vacations, speculation, and sports, strengthening your psychic abilities and intuitive insight into others' motives. Although you're normally much more secretive, if you can tap into these qualities instead of showing your hard-driven mindset, those who know you will warm up to your newly exposed problem-solving style. Neptune wants you to get in touch with your inner dreams and include more of your insightful gifts in collaborative dealings. Cryptic Neptune captures your soul and encourages you to become smitten with friends, lovers, and traveling companions. You may even snag a new line of work that incorporates spiritual interests and benefits charitable causes. Find that aha moment in your solar plexus that tells you that you have discovered your true purpose. Saturn in Pisces shows up in this same solar fifth house in March to validate your feelings and reframe the way you express responsibility. Scorpios born between November 14 and 21 see the most activity from Neptune this year.

Pluto

Since late January 2008, Pluto, the planet of deep psychology, has been firmly planted in Capricorn and your solar third house, which relates to communication, contracts, education, electronic equipment, learning options, your mental capacity, neighborhood dealings, siblings and cousins, and transportation. During this long passage, you may have uncovered blocks to successful dealings in these areas or recognized that people in your circle are undergoing challenges connected with these themes. The planet of transformation allows hidden elements to surface during the year. Those affiliated with this house may divulge secrets and ask you to maintain confidentiality. No topic is off limits, but what you do with it is. If you experience a buildup of stress, you could put a strain on your mental health and need an outlet to unwind. Release what is blocking your subconscious mind through meditation and yoga. Resolve to manage everyday stresses and meet setbacks with insight and a broad array of solutions. Transform your fears.

Pluto, the change agent, makes a brief entry into Aquarius starting on March 23. It turns retrograde on May 1 in the first degree of Aquarius and returns to Capricorn on June 11 to complete the remaining months of its cycle, which officially ends in November 2024. Scorpios most affected by this Pluto-in-Capricorn windup are those born between November 19 and 22. Scorpios born on October 22 or 23 feel the impact of a brief teaser when Pluto occupies Aquarius from March 23 through June 11. Add new skills to your portfolio that address your preparation to achieve long-range goals and career aspirations. You can expect change this year if your birthday falls on the dates mentioned above, as Pluto helps you to eliminate hidden baggage and aids you in releasing what's been stuck in your head that no longer has a purpose. Notice the warmer tones in relationships.

How Will This Year's Eclipses Affect You?

In 2023 a total of four eclipses occur: two Solar (New Moon) Eclipses and two Lunar (Full Moon) Eclipses, which create intense periods that start to manifest a few months before their actual occurrence. Two of the eclipse signs are changing this year. The first eclipse occurs in your solar sixth house, the second in your solar first house, the third in your solar twelfth house, and the final eclipse in your solar seventh house. Eclipses unfold in cycles involving all twelve signs of the zodiac, and usually occur in pairs about two weeks apart. Don't fear eclipses—think of them as growth opportunities that allow you to release old and outworn patterns. They often stimulate unexpected surprises and windfalls. The

closer an eclipse is to a planet or point in your birth chart, the greater the importance of the eclipse in your life. Those of you born with a planet at the same degree as an eclipse are likely to see a high level of activity in the house where the eclipse occurs.

The first Solar Eclipse of 2023 takes place on April 20 in Aries and your solar sixth house of daily routine, health, nutrition, work environment, colleagues, organizational aptitude, and animal companions. When this eclipse hits, you could be surprised by what you discover regarding the efficiency of work practices, staff interaction, and the commitment to meeting work timelines. Find benefit from listening to helpful feedback, strengthen communications, and discuss critical goals. If challenges emerge, address them immediately to sidestep misunderstandings or avoid inconvenient delays.

Two weeks later, on May 5, the first Lunar Eclipse of the year takes place in Scorpio and your solar first house of action, self-interest, assertiveness, independence, and passion. You'll feel energized and eager to embrace new pathways. Take advantage of personal leads you receive through trusted networks. Embrace newfound optimism with the liberating choices you make while creating successful, change-oriented enterprises.

On October 14 the second Solar Eclipse of 2023 takes place in Libra and your solar twelfth house of introspection, activity behind the scenes, healing your mind and body, mystical moments, psychic impressions, secrets, and recovery. Enjoy some much-deserved quality downtime to reflect on next steps and plan for your future. Take care of any lingering effects of illness you experienced in the recent past, and take care of those in your circle who may be ill. Work on your resume if you are contemplating a job change. Consult quality experts if you need help sorting out key areas of your life.

The year's final eclipse is a Lunar Eclipse on October 28 in Taurus and your solar seventh house of personal and business partners, collaborators, cooperators, roommates, legal or medical professionals, therapists, open enemies, and the public. This eclipse brings opportunities to review the status of relationship issues you examined last fall and note how well targeted decisions aided in healing sore spots that resulted in more loving or compatible relationships. If the year has led to painful breaches in understanding, you may be making plans to opt out of the personal or business relationships.

Scorpio | January

Overall Theme

This month you experience the shift of three retrograde planets that delayed plans in recent months. Energetic Mars in Gemini goes direct in your solar eighth house of financial matters on the 12th, enabling loan repayment. Negotiation resumes when Mercury in Capricorn moves forward on January 18 in your solar third house, and erratic Uranus in Taurus shakes loose in your solar seventh house of partnerships on January 22.

Relationships

At a dinner with your boss on the 8th, you may learn confidential details about organizational changes and your role in the operation. Convey optimism about your work environment. You're hosting family from a distance on the 21st and look forward to entertaining them, feasting on favorite dishes.

Success and Money

If you're shopping for bargains, grab your partner and scoop up items on the 2nd, when stores mark down prices on household goods and holiday dinnerware. A surprise awaits you on the 30th when you learn the size of the upcoming raise that is tied to a recent promotion.

Pitfalls and Potential Problems

The Friday night Cancer Full Moon of January 6 brings surprises when retrograde Mercury opposes it. The party you were supposed to attend is several tables short of accommodating invited guests. Meanwhile, weather conditions force several guests to cancel due to road hazards. Be glad you're not hosting the event. A scheduled staff meeting on the 9th is cut short due to missing information and reports.

Rewarding Days

2, 8, 21, 30

Challenging Days

4, 6, 9, 16

Scorpio | February

Overall Theme

Tension creeps into the organizational arena during the week of the Leo Full Moon on the 5th, giving you a few tight spots to work through with colleagues over creative differences. With the challenging lunar aspects on the 8th, expect a dispute over political differences with a friend to evolve. Help an elderly neighbor with an outdoor chore such as snow or leaf removal.

Relationships

Take a long-distance trip early in the month to visit relatives who have been asking to spend time with you. Bond with siblings who spend a long weekend with you on the 17th and celebrated delayed Valentine's Day plans with you, enjoying a lively time and sharing loving gestures. The February 20th New Moon in Pisces and your solar fifth house rewards you and your partner with private, intimate moments.

Success and Money

Travel bargains net fares you're willing to pay around the 2nd, along with package deals that offer attractive perks. Contracts involving a car or home purchase come through. Sign papers during the weekend of the 17th. Work diligently with coworkers to find qualified candidates to fill newly created positions after February 22.

Pitfalls and Potential Problems

Clarify confusing information for a relative on the 16th, when an exaggerated account of an incident gets out of control. Lunar aspects on the 25th irritate your partner, who could use a supportive message and a compliment to lift spirits. Encourage cooperation to heal hurt feelings.

Rewarding Days
2, 10, 17, 22

Challenging Days
5, 8, 16, 25

Scorpio | March

Overall Theme
When Venus moves into Taurus on the 16th, your solar seventh house comes alive with passion and a desire to please your mate. That magic time starts on March 17, allowing you to exude your sexy charm and loving gestures. Single Scorpios have the perfect opening to mingle at happy hours and parties in search of an eligible partner.

Relationships
Travel on the 2nd, an excellent day to visit parents or invite them to enjoy an outing or a meal or celebrate an important milestone. The romantic vibes of the 24th create the perfect opportunity for a date night with your partner. Ask another couple to join you at a popular musical venue.

Success and Money
You have done your job well and finances are flourishing. Spend some of your cash on upgrading your wardrobe and pampering your body with an updated hairstyle, a manicure, or a massage. Look your best at a job interview during the week of the 19th. Shop for jewelry on the 19th and make an offer on a ring for your loved one.

Pitfalls and Potential Problems
Annoyance creeps in on the 5th over mistakes in your work environment that seem unnecessary if sloppy work had been monitored for quality control. Aspects to the March 7th Virgo Full Moon create tension that affects clear communication and confuses the selection of workable solutions. Listening skills suffer when Mars squares Mercury in Pisces on the 16th.

Rewarding Days
2, 17, 19, 24

Challenging Days
5, 7, 16, 26

Scorpio | April

Overall Theme

Venus in Taurus livens up your solar seventh house of partners, creating romance and joyful moments in your love life. Single Scorpios could meet a future mate. The Aries New Moon on the 20th is the year's first Solar Eclipse, conjunct Jupiter in your solar sixth house, releasing news of imminent changes in your work environment.

Relationships

Siblings visit you around the 12th, sharing food and fun as well as discussing pending family matters involving parents that need attention. Cooperation shines through and you agree to meet with additional relatives around the 15th to put plans in motion. Celebrate with a child whose achievements bring accolades on the 17th.

Success and Money

Jupiter in Aries leads you to the successful purchase of kitchen equipment and appliances when vendors tempt you with sale prices that are hard to pass up. Grab your partner and decide on the model. Good news from lenders arrives the week of the 23rd, allowing you to submit paperwork and pursue a planned purchase.

Pitfalls and Potential Problems

Members of a professional organization argue over differences in priorities on the 3rd and could be looking for a scapegoat, even talking behind your back. Avoid difficult exchanges, especially until after the 6th, when the Full Moon in Libra occurs in your solar twelfth house of secrets. Mercury goes retrograde in Taurus on the 21st, potentially leading to garbled explanations of conditions and poor advice.

Rewarding Days

12, 15, 17, 23

Challenging Days

3, 6, 14, 21

Scorpio | May

Overall Theme

Following the Lunar Eclipse in your sign on May 5, you'll attract the attention of individuals in your circle as well as strangers seeking a place in your world and wanting to know what you offer. Doors open and most paths lead to money and prestige.

Relationships

Children plan a Mother's Day celebration on the 14th that includes family from different generations. Enjoy the rapport. The Taurus New Moon in your solar seventh house on the 19th truly represents a new beginning for either your existing marriage or a wedding if you are headed for the altar. Collaborate with friends on the 28th to finalize upcoming vacation plans for agreeable dates and venues.

Success and Money

Business travel highlights primary activity around the 9th, when new initiatives call for short implementation time and smooth resolution of loose ends. You easily handle complex strategies that boost your earning power. Take advantage of travel bargains and start looking at options for a vacation in July.

Pitfalls and Potential Problems

Pluto turns retrograde on the 1st in Aquarius and your solar third house, coinciding with a need to look closely at contracts related to business projects. Assess funds needed to cover housekeeping items. The Lunar Eclipse of May 5 in Scorpio affects your partnership sector. Discuss vacation plans with your partner.

Rewarding Days

9, 14, 19, 28

Challenging Days

1, 5, 11, 25

Scorpio | June

Overall Theme

Your organizational environment may be in turmoil all month, with the passage of Mars in Leo clashing with your Sun for the duration. By the time Mars lands on the transiting Moon on the 22nd, you'll be ready to engage a mediator to defuse the hostility in the air. Your financial picture feels the sting when the Full Moon on the 3rd in Sagittarius and your solar second house sours spending plans due to a barrage of stressful transits.

Relationships

Interactions with relatives provide pleasant interludes when you get together with siblings for a weeknight social event on the 6th and with children for an enjoyable outing on the 11th. Pamper your partner on the 17th with a leisurely date night that features dining and intimacy.

Success and Money

On the 6th you're able to assist your community by agreeing to reframe existing bylaws that seem outdated for current needs. Jupiter's recent entry into Taurus and your solar seventh house nets a salary increase for your partner that generously acknowledges work accomplishments and supports mutual goals.

Pitfalls and Potential Problems

The June 3rd Full Moon in Sagittarius is volatile. You can't seem to settle differences with siblings and family from the 3rd through the 5th, when unfavorable aspects to your Sun strike a nerve. When Saturn in Pisces makes a retrograde station on the 17th, a romantic prospect may unexpectedly cancel a planned date.

Rewarding Days
6, 11, 15, 28

Challenging Days
3, 17, 22, 26

Scorpio | July

Overall Theme

The Full Moon in Capricorn on July 3 occurs in your solar third house. Instead of traveling over the 4th of July, why not participate in local celebrations and make your gathering simple yet enjoyable? Combine takeout with favorite barbecue choices to keep cleanup at bay, and serve a sparkler cake for the nation's birthday while you watch fireworks from the comfort of your patio.

Relationships

The theme this month is social invitations, especially from the 5th through the 31st. Vacation time looks good after the Cancer New Moon on the 17th. Out-of-state reservations with friends result in surprises and a feeling of finding the "happy place" you've been hoping to discover. Meet a cousin or sibling for lunch on the 31st.

Success and Money

Rapport with personal and business partners exceeds expectations, leading to a discussion about pursuing a new cooperative venture. You'll win points with your boss by taking the lead on preparing a proposal. Praise children for their success in summer sports leagues or activities.

Pitfalls and Potential Problems

The 19th is testy and not a good day to meet with your boss to discuss a money issue. When Venus goes retrograde in your solar tenth house on the 22nd, you discover a funding issue with an important project that is temporarily tabled. On the 21st, too many members of a professional group are no-shows, forcing cancellation of a vote on project viability.

Rewarding Days

7, 11, 17, 31

Challenging Days

3, 5, 19, 21

Scorpio | August

Overall Theme

Your best week to schedule a vacation is the week of the 13th, when you and your partner join family or friends for the perfect seashore trip at a location that offers plenty of eating spots and entertainment to please individuals in all age groups. Two Full Moons this month in Aquarius and Pisces, on August 1 and 30, stimulate emotions.

Relationships

Children look forward to a zoo or amusement park visit around the 4th. Older children may prefer museums with a scientific theme. In-laws visit after the 13th and may join you in vacations plans. They'll enjoy historical attractions that shed light on inventions and living conditions.

Success and Money

Many a Scorpio is paying the tuition bill around the 10th, as children head back to college and double-check rooming accommodations. Your knack for solving puzzling problems saves the day in a work setting on the 23rd, and you do it without pointing a finger or showing annoyance. Your boss comments favorably and points you toward job announcements in your company's recruiting pipeline.

Pitfalls and Potential Problems

Don't start travel on the 1st, when the Aquarius Full Moon clashes with Jupiter and Uranus in Taurus, your opposite sign. Start no new projects nor travel when Mercury in Virgo goes retrograde on the 23rd and disrupts plans. Uranus in Taurus shakes up the status quo starting on the 28th, moving retrograde until January 2024.

Rewarding Days

4, 13, 18, 27

Challenging Days

1, 3, 10, 28

Scorpio | September

Overall Theme

Planetary stations this month facilitate implementation of goals. First Venus in Leo goes direct on the 3rd, giving your solar tenth house financial support for new initiatives. Then your well-developed sixth sense is powerfully activated on the 15th after Mercury goes direct in Virgo. Act on your hunches regarding a friend's request.

Relationships

Romance your partner on the 20th, when positive planetary aspects increase vibrations of love. Follow through with the promise of a mini vacation on the 14th that includes your partner and children for a wilderness adventure. Connect with a sibling or favorite cousin, especially on the 23rd, when you might be hosting a sports weekend with your children, and show support for favorite teams.

Success and Money

A tip from a friend leads to a membership in a highly regarded professional group whose humanitarian causes interest you. The initial entry leads to a whole new network of like-minded people whose passion for going the extra mile matches yours. Share ideas and strategies for their game changing opportunities.

Pitfalls and Potential Problems

Expansive Jupiter goes retrograde in Taurus on the 4th. Don't take the bait on the 7th on a too-good-to-be-true investment spiel that promises an astronomical return on your dollar. The Aries Full Moon in your solar sixth house on the 29th makes you sensitive to the undercurrent in your workplace. Ask the right questions, and the answers you seek will pay off within a few days.

Rewarding Days

9, 14, 20, 23

Challenging Days

4, 7, 12, 29

Scorpio | October

Overall Theme

When Venus in Virgo enters your solar eleventh house on the 8th, the pace of your social life picks up steam and invitations abound. Enjoy the rapport and fun with friends by joining them for tasty meals at your favorite eateries or in their homes. Include fall themes when entertaining in your home.

Relationships

Acknowledge meaningful relationships that influence your life this month. Financial experts lead the pack, friends and professional associates sing your praises, and neighbors are in your corner for the insightful way you manage neighborhood problems. Joy in your children's accomplishments gives you proud moments, especially on the 24th, when a school award changes a child's future.

Success and Money

On the 11th, celebrate your generous raise with loyal friends who acknowledge your outstanding performance. The Solar Eclipse on October 14 in Libra and your solar twelfth house of privacy gives you more time to produce innovative products and select a launch date for a high-content project. Share insight with your team on the 21st.

Pitfalls and Potential Problems

After being retrograde since May 1, Pluto in Capricorn turns direct on the 10th in your solar third house. You're ready to unload exhausting mental baggage. Let it go before the final Lunar Eclipse of 2023 on October 28 in Taurus, especially if your partnership house has been tension-filled. Monitor financial dealings on the 18th by checking numbers carefully.

Rewarding Days
4, 8, 21, 24

Challenging Days
1, 7, 18, 23

Scorpio | November

Overall Theme

A short business trip could be on tap for you around November 2–3, when you evaluate progress on new initiatives. Those of you born between November 12 and 14 benefit most from the Scorpio New Moon on the 13th. If you're hosting Thanksgiving dinner, send invitations early to all guests to make sure they can RSVP on time.

Relationships

If you love to entertain at home, decide whether you need help preparing courses and ask accomplished cooks to help you. Out-of-town guests begin to arrive around the 17th. A sibling agrees to prepare desserts and offers options. Show gratitude to the worker bees who help you. Invite a couple of work colleagues to join you.

Success and Money

Saturn in Pisces moves direct in your solar fifth house on the 4th, clearing space for single Scorpios to meet or get to know attractive potential partners. Use bonus money to start holiday shopping. Work with community organizers to provide a delicious Thanksgiving feast for those in need. Round up committed volunteers.

Pitfalls and Potential Problems

Both Mercury and Mars are conjunct in your sign and oppose Uranus in Taurus though the 11th, a potentially exhausting scenario that is known to serve up unanticipated problems. Keep your calendar light. The Gemini Full Moon on the 27th in your solar eighth house suggests you confer with your partner before purchasing expensive gifts. Use cashback points and credit rewards.

Rewarding Days

2, 13, 17, 22

Challenging Days

11, 23, 25, 27

Scorpio | December

Overall Theme

Take the time to complete your holiday shopping early in the month and get packages and greeting cards ready for mailing. Find discount deals online and take advantage of free gift-wrapping and shipping options. Satisfy friends with a sweet tooth by sending treats that include baked goods, candy, and fruit ensembles.

Relationships

Friends, siblings, children, lovers, and partners ultimately benefit from December's endearing theme of love and togetherness. Transiting Venus in Scorpio in your solar first house through the 29th provides options to bond with your partner and children. Enjoy seasonal entertainment on the 18th and 22nd.

Success and Money

You work with others committed to embracing the spirit of the season on the 5th to generously support your favorite charity. Saturn in Pisces transiting your solar fifth house brings recognition for entrepreneurial achievement and a substantial bonus for your efforts. Spend some of it on a gift for your partner to express the love that shines in your heart.

Pitfalls and Potential Problems

When Neptune in Pisces goes direct on December 6 in your solar fifth house, you may discover that someone you've been dating has not been truthful about key information. Mercury goes retrograde in Capricorn on December 13 in your solar third house right after the December 12th Sagittarius New Moon. Local travel and plans are subject to delays. Jupiter in Taurus resumes direct motion in your solar seventh house on December 30, aiding you in launching new goals in 2024.

Rewarding Days

5, 14, 18, 22

Challenging Days

6, 8, 13, 16

Scorpio Action Table

These dates reflect the best—but not the only—times for success and ease in these activities, according to your Sun sign.

	JAN	FEB	MAR	APR	MAY	JUN	JUL	AUG	SEP	OCT	NOV	DEC
Move			2		9			13			2	
Romance	2		17	23		15						22
Seek counseling/coaching		17			28		31		23		22	
Ask for a raise										21		
Vacation		2		17		11	17		9			18
Get a loan	30							27		4		

Sagittarius

The Archer
November 22 to December 21

↗

Element: Fire

Quality: Mutable

Polarity: Yang/masculine

Planetary Ruler: Jupiter

Meditation: I can take time to explore my soul

Gemstone: Turquoise

Power Stones: Lapis lazuli, azurite, sodalite

Key Phrase: I understand

Glyph: Archer's arrow

Anatomy: Hips, thighs, sciatic nerve

Colors: Royal blue, purple

Animals: Fleet-footed animals

Myths/Legends: Athena, Chiron

House: Ninth

Opposite Sign: Gemini

Flower: Narcissus

Keyword: Optimism

The Sagittarius Personality

Strengths, Talents, and the Creative Spark

No sign has a better handle on absorbing different ways of thinking than you, Sagittarius. You challenge yourself to live for long stretches among those with unfamiliar customs or vistas, determined to understand what drives people from other cultures and hear their life stories. You most definitely like to expand your borders, and many of you live far from your place of birth for long periods of time. It's not unusual for you to be gone for decades and then return in later years to the location of your birth. Jupiter rules your sign, attracting you to travel and ventures that broaden your life experience. Sagittarius is known as the sign of the Archer, with the symbol of the Centaur, a mutable fire member of the zodiac and ruler of the solar ninth house of the higher mind, religion, spirituality, the clergy, advanced education, law, publishing, in-laws, foreigners, and travel to distant places. With expansive Jupiter in charge, you enjoy the lead role of educating yourself and others in life's potential by exploring new mental concepts, discovering the mysteries of nature, acquiring multiple degrees, and appreciating the many choices available to you.

You are ever a truth seeker honoring the mission to expand your consciousness and discover a deeper passion for life. When considering a career choice, you may be captivated by the entire legal system, including criminal and civil courts, civil rights, and judges who hand down decisions. No wonder you like to ask probing questions. More than likely you studied more than one language and usually prepare for foreign travel by taking a crash course in the language spoken in the country you're visiting to be able to communicate and understand important customs of the region. You prefer rich colors like dark blues, browns, purples, and deeper green shades. You honor the mission to expand your consciousness. Most of you can be very straightforward and freely express your opinion, often shocking others in your circle with your blunt remarks.

Intimacy and Personal Relationships

You study the people you meet to get a handle on what makes them unique. They ultimately enjoy your sense of humor and conversational wit when you share stories of your adventures. Associates describe you as popular with friends, coworkers, and most people who cross your path. You collect more than your share of friends and prefer to have one of them tag along with you on a trip or to a seminar. A prerequisite is that you can share your inner feelings with them, and they know that they can count on you for support in a pinch. You believe deep friendship precedes a love relationship, and until you find it, you delay committing to an individual who might attract you. Sometimes you enjoy playing the field and often marry later in life. When you marry young, the relationship often falls apart, and the duality of your sign brings multiple marriages. You are often attracted to Gemini, your opposite sign, who appreciates your passion, playfulness, and sense of adventure. The two other air signs, Libra and Aquarius, make excellent matches and could start out as best friends. You have chemistry with Aries and Leo, too, who are seldom boring. You'll probably struggle with Pisces and Virgo, who prefer scheduled interactions and no guesswork. You make sure your children receive a fine education and encourage them to participate in creative or sports-related extracurricular activities. If you're in the market for a new love this year, book an enjoyable trip.

Values and Resources

You're on the lookout for a career that includes travel and a variety of training opportunities that suit your versatile nature. Education is your jam, and even if your profession isn't teaching, people learn from you. You've been called a perpetual student and rarely let a year go by without enrolling in a fascinating learning opportunity. Staying chained to a desk or interacting in the same daily environment bores your restless spirit. An attractive option is one that gives you maximum autonomy to perform your unique skills creatively. Sagittarians either adhere to strong formal religious practices or embrace a holistic, metaphysical philosophy that matches their spiritual outlook. You admire those with a generous spirit and value their loyalty, displaying enthusiasm and showing adaptability when circumstances change considerably. You treasure close friendships with individuals you rarely see but whose bonds are long-lasting, and rekindle their fire in a moment's notice.

Blind Spots and Blockages

Reminders about managing your responsibilities push your buttons and sour your attitude toward your job. The concept conjures up an image of the boss looking over your shoulder and prodding you to get moving on finishing assignments, something that shatters your spirit and translates to a vote of no confidence. You have plenty going on in your head yet often fail to keep a visible timeline that shows what has been accomplished. Tasks fall between the cracks until you discover there's a missing link that has to be adapted to cohesively fit into the assignment. You also have a tendency to run late for meetings, appointments, and dinner dates, much to the consternation of those you keep waiting. At times, excessive talking distracts you and annoys your boss, especially if you are delivering a presentation and keep going off topic, running out of time to present information that should have been shared.

Goals and Success

Those of you with excellent writing skills present ideas and successfully mold the opinion of readers by formally publishing books, articles, guides, and pamphlets that show the way you have mastered the intent of the solar ninth house: to educate and influence thinking patterns. Now more than ever it's time to show others the way. With a wealth of information flowing from the impact of COVID-19, you have abundant material ready to be told to engage interested parties. If the pandemic affected your career path in any way, as it did for many in 2022, think about using one of your related skills like broadcasting to air public service announcements, narrate documentaries, or run community meetings. The way business is done may change drastically and call for social and workplace change, a passionate interest of yours that you could tackle especially if you have a competent assistant available to keep you on track.

Sagittarius Keywords for 2023
Venture, vision, voyage

The Year Ahead for Sagittarius

In 2023 two eclipses occur in fixed signs, Scorpio in the spring and Taurus at the end of October. A new eclipse sequence begins on April 20 in Aries, with one in its opposite sign of Libra in mid-October. Find your sense of humor before venturing full steam ahead to pursue pressing issues that are waiting for you. Mars in Gemini ends a retrograde period in your solar seventh house on January 12, putting an end to impulsive action regarding relationship goals that affect personal and business partnerships. Mercury in Capricorn goes direct on January 18 in your solar second house, ending delays around receiving your paycheck on time and engaging in developmental opportunities. Pluto in Capricorn in late degrees occupies this same solar second house until March 23, when it transitions into Aquarius for several months.

You let out a sigh of relief when Uranus in Taurus in your solar sixth house turns direct on January 22, clearing a path for exploring new opportunities in your work environment, improving your health, and organizing your daily environment to operate more efficiently. For the first part of the year, Jupiter, the planet of expansion, is in Aries and your solar fifth house of children, entertainment, recreation, romance, sports, and risk-taking, planting seeds in your active mind to consider independent contracting while the dust settles in the employment arena. On March 7, transiting Saturn in Aquarius finishes its two-and-a-half-year tour of duty in your solar third house, where you dealt with communication issues that affected education, community affairs, local travel, interaction with relatives, and electronic systems. The planet of restriction then moves into Pisces and your solar fourth house, where you'll examine domestic matters with household members, parents, and anyone else who lives with you.

Jupiter

For the first part of 2023, Jupiter occupies Aries and zooms through the solar fifth house of children, amusements, entrepreneurial ventures, recreation, risk-taking, romance, sports, and vacations. Jupiter affects every degree of Sagittarius through May 16, when it moves into Taurus and your solar sixth house, the environment where you use your blood, sweat, and tears to accomplish assignments, improve your health, prepare nutritious meals, collaborate with workmates, care for animal companions, and organize your work space and plans. What contributions are you making to improve conditions for humanity as you clean up the post-coronavirus environment? Did you add credentials to your skills portfolio? You have options for making the environment healthier and more efficient. If you want to make a job change, expand your circle of influence through professional memberships, neighborhood associations, clubs, peer groups, and volunteer services. When Jupiter begins its rapid trip through Taurus, it pauses for a few months by going retrograde on September 4 and turning direct on December 30. Those of you born between November 22 and December 9 see the most action while Jupiter is in Taurus.

Saturn

At the beginning of 2023, the planet of restriction continues its intense journey in Aquarius and your solar third house of advertising, communication, contracting, education, electronics, mental outlook, community and neighborhood activity, transportation (including vehicles), machinery, and relationships with cousins, siblings, and neighbors. Saturn insists on added discipline to follow through on agreements you forged that are ready for action and commitments that are going to bring you increased responsibilities as a result of higher demand for your services. Analytical positions emerge, giving you attractive choices. Those of you born between December 14 and 21 see the most action while Saturn wraps up its cycle in Aquarius. Authorities in charge notice your skillful application of processes that added value to each project phase.

Saturn moves into Pisces on March 7 in your solar fourth house of domestic matters, home, family, parents, home-improvement projects, and the daily life of residents in your home. Be prepared to adjust routines and lay down new expectations for household members. While Saturn is in this house, you'll be pushed hard to adapt to health conditions or a changing outlook for family members. You could also decide to start a home-based business to fulfill a long-held dream. If you write, you may possibly take on freelance assignments but will do this successfully only if you apply strong discipline to meeting timelines. During the remaining nine months of 2023, Saturn most affects those of you born between November 22 and December 1. You'll welcome the chance to create a new product, assess the strength of your skills, and take a mental health break via a vacation before launching a new enterprise. Share goals with those who support your vision.

Uranus

If you were born with natal planets in Taurus, you may have noticed how they clash with your unhurried style, especially while Uranus in Taurus has been in residence in your solar sixth house of daily routines, fitness, health, healing, nutrition, organizational style, animal companions, coworkers, and approach to work since May 2018. How have you dealt with the signature chaotic antics of Uranus? The delays in matters related to your solar sixth house will soon be behind you. You will have one more Taurus eclipse here on October 28, which could play out through spring of 2024. It could open your eyes to new possibilities that stimulate your spirit. What if multiple offers surface for you? If you were born between December 7 and 17, the planet of wild rides and disruption has the greatest impact on your brilliant mind and complicated routines. The year starts out with Uranus in retrograde motion, going direct on January 22 and shaking up the energy in your work and health-oriented solar sixth house. No doubt you will experience a few unanticipated quirks or puzzling challenges that will influence your decision to scope out new work opportunities. The unpredictable planet will move into retrograde motion on August 28 in Taurus and go direct on January 27, 2024. Stay calm as the predictable Uranian blasts shake up your work world by showing your light side to authorities and employees who appreciate your unrelenting charm.

Neptune

Enjoy a spiritual interlude when Neptune in Pisces stimulates action in 2023 in your solar fourth house of domestic matters, home, family, parents, home-improvement projects, and the daily life of those who live with you. Reflect on what you've experienced with this complex yet inspiring energy since April 2011. Realize that glamorous Neptune has been getting in the way of your abstract mind, and that has created a significant amount of daydreaming time you've allocated to spend on these reveries. Be a good listener this year and show compassion, a Neptune trait that is essential to healing family ties and stimulating teamwork in accomplishing mutual goals.

Saturn in Pisces shows up in this same solar fourth house in March to help you validate your feelings and reframe the way you take responsibility, maybe now through healing hearts, minds, and attitudes. Learn to trust your instincts as you work with Saturn in Pisces to find a meaningful strategy for bringing important focus to family interests. Manifest ongoing humor to keep others from sinking into an abyss of sadness when they hear about the death or illness of contacts. Work with loved ones when learning of new anxieties and share information on emerging treatments and procedures that could be helpful to all. Keep an eye on drinkers or those who take medications to make sure dosages are effective. Let Neptune help you get ahead by putting you in touch with dreams for your family as you use your astute mind to restore unity in the home. Use your psychic gifts that give you a nudge until you get that strong gut feeling. Voilà! Discover your true purpose with your family.

Sagittarians born between December 14 and 21 see the most activity from Neptune this year. Use your abundant healing energy.

Pluto

Pluto in Capricorn first appeared in 2008 in your solar second house of assets, income, money you earn and how you spend it, what you value, and self-development interests. Pluto is winding up this long passage and directs you to address old issues you've held on to in this important house, making sure you are clear about your intentions and have let go of fears regarding earning power and personal advancement. Move toward release by examining any baggage still affecting your financial security needs, and let the Pluto-driven karma cleaners dispose of any anxiety. Address any remaining aggravations. Pluto creates intensity in financial relationships that show up as power struggles and may lead to unpleasant confrontations. What's it like for you this year? Let go of painful issues to welcome regeneration of your attitude toward money. Pluto is visiting the final degrees of Capricorn in this long transit, which finally wraps up in November 2024. Pluto affects you mildly this year if you're a Sagittarius born between December 18 and 21, the dates most affected by this transit. Pluto makes a brief entry into Aquarius starting on March 23. It turns retrograde on May 1 in the first degree of Aquarius and returns to Capricorn on June 11 to complete the remaining months of its transit, which officially ends in November 2024. Sagittarians born between November 22 and 24 feel the impact of a brief but harmonious teaser when Pluto occupies Aquarius from March 23 through June 11. Start thinking about communication priorities, your mental outlook, neighborhood conditions, and local travel and transportation during this period.

How Will This Year's Eclipses Affect You?

In 2023 a total of four eclipses occur: two Solar (New Moon) Eclipses and two Lunar (Full Moon) Eclipses, which create intense periods that start to manifest a few months before their actual occurrence. Two of the eclipse signs are changing this year. The first eclipse occurs in your solar fifth house, the second in your solar twelfth house, the third in your solar eleventh house, and the final eclipse in your solar sixth house. Eclipses unfold in cycles involving all twelve signs of the zodiac, and usually occur in pairs about two weeks apart. Don't fear eclipses—think of them as growth opportunities that allow you to release old and outworn patterns. They often stimulate unexpected surprises and wind-falls. The closer an eclipse is to a planet or point in your birth chart, the greater the importance of the eclipse in your life. Those of you born with a planet at the same degree as an eclipse are likely to see a high level of activity in the house where the eclipse occurs.

The first Solar Eclipse of 2023 takes place on April 20 in Aries and your solar fifth house of children, amusements, romance, sports, speculation, and vacations. Expect pressure from any pending relationship matters to come up, and take the time to examine what you can do to solve problems. Strengthen bonds and work on mutual goals. If surprises hit, discuss workable solutions and call a truce. Hire qualified consultants if you need help managing critical relationships.

Two weeks later, on May 5, the first Lunar Eclipse of the year takes place in Scorpio and your solar twelfth house of recovery, healing, hospital visiting, metaphysics, enemies, psychic insight, secrets, and charities. Working in seclusion prepares you for emerging projects that may include significant writing goals. You like to dig deep to uncover good material that solves mysteries, features human interest stories, or perhaps shows how others worked through the pandemic, kept their jobs, and improved their health during this world-changing phenomenon.

On October 14 the second Solar Eclipse of 2023 takes place in Libra and your solar eleventh house of associations, friends, goals, groups, and humanitarian interests. If you have planets in the eleventh house in your birth chart, the pressure is on you to keep goals on track, monitor funds, take on initiatives that reflect your personal philosophy, and balance your work with festivities that complement these themes. You'll gain insight into special people and have opportunities to strengthen networks. Enjoy the harmony that accompanies doing work you enjoy.

The year's final eclipse is a Lunar Eclipse on October 28 in Taurus and your solar sixth house of daily routines, fitness, health, nutrition, and teamwork. The intensity of this eclipse could bring a heavier workload your way, when authority figures assign you to tasks that maximize your talent in communicating, problem-solving, and collaborating with teammates. When you take a day off, you'll benefit from scheduling medical and dental checkups. Although you're tired of the unexpected jolts that interfere with your plans because of the presence of Uranus in Taurus in this house, you can be very proud of what you accomplished in trying times. Maintain a cheerful mindset as you celebrate success.

⤳ Sagittarius | January ⤳

Overall Theme

Mars in Gemini goes direct in your solar seventh house on the 12th, acknowledging front-burner partnership matters that have no steam. Give them a nudge to implement plans after January 18, when Mercury goes direct in Capricorn in your cash-infused solar second house that funds your anticipated winter getaway.

Relationships

January is the perfect month to renew love and bond with your partner, immediate family, and siblings. It's date night for you and your honey on the 3rd. Invite siblings for a home-cooked meal and games on the 21st, and save the 24th for an early movie and dinner with your partner and children. Treat visiting in-laws to a night at the theater on the 8th.

Success and Money

Wait until after the January New Moon in Aquarius on the 21st to pay off credit cards with a generous holiday bonus. Your solar third house shows an increase in local travel and participation in a weekly seminar that offers timely self-help tips to give your personal style a lift in the new year. Complete a project proposal after the 22nd, when Uranus in Taurus goes direct.

Pitfalls and Potential Problems

Hang on to your wallet on the January 6th Full Moon in Cancer to avoid overspending on items that are subject to further price clearances. Watch weather conditions on the 9th, when an ice storm could delay the start of business or pleasure travel. Friends may cancel a planned dinner on the 14th.

Rewarding Days

3, 8, 21, 24

Challenging Days

4, 6, 9, 14

↗ Sagittarius | February ↗

Overall Theme

You could experience more travel than usual when the February 5th Full Moon in Leo occurs in your solar ninth house and creates a few unexpected conditions. Don't leave on that date, since aspects are unpredictable. Instead, put a value on how well you can analyze shaky conditions that plague relationships by expressing comforting words of support.

Relationships

Friends are game for a bit of early Valentine's Day celebrating on the 10th. Find a venue that offers tasty food and entertainment, especially dancing. Invitations come at you rapidly and your social life escalates after the 15th. The 22nd is ideal for accepting a date with someone you admire for a romantic midweek rendezvous.

Success and Money

Financial news pleases you on the 2nd, when you receive attractive proposals for remodeling your family room. Select a favorable start date for this long-desired project. The New Moon in Pisces on the 20th focuses on using salary and bonus increases that mesh with upcoming plans. Select materials and purchase them through your contractor for maximum discounts after the 17th.

Pitfalls and Potential Problems

Work-related tension leads to uncertainty on the 7th over differences in funding projections and details of the project's cost-benefit analysis. The 8th is no better, when you meet with the work team and find opposing viewpoints on the value and scope of the work. By day's end, discussions move to a sweeter place, netting a vote of confidence.

Rewarding Days

2, 10, 17, 22

Challenging Days

5, 7, 8, 25

Sagittarius | March

Overall Theme

You're getting bored with the monotonous routine of start-up tasks that occur when you take on a new project. Be sure you don't get sidetracked if Uranus in Taurus gets antsy in your solar sixth house of daily routines. Inevitably your boss will hand you extra responsibilities and you'll feel like you're riding a roller coaster.

Relationships

Single Sagittarians get to play the field, finding kindred spirits at happy hours or company functions. Those of you who already have partners and children gather on the 19th with fun, games, and a takeout meal. When the Aries New Moon shows up in your solar fifth house on the 21st, your social sector gets attention with invites to movies, shows, and sporting events.

Success and Money

Jupiter in Aries in your solar fifth house brings quality time to bond with children and participate in their interests. Some of you may give birth. You make connections with entrepreneurial types and consider collaborating on a popular enterprise. Use the cash you set aside to surprise your partner with a mini vacation.

Pitfalls and Potential Problems

Relatives at a distance could cause you concern related to health matters on the 5th. Suggest holding a Zoom call to discuss details. Don't let the Virgo Full Moon on the 7th interfere with meeting plans for your team. Aspects are harsh, so keep the agenda light and agree to assign tasks to discuss at the follow-up meeting.

Rewarding Days

2, 15, 19, 21

Challenging Days

5, 7, 16, 26

Sagittarius | April

Overall Theme

When a fiery Sun, Moon, Mercury, and Jupiter on April 1 resonate with your Sagittarius Sun, expect a few April Fools' jokes from friends. You'll undoubtedly reciprocate. Select a favorite bistro and mingle with a few kindred spirits on this breezy Saturday night to relax over delicious food and drink.

Relationships

Financial advisors come through for you when you seek advice on the 12th and feel strong appreciation for the expertise of astute money managers. Siblings gather on the 15th and talk leads to summer vacation plans and reunions. Agree to poll missing family members for their input. You and your partner share deep feelings and assess new goals on the 23rd.

Success and Money

The very first Solar Eclipse of the year falls in your solar fifth house on the 20th conjoined to Jupiter in Aries, marking an opportune time to look at college options for your senior, gymnastic lessons for your children, and an idea-stimulating seminar for your entrepreneurial pursuits.

Pitfalls and Potential Problems

The April 6th Full Moon in Libra and your solar eleventh house has a disappointing outcome. Without your knowledge, members of a professional group have met separately to weigh in on a humanitarian initiative you thought was a go, and decided to drop it from further action. Mercury in Taurus turns retrograde in your solar sixth house on the 21st, alerting you to a possible change in plans.

Rewarding Days

12, 15, 20, 23

Challenging Days

1, 3, 6, 14

Sagittarius | May

Overall Theme

May's planetary activity could become erratic. The May 5th Lunar Eclipse in Scorpio in your solar twelfth house of behind-the-scenes activity opposes Uranus in Taurus in your solar sixth house of daily routines. Simultaneously, Mercury is retrograde in your solar sixth house until May 14, and Jupiter is moving there on May 16. Be prepared for disclosure of workplace and health secrets.

Relationships

Financial experts provide advice and assistance to your money and estate transactions from the 9th through the 12th. See a doctor and schedule tests to examine a bothersome ailment during the week of May 18. You and your boss enjoy a productive lunch on the 28th, discussing emerging plans to add revenue to the company's assets that includes a new role for you.

Success and Money

Mercury moves direct in Taurus and your solar sixth house on the 14th, followed by Jupiter's entry there on the 16th, making this an excellent time for landing plum assignments and using unique skills as you take the lead in managing critical projects. On the 18th you could be offered a supervisory position to get acclimated for upcoming company expansion. Teammates offer a vote of support.

Pitfalls and Potential Problems

Pluto in early Aquarius goes retrograde on the 1st in your solar third house, possibly leading to the cancellation of a course you planned to take to build technical credentials. Stay neutral on the 25th when visiting relatives squabble over old family history and their stubbornness ends in a stalemate.

Rewarding Days

9, 13, 18, 28

Challenging Days

1, 3, 11, 25

Sagittarius | June

Overall Theme
Get ready for travel to a vacation destination at a location you've never visited with your partner around the New Moon in Gemini on the 18th. Clear some space around the 27th for a few days of impromptu rest and recreation while you hit the local scene for some family fun. Confirm reservation details for upcoming travel.

Relationships
Family members are caught up in summer plans during the week of the 11th and ask you to join them for a few days. You and your partner are ready for adventure on the 16th and may take a side trip in advance of your island vacation. Friends organize a midweek ballgame around the 27th, asking you to play on the team.

Success and Money
You're feeling a little bit richer on the 2nd due to the bonus money you'll receive that reflects excellent performance and teamwork on a highly visible project. You can put that promised bonus toward your pool or other home purchases. Say yes to the catered buffet lunch that honors employee performance at mid-month.

Pitfalls and Potential Problems
The psychic sign of Pisces has high activity this month. Setback-oriented Saturn slips into retrograde motion on the 17th in Pisces, possibly delaying the implementation of plans to install a swimming pool. Contractors hope to do damage control. On the 30th, Neptune in Pisces turns retrograde in your solar fourth house until December 6, creating confusion over relocation plans of resident family members.

Rewarding Days
11, 16, 18, 27

Challenging Days
4, 6, 22, 26

Sagittarius | July

Overall Theme
Consider staying in your local neighborhood over the 4th of July holiday. The lunar aspects do not favor travel and indicate that your best time will be celebrating at home base through July 7. The Capricorn Full Moon on the 3rd is a mixed bag and opposes the Sun and Mercury. Don't hang out with any wet blankets.

Relationships
Family members are grateful for the holiday theme you selected for home-based celebrations from the 1st through the 4th. Invitations from coworkers on the 11th can be a blast. Accept an invitation from a friend to go horseback riding during that week. Excite children with a day of play at a favorite amusement park before the 11th.

Success and Money
The July 17th New Moon in Cancer has a powerful place in your solar eighth house of joint income. The second half of July proves to be a powerful money magnet. By month's end you're looking at a couple of job opportunities compatible with your resourceful resume. Congratulate yourself on reaching sound financial footing after a couple of rough years.

Pitfalls and Potential Problems
On the 22nd, the love planet Venus turns retrograde in Leo and your solar ninth house and sends mixed signals regarding a love interest you met while traveling. While you communicated frequently in the early stages, you haven't been able to connect lately and phone calls go unreturned. Your prospective mate appears to lack interest.

Rewarding Days
7, 11, 17, 31

Challenging Days
3, 5, 19, 22

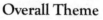 # Sagittarius | August

Overall Theme

Let's see how you handle an overload of lunar activity this month when you experience two Full Moons. The Moon turns full in gregarious Aquarius and your solar third house on August 1. Testing communication assets is not a good move since the Moon receives opposition and inconjunct aspects from multiple planets, resulting in stressful conversations. The second Full Moon occurs in Pisces and your solar fourth house of home on August 30.

Relationships

A older person sends you flowers on the 4th in gratitude for your help on an eldercare initiative. Lovely Venus aspects set a romantic tone on the 13th in your sensual solar eighth house, inspiring you to offer your love partner an elegant meal that reflects an intimate mood. Accept an invitation from your boss to attend a ballgame on the 18th, a day when engaging conversation is a go.

Success and Money

You experience enthusiasm and gratitude at a high level for the meaningful visionary work you've accomplished and the acknowledgment of quality performance from your boss. Your money houses show plentiful resources for you and your partner. When your cousin arrives in town unexpectedly, be sure to alter plans and enjoy the company.

Pitfalls and Potential Problems

You're wise to postpone a personal or local business trip on the 1st due to Mercury in Virgo's opposition with Saturn in Pisces. When Uranus in Taurus goes retrograde on the 28th in your solar sixth house of routines, expect unforeseen problems to disrupt your schedule.

Rewarding Days

4, 13, 18, 24

Challenging Days

1, 3, 10, 28

☓ Sagittarius | September ☓

Overall Theme
Work dominates your activity this month while important planetary stations take place. Pace yourself. Venus in Leo goes direct in your solar ninth house on September 3, clearing the way to pursue studies, business travel, or romance. Jupiter in Taurus turns retrograde in your solar sixth house on the 4th until December 30. Mercury moves direct on the 15th in Virgo and your solar tenth house.

Relationships
The first week of September unites your work team to strategize over details of a critical short-term project. Around the 14th, management calls employees together to make assignments and review the projected timeline. Connect with friends on the 16th for a special dinner to kick off the fundraising initiative for a charity's year-end campaign.

Success and Money
Financial matters progress smoothly this month due to closer monitoring of expenses and reduced loan balances. Discuss information regarding tuition costs for a teen looking to start college next year, sharing the maximum budget you have for funding this expense. The 23rd is a good day to comparison shop for a replacement television.

Pitfalls and Potential Problems
Don't let children talk you into a one-day trip on the 2nd, when your impulsive plans disconnect with a jarring Saturn-Mars aspect. On the Aries Full Moon of the 29th, a child could ask you to purchase another vehicle in exchange for running household errands and maintaining the car's upkeep.

Rewarding Days
8, 14, 16, 23

Challenging Days
2, 7, 17, 29

Sagittarius | October

Overall Theme

When the final Solar Eclipse of 2023 occurs in Libra and your solar eleventh house on October 14, you discover that a friend or professional colleague means much more to you. That's great news if you're single, Sagittarius, but if you're already taken, complications set in immediately. With Mercury moving into this house, you'll have lively conversations and copious social invitations.

Relationships

Intimate relationships bond on the 4th when you and your partner share feelings and gratitude for the strength of your connection. With the Moon and Venus transiting your solar tenth house on the 10th, you'll rave over the harmonious exchange of information, reports, and financial strength that your CEO shares at a meeting.

Success and Money

The final Lunar Eclipse in Taurus and your solar sixth house on the 28th makes you the logical candidate for an important position that opens up this month. Get your resume ready. Contact you made earlier this year proves valuable in both your job and your professional affiliations. Be sure your boss has a copy of the insightful vision paper you developed for a current assignment.

Pitfalls and Potential Problems

When Pluto turns direct in Capricorn on October 10 in your solar second house, you're able to confirm that you have lucrative assets and won't need to tap your home equity to replace furniture. Leave work early on the 18th when testy lunar aspects kick in, exhausting and depleting your energy.

Rewarding Days

4, 10, 14, 24

Challenging Days

1, 7, 18, 23

✗ Sagittarius | November ✗

Overall Theme

Start holiday shopping on the 2nd and don't forget your list. Tackle some purchases online with vendors who offer free gift wrapping and shipping. Write a check for a favorite charity that feeds those without a home to brighten spirits and create memories. The New Moon in Scorpio and your private solar twelfth house on the 13th creates space to write greeting cards and wrap presents for early mailing.

Relationships

Take a dating relationship to the next level if you're a single Sagittarius by setting a place at your Thanksgiving table for your new love interest. Welcome children who live out of town to your holiday feast and surprise any grandchildren with favorite treats. If they arrive by the 22nd, they can help you make desserts. Cherish the hearts and minds of those present.

Success and Money

You score big in the financial department on the 2nd and 17th when you spend set-aside funds on holiday gifts and receive a rebate check from a refinancing transaction. The company owner lauds your efficiency in job performance on the 7th. Enjoy the holiday bonus surprise.

Pitfalls and Potential Problems

Saturn in Pisces turns direct on the 4th in your solar fourth house, redirecting the flow of family activity to meet household goals. Although you may be tempted, leave politics out of Thanksgiving dinner conversations on the 23rd, since the Moon in Aries receives barbs from the opposition of Venus in Libra. Festive music breaks the ice.

Rewarding Days

2, 7, 17, 22

Challenging Days

4, 11, 23, 27

Sagittarius | December

Overall Theme

Let the parties begin with festive events scheduled between the 5th and 7th hosted by your employer and professional groups who extend gratitude for support and service. Wait until the 14th to complete last-minute shopping. You'll be all business until then, clearing away unfinished work and using leave to enjoy a sea voyage once Neptune goes direct in Pisces on the 6th.

Relationships

Buy gifts for the community angel tree and visualize the deserving children who receive them that you meet through charitable institutions. Cherish your favorite people and spend quality time with them. Remember work colleagues with gifts or invitations for meals. Spend quality time with your partner and celebrate optimism in the new year.

Success and Money

Jupiter now transits your solar sixth house, reminding you that your mental acuity and wit lift the team spirits of those committed to the completion of critical work well ahead of schedule. Leaders acknowledge performance excellence in the communication and contracting arena. Set funds aside for investing in savings accounts using your bonus award.

Pitfalls and Potential Problems

Neptune goes direct in Pisces on the 6th in your solar fourth house, clearing away confusion over family members' tentative moving or travel plans. Mercury slides into retrograde motion in Capricorn on the 13th, not an ideal day to purchase systems equipment for a holiday gift. Prosperity-oriented Jupiter goes direct in Taurus on the 30th, looking for a windfall in 2024.

Rewarding Days

6, 7, 14, 30

Challenging Days

3, 8, 13, 26

Sagittarius Action Table

These dates reflect the best—but not the only—times for success and ease in these activities, according to your Sun sign.

	JAN	FEB	MAR	APR	MAY	JUN	JUL	AUG	SEP	OCT	NOV	DEC
Move			21						14			
Romance	3			23		27	17			4	2	
Seek counseling/coaching		10			18			4		10		7
Ask for a raise			2		28			24	8			
Vacation	21					18	11				22	
Get a loan		2		12								14

Capricorn

The Goat
December 21 to January 20

♑

Element: Earth	Glyph: Head of a goat
Quality: Cardinal	Anatomy: Skeleton, knees, skin
Polarity: Yin/feminine	Colors: Black, forest green
Planetary Ruler: Saturn	Animals: Goats, thick-shelled animals
Meditation: I know the strength of my soul	Myths/Legends: Chronos, Vesta, Pan
Gemstone: Garnet	House: Tenth
Power Stones: Peridot, onyx diamond, quartz, black obsidian	Opposite Sign: Cancer
	Flower: Carnation
Key Phrase: I use	Keyword: Ambitious

The Capricorn Personality

Strengths, Talents, and the Creative Spark

Although you may be shy in your youth, you are among the most ambitious astrological signs. Obedient to a fault in your younger years, you're capable of manifesting unbeatable accomplishments that make you the competitive head of the pack once you learn to master the rules and regulations that society and your workplace demand. You're willing to take baby steps to gain knowledge and years of experience in order to build confidence and develop a reputation for achieving your objectives. Capricorn is the sign of the Goat, the third earth sign and the fourth cardinal sign of the zodiac, and the natural occupant of the solar tenth house of career, status in life, ambition, authority and father figures, government, maturity, recognition of achievement, and the path to success. Saturn rules your sign and plays a lead role in attracting you to a variety of challenges in matters of expertise, fame, and influence. Supporters say you are driven by the desire to improve yourself both mentally and physically on your quest to realize goals and dreams. Your sign rules the bones, hair, joints, knees, skeletal system, skin, and teeth. Your colors are black, dark blue, garnet, gray, navy, evergreen, and brown.

Troubleshooting, problem-solving, and upward movement drive your personality. In many cases your employment experience started early, sometimes before you entered your teens. You might have been the kid in your neighborhood selling greeting cards door-to-door in fifth grade because your parents told you to get a job to earn money for school expenses. By the time you got to high school, you may have learned so much about money management that you were capable of taking inventory of goods on hand and making recommendations about what products should be reordered for the business to keep the customers happy. From your first employment experience, you have been drawn to and willing to take on leadership roles as you climb the mountain to success.

Intimacy and Personal Relationships

A quote I wrote for *Llewellyn's Moon Sign Book* years ago seems to mirror your take on the importance you place on close connections: "Each relationship you have with another person reflects the relationship you have with yourself." While it's true that you tend not to be the first in your group to head for the altar, your secret wish is to have a partner who makes you feel emotionally secure. Your friends and companions represent the needs you want to fulfill. You are very loyal toward them and would do anything to help them succeed. Those who know you well appreciate your ironic and subtle humor and ability to laugh at yourself. Although often reserved in showing outward signs of affection in public, you are deeply romantic, with a strong, sexy side that you demonstrate passionately to your partner. Water signs like Scorpio and Pisces make excellent mates, along with Cancer, your opposite sign, who shares your love for a beautiful home and financial security. Taurus is a good fit, too. Children know they are loved and enjoy the special attention you pay to their accomplishments and educational interests.

Values and Resources

Achievement is a driver of your psyche. Responsibility speaks volumes to you, and the more of it you have, the happier you are with your work. With Saturn as the ruler of your solar tenth house, you expect to be recognized for what you accomplish and rewarded appropriately. You keep clippings of news articles, press releases, and transcripts of speeches that showcase your work, and proudly display photos and awards of these career highlights. Whether you're the chief dispatcher in a transportation venue or the commanding officer in a military arm, you thrive on following rules and regulations and expect the same of others who report to you. With a competitive spirit that others notice, your performance and trust win the respect of authority figures, bosses, father figures, law enforcement officers, and government officials. Outstanding relationships with organizational VIPs motivate you to go out of your way to give the company a good name, meet deadlines, and accomplish agreed-upon goals. You also place special value on older people and their needs regarding their status as the institutional memory in the work arena. You frown on evidence of ageism toward older workers and have been known to defend performance when less experienced employees criticize practices. Others laud your commitment to your work and your follow-through to keep others in the loop on projects.

Blind Spots and Blockages

Impatience is one of the criticisms others make of your stern taskmaster persona. They say you run a tight ship when you hold a meeting, and would be more productive if you offered more opportunities for participants to engage in discussions about assignments, productivity, and pitfalls. Employees sometimes complain that you don't share the workload by delegating enough of it so subordinates have better growth opportunities. You have problems with slow pokes who always have excuses for not getting to work on time or meeting deadlines. Although this behavior is annoying, why not talk one-on-one with the individual instead of lecturing to everyone about the source of the slowdown? A bigger problem is in not tolerating the differences in work styles or understanding that not everyone in your work group is a workaholic, a criticism others have of you. Some of you are known to send messages in the middle of the night, elaborating on assignments, which could be perceived as intrusive on another's personal time. Take a breath and wait until morning.

Goals and Success

For ambition-minded Capricorns, the year ahead is tailor-made to stir up your solar tenth house of career and bring opportunities for success and accomplishment. You could be the favorite of your boss, become a new administrator or supervisor, or take on additional family responsibilities. You thrive on setting goals and staying on top of the steps you're taking to achieve them. When work piles up, you are one of the first to pitch in and lend a helping hand, whether you are the boss or the new hire learning the ropes. You enjoy freedom in your work, and few are as adept at multitasking than you. When you have the license to structure your workload, you excel in whatever you undertake. With a micromanager looking over your shoulder, you feel underappreciated. Autonomy gives you that rare air to breathe through problems and create innovative products and solutions. Opportunities for continuous growth and improvement nurture your soul and bring out the magnificent talent you were born with and cherish.

Capricorn Keywords for 2023
Occupation, orderliness, outcome

The Year Ahead for Capricorn

Keep your eye on Uranus in Taurus as it continues to disrupt the status quo in your solar fifth house while retrograde until it turns direct on January 22. Examine this house for signs of significant activity related to children, romance, social life, and travel. By mid-May, Uranus will have the company of Jupiter in Taurus through the end of the year. Your solar first house continues to host transiting Pluto in Capricorn, reminding you to rid yourself of any remaining blocks to freedom that keep you trapped in undesirable patterns. Mercury is here in Capricorn in retrograde motion as the year gets underway and adds perplexing questions to decisions you'll reach after the planet of communication goes direct on January 18. Pluto will make a teaser appearance in Aquarius in your solar second house for a few months starting on March 24. Expect new insights regarding financial matters connected with income, allocations, and lenders.

At the beginning of the year, Saturn in Aquarius occupies your solar second house of income, money you earn, resources, bonuses, and self-development. On March 7 Saturn moves into Pisces and your solar third house of communication, community, electronic equipment, neighbors, siblings, and transportation. While in Aquarius, the planet of restrictions reminds you to release any lingering blind spots that restrict the use of personal income and purchasing power. When Saturn moves into Pisces for its two-and-a-half-year cycle, it will stimulate your intuitive powers and inspire your psychic senses to open up.

Jupiter

The big-hearted planet of prosperity starts out the year in Aries and your solar fourth house of home, family, base of operations, and household conditions. You may be treated to greater harmony at home this year, with healthier relationships and stronger bonds. With Jupiter in this house, you may add rooms, remodel space, or paint the exterior if household projects are in your plans. This planet dropped hints for several months last year alerting you to how conditions might change by adding people to your family or saying goodbye when children leave to do their own thing. Take action now if you have projects you want to accomplish. Get in touch with key people to estimate the costs and time frame for the work. Once Jupiter makes its move into Taurus on May 16, it spends the rest of 2023 in this sign and your solar fifth house of children and their needs, recreation, romance, your social life, sports, teaching, and vacations. Those of you wishing to expand your family may welcome a new baby during 2023 or announce a pregnancy. Expand your entrepreneurial talent as well and grow your circle of contacts. During Jupiter's rapid trip through Taurus, it takes a timeout by going retrograde on September 4 and turns direct on December 30.

This opportunity-driven planet occupies your solar fifth house for seven months this year, finding ways to give you more time for adventure, help you cherish your children and their gifts, and start dating again if you are single. Those of you born between December 22 and January 7 will see the most action from this year's Jupiter in Taurus transit.

Saturn

As you usher in 2023, Saturn, the planet of responsibility and hard work, makes progress in its journey through Aquarius and your solar second house of assets, earned income, compensation for goods and services you provide, commissions, earned income, financial resources, self-development, and people affiliated with banking and lending institutions. Since the end of 2020, Saturn has filled your life with both windfalls and hard lessons that have restricted the flow of cash or prevented easy wins in the money department. You'll be relieved to know that these painful restrictions are moving toward closure in March. Those of you born between January 12 and 20 see the most action as Saturn wraps up its cycle in Aquarius. When Saturn moves into Pisces and your solar third house on March 7, you experience a high degree of activity in your neighborhood and with all things related to communication and networking, local travel, and educational pursuits, interaction with siblings, and matters connected with contracts, equipment, and transportation. In Pisces, Saturn may ease up on fussing over petty details but will expect you to take orderliness seriously as you take a closer look at contractual agreements, availability of talent, timelines, and compatible alliances. Continue to adapt to changing work conditions and the influx of new key people. During the remaining nine months of 2023, Saturn most affects those of you born between December 21 and 30. You'll welcome a chance to be more autonomous in your work, assess work details, take a break to refresh your mind and body, and discuss goals with members of your team.

Uranus

Your solar fifth house of children, amusement, lovers, recreation, social life, sports, and vacations has been subject to a number of demands and disruptions on your time with the transit of Uranus in Taurus here since May 2018. Along with two eclipses in Taurus last year and another occurring in late fall in 2023, this house has been excessively activated, full of surprises related to those in your circle, and disruptive of plans you may have initiated regarding projects, recreational pursuits, spending quality time with children or students, and a pending engagement for single Capricorns. You appreciate security, and Uranus, even in a sign compatible to yours, is likely to deny it. Establishing solid communication links to those connected with this house are a must. Be sure to include it as part of your current plans. Take exercise seriously, add downtime to each day, and ditch your workaholic Capricorn reputation by surprising coworkers with an invitation to lunch. Show your lighter side and pursue humanitarian goals that better serve your current needs. Those of you born between January 5 and 15 experience the most interaction from this year's Uranus transits. After mid-May, Jupiter in Taurus favors increasing harmony and productive outcomes.

Neptune

The charming and slow-traveling planet Neptune continues its long transit through Pisces and your solar third house that began in April 2011. What a year to showcase your quest for a new occupation! Planetary alignments offer favorable conditions for embarking on creative, eye-catching projects, educational pursuits, and venues that compatibly accommodate local travel plans. Your idea of a perfect conference location with harmonious vibes is one near a body of water like a lake or the ocean that features soothing sounds and enhances your focus, taking your intuition up a few levels. With Saturn transiting this same solar third house in Pisces simultaneously, you'll take on increased responsibilities that produce self-help seminars, relaxation routines, and mediation training designed to help others cope with adjustments in routines. Take the time to analyze problematic work conditions. Strengthen communication related to any fractured relationships and clear the air to give yourself a fresh start in 2023. Seek out freelancing assignments while you pursue a new job that interests you. If you write for a living, you have an opportunity to create a deeply spiritual article that may be the vehicle that interests publishers in a book deal. Those of you born late in the Capricorn cycle (between January 12 and 19) have Neptune in Pisces making an easy sextile aspect to your Sun this year.

Pluto

Your solar first house holds Pluto, the only outer planet transiting the sign of Capricorn this year. The first house relates to adaptability, assertiveness, innovation, passion, personality, and self-image. Pluto here gives your mind a thorough workout. This transformative planet has been aiding you in dislodging stuck parts of your psyche ever since it first showed up in your house of individuality in 2008. Perhaps transiting Pluto has helped you identify sources of doubt and people who want to control you and your decisions. The first house is action-oriented, so it's time to get moving and use your perceptive analytical skills. Self-examination will help you see who or what is interfering with your desire for freedom. You dislike waiting, so you may have solved several of the most annoying matters over the last fifteen years. If some of them linger, you can call on the karma-cleaning side of Pluto to identify the missing links. If you are ignoring the obvious, it's possible that will have a huge wake-up moment by the end of 2024.

While in Capricorn, Pluto conjuncts your Sun with pressing challenges if your birthday falls between January 17 and 20 or you have late-degree Capricorn planets in your birth chart. Pluto makes a brief entry into Aquarius starting on March 23. It turns retrograde on May 1 in the first degree of Aquarius and returns to Capricorn on June 11 to complete the remaining months of this transit, which seems endless since it really doesn't end until the full cycle wraps up in November 2024. Capricorns born on December 21 or 22 feel the tension of the brief teaser period of Pluto in Aquarius in your solar second house of assets and money.

How Will This Year's Eclipses Affect You?

In 2023 a total of four eclipses occur: two Solar (New Moon) Eclipses and two Lunar (Full Moon) Eclipses, which create intense periods that start to manifest a few months before their actual occurrence. Two of the eclipse signs are changing this year. The first lands in your solar fourth house, the second in your solar eleventh house, the third in your solar tenth house, and the final eclipse in your solar fifth house. Eclipses unfold in cycles involving all twelve signs of the zodiac, and usually occur in pairs about two weeks apart. Don't fear eclipses—think of them as growth opportunities that allow you to release old and outworn patterns. They often stimulate unexpected surprises and windfalls. The closer an eclipse is to a planet or point in your birth chart, the greater the importance of the eclipse in your life. Those of you born with a planet at the same degree as an eclipse are likely to see a high level of activity in the house where the eclipse occurs.

The first Solar Eclipse of 2023 takes place on April 20 in Aries and your solar fourth house of home, foundation, family, and current conditions related to the structure and temperament at home base. If you have planets in this house in your birth chart, expect revelations related to ongoing themes as you discover insights into those you live with. Assess and strengthen communications, share leisure moments and quality time, and embrace the love principle. Complete work on household projects. Build happiness through enjoyable, harmonious conversations that are tension-free.

Two weeks later, on May 5, the first Lunar Eclipse of the year takes place in Scorpio and your solar eleventh house of friends, groups, associates, goals, plans, and dreams. During this cycle you're able to eliminate unfulfilling membership links that waste your time and leave you exhausted. Search for worthy causes and join a socially conscious group that matches your philosophy and helps others enjoy a meaningful life. Promote examples of how people improve their status quo and how their experience makes a successful difference. Support initiatives that bring unity and cooperation to future generations.

On October 14 the second Solar Eclipse of 2023 takes place in Libra and your solar tenth house of career, authority figures, ambition, achievement, and organizational and related conditions. When an eclipse lands in this house, you'll be reminded to honor commitments or develop new ones. Accountability and responsibility drive your aspiration for being promoted in your work, elevating your status, and increasing earning power. Refine critical goals that lead to greater productivity and establish new work norms that mesh with the shifting work culture. If you are anticipating a career change, enlist the help of an experienced coach.

The year's final eclipse is a Lunar Eclipse on October 28 in Taurus and your solar fifth house of children, amusements, romance, social life, sports, and speculation. Although you may be exhausted from the unanticipated disruptions that interfered with your plans due to the presence of Uranus in Taurus in this house, enjoy new connections coming into your life that bring you greater happiness, enjoyment, and love. Spend worthwhile time and energy on strengthening bonds, finding solutions to problems, and enjoying downtime that includes happy surprises. Taurus is compatible with your sign. For the best outcome, include fun, relaxation, and romance on your stimulating agenda.

Capricorn | January

Overall Theme

While Jupiter in Aries resides in your solar fourth house through May 16, family matters, your home, and household improvements claim the spotlight. Take a look at conditions surrounding older relatives, such as parents, to make sure health matters are under control. Treat younger children to a favorite entertainment venue before they return to school.

Relationships

When you head back to work after the holidays, relationships with coworkers reflect an upbeat tone when a positive attitude demonstrates a can-do spirit on the 3rd. Invite siblings and cousins on the 24th for a lively gathering with dinner and favorite games.

Success and Money

Shop till you drop with generous gift cards to favorite shops for clothing and appliances that made their way to you last month over the holidays. Schedule a restaurant meal with your family on the 21st, when a popular venue has entertainment and post-holiday treats they can all enjoy! Smile when you discover your savings account has a higher balance than expected due to increased interest earnings. Mercury's station to move direct in Capricorn on the 18th paves the way for executing pending financial plans.

Pitfalls and Potential Problems

Mars in Gemini goes direct on the 12th, energizing your delegation style at work and giving you the go-ahead to implement a space reorganization project you had to postpone in October. Table travel until after Uranus in Taurus turns direct on the 22nd. The Cancer Full Moon on the 6th brings out your partner's sensitive feelings and affects yours, too.

Rewarding Days

2, 3, 21, 24

Challenging Days

4, 6, 14, 16

Capricorn | February

Overall Theme

With no retrograde planets to battle this month, use this agreeable period to participate more with personal and business partners and their interests, renew ties with authority figures, and bond with various family members. Make reservations for a romantic date night with your partner and share loving feelings on the 2nd.

Relationships

Venus is in compatible Pisces through the 20th, offering perfect opportunities to bond with your partner, plan a Valentine's Day celebration, or enjoy a weekend getaway to lift your spirits and energize your passion. Jupiter and Mars work in harmony to build rapport among work groups and tackle important projects. Romance looks promising on the 2nd and 22nd.

Success and Money

You're pumped to meet established timelines this month, and the management team notices the effective delivery. Take advantage of your most productive cycle, which occurs around the Pisces New Moon on the 20th. Volunteer to work on tasks with the highest priority. Share your best strategies with your boss around the 22nd and earn more respect for your objectivity.

Pitfalls and Potential Problems

You and your mate bicker over money matters on the Leo Full Moon of the 5th. Overspending is a sore spot. Relatives at a distance could be argumentative on the 7th, a day when you feel tired and not up for an annoying debate. Confirm your reservation before heading to brunch with a friend on the 12th.

Rewarding Days

2, 10, 18, 22

Challenging Days

5, 7, 12, 25

Capricorn | March

Overall Theme
Venus in Taurus lights up your romantic world on the 16th, and socializing with favorite people increases. Your calendar fills up fast, with dates if you're single or with meals, movies, or concert venues with close associates. Spend money on a trendy haircut, a new outfit, and stylish shoes to make a statement.

Relationships
Home is where the heart is, with Venus and Jupiter making strong connections among family members. Friends could visit on the 11th, and if you're unattached, it could be love at first sight with a new acquaintance you meet through one of them. If you're already attached, the 24th works well for intimacy with your partner—strew the rose petals and open a bottle of expensive wine.

Success and Money
The New Moon in Aries and your solar fourth house on the 21st draws attention to home-based decorating changes when you and your partner discuss pending design plans. Finances look favorable to fund your dreams. Meet with contractors for estimates and a start date before Mercury goes retrograde in Taurus on April 21.

Pitfalls and Potential Problems
Be sure to avoid a testy Virgo Full Moon confrontation with a child or mate on March 7. Relentless harping and arguing gets in the way of listening to proposed solutions. Insist on a timeout. Review your position, suggesting options before the 16th, when Mars is at odds with Mercury.

Rewarding Days
6, 11, 19, 24

Challenging Days
5, 7, 16, 21

Capricorn | April

Overall Theme

The April 6th Full Moon in Libra highlights your solar tenth house, bringing attention to career goals, ambition, and critical matters in your employing organization. You'll have to use some of your colossal management skills this month to work on these tasks while you juggle unexpected expenses, challenging household setbacks, and misplaced personal property related to home renovations.

Relationships

Travel and a short getaway are perfect venues for bonding with your partner and other close relatives around the 22nd. Show out-of-towners the beautiful attractions nearby and treat them to local cuisine specialties and music. Accept an invitation from neighbors to a celebratory dinner around the 21st, and enjoy the warmth and congeniality they offer.

Success and Money

The Aries New Moon on the 20th is the year's first Solar Eclipse and conjoins Jupiter in late Aries in your solar fourth house, as details emerge related to ongoing household projects. You could receive a raise or promotion around the 15th. On the 23rd, you're elated by the team's strong rapport on a taxing project that demonstrates the commitment of skilled employees.

Pitfalls and Potential Problems

Check invoice details, contracted work timelines, and materials. Proof-read the contract carefully before signing and insist on periodic inspections of work. Don't release funds incrementally without checking job status. Mercury goes retrograde in Taurus on the 21st, potentially leading to mixed messages, incomplete orders, missing mail, and postponement of plans.

Rewarding Days

15, 17, 20, 23

Challenging Days

3, 6, 8, 21

Capricorn | May

Overall Theme

Personal relationships dominate the landscape this month, with multiple relatives competing for your time. As you examine your workload and household chores that are piling up, decide what you can accommodate and when. Unplanned work initiatives demand your attention as you develop a plan to spread out the tasks among capable experts.

Relationships

Neighbors want your opinion about disruptive activity taking place on your block. Listen but don't pass judgment until you research circumstances. Book a short getaway with your love partner around the 23rd, when your schedules sync and you are ready for relaxing alone time. Mercury turns direct in Taurus on the 14th, clearing a path for checking out summer family vacation venues.

Success and Money

The Taurus New Moon in your solar fifth house on the 19th leads to adjusting recreational plans with a child as a result of new study demands and preparation for important scholastic tests. A scholarship is possible. Spot-on solutions you shared with management pare down the spending costs of an important phase of a contract after May 28.

Pitfalls and Potential Problems

Pluto turns retrograde on the 1st in Aquarius and your solar second house, coinciding with a need to look closely at expenses related to project costs and overruns. The Lunar Eclipse on the 5th in Scorpio puts the kibosh on Friday plans when an upset friend cancels without an explanation. Workplace tension increases on the 31st.

Rewarding Days

9, 14, 18, 23

Challenging Days

5, 11, 25, 31

Capricorn | June

Overall Theme

Throughout June, Mars energizes your solar eighth house in Leo, enticing you with lucrative deals, attractive goods, and dazzling ways to spend your money on luxurious gifts. When Venus joins Mars in Leo on the 5th, ardor flares and romance fills your heart with love and indulgence for your sweetheart.

Relationships

The 11th favors communication with siblings, cousins, and neighbors. Balance the load your wallet can bear if you're asked to spearhead a gathering. Ask those questions about willing participants sharing expenses. Clear your calendar around the 15th to enjoy quality time with your children at outdoor venues, including swimming, horseback riding, and biking.

Success and Money

Jupiter's transit of your solar fifth house in Taurus attracts entrepreneurial opportunities and requests for your resume. Networking around the 2nd exposes you to a variety of professional connections all month. One of them could actively recruit you for a new position. The salary increase offers a sizable cushion, yet your gut tells you to explore details thoroughly. Banking earned bonuses is a sound move. Your boss shows support around the 27th.

Pitfalls and Potential Problems

With Sagittarius on the cusp of your solar twelfth house of healing, you'll need to be vigilant about the dates to avoid surgery or treatment for critical ailments. Avoid the 3rd (Full Moon in Sagittarius), the 17th (when Saturn turns retrograde in Pisces), and the 30th (when Neptune in Pisces stations to move retrograde in Pisces). Protect your femur bones and thighs.

Rewarding Days
2, 5, 11, 27

Challenging Days
1, 3, 17, 30

Capricorn | July

Overall Theme

If your Capricorn birthday falls opposite the Cancer New Moon of July 17 in your solar seventh house, the rest of the year can be exceptionally important for you, since Pluto now occupies the late degrees of Capricorn and affects how you are handling partnership and domestic matters.

Relationships

Invitations pour in from cousins, siblings, and neighbors, especially during the first ten days of the month. By the 12th, you're spending quality time on vacation with your children, lover, mate, or traveling companions. Business partners invite you to dinner mid-month. Family members visit you, and you fondly recall old memories and your childhood home. Be a gracious host.

Success and Money

Money continues to accumulate this month, with the exception of the 5th and 19th, two dates that suggest curbing spending and checking for errors in financial transactions. Your partner is likely to earn a generous bonus, which pays off after the 17th. Your heart swells with pride over your children's accomplishments. Be generous with kudos.

Pitfalls and Potential Problems

For a few days surrounding the 4th of July holiday, be content to downplay celebrations due to disruptive weather changes and erratic emotional behavior from key individuals in your circle. Avoid travel on the 21st. Venus goes retrograde in Leo and your solar eighth house on the 22nd. Be warned and don't invest in a risky venture.

Rewarding Days

7, 12, 17, 31

Challenging Days

5, 19, 21, 22

Capricorn | August

Overall Theme

Your solar second and third houses get busy, with two Full Moons in two different signs this month. You could be deliberating over whether to spring for an expensive vacation or buy a new vehicle. Your family lobbies for a nice getaway when the Aquarius Full Moon shines on the 1st. Can you do both? Take a vote.

Relationships

This month favors bonding with relatives and neighbors. After postponing vacations for the last few years, you're ready to hold a reunion to gather kin together for sun, fun, and hugs while you reminisce and share family news. Make every moment count. The 17th favors romance with your mate.

Success and Money

While crunching numbers on the 9th, you discover extra cash to cover bills and fund travel plans. Pay children's school expenses early before temptation sets in while you're vacationing. Neighbors invite you to participate in a block party on the 4th.

Pitfalls and Potential Problems

When Mercury in Virgo goes retrograde on the 23rd, adapt plans to accommodate delays or travel snafus. The unpredictability of Uranus in Taurus on the 28th flares when the planet turns retrograde and clashes with activities you planned for your children. Stay home on the 25th to rest and recover.

Rewarding Days

9, 13, 17, 18

Challenging Days

1, 10, 25, 28

Capricorn | September

Overall Theme

The New Moon in Virgo on the 14th falls in your solar ninth house, suggesting that you give yourself a short break since Mercury, Jupiter, and Uranus are in compatible earth signs and favor enjoyable routines. When Venus goes direct in Leo on the 3rd in your solar eighth house, you can resume shopping for a good deal on the vehicle you desire.

Relationships

Getting children settled in school or enrolling in a desired class for yourself takes up considerable time from September 4 to the 12th. Distant relatives contact you to set up a fall visit. A work executive hosts a gathering on the 16th and invites you and your partner to dinner. Members of a professional group invite you to join them on the 20th. Be sure to attend, since you are a stakeholder in the direction they are promoting for a humanitarian project.

Success and Money

Networking and making yourself available for business and social events pays off when you hear about new employment opportunities and position turnover in the management ranks of your employing organization. Your dollar goes far when negotiating a fair price for a big-ticket item.

Pitfalls and Potential Problems

Jupiter goes retrograde in Taurus on the 4th, affecting social plans over the holiday weekend. Sign loan documents after Mercury turns direct in Virgo on the 15th to avoid intense haggling over the price. The price of vehicles has increased. Make a firm offer to the dealer.

Rewarding Days

3, 14, 16, 20

Challenging Days

4, 7, 17, 29

Capricorn | October

Overall Theme

Your career takes on new life this month when the Solar Eclipse in Libra occurs in your solar tenth house on the 14th. Could there be a promotion in your future when nods of approval for your work result in greater support from the executive team? Outshine the competition with your strategic insight and problem-solving expertise.

Relationships

Work relationships with peers reveal your compatibility with staff, who laud your organized leadership style during a monthly meeting around the 4th. Expressions of love abound when Venus in Virgo enters your solar ninth house on the 8th. You and your partner schedule a short getaway around the 24th. Schedule a conference call with an ailing family member before you leave.

Success and Money

During a long-distance business trip, colleagues inform you that your name is in the pipeline to become the next division head. While on temporary duty, you receive a performance award from the chief officer who has been working with you remotely in challenging times. You'll know what to do with the generous cash bonus.

Pitfalls and Potential Problems

Pluto in Capricorn turns direct on the 10th in your solar first house, releasing frustration over having to table project plans and adjust goals since April. The final Lunar Eclipse of 2023 occurs on October 28 in Taurus and your unusually active solar fifth house, which also currently holds disruptive Uranus and transiting retrograde Jupiter. Watch for unplanned expenses.

Rewarding Days

4, 8, 14, 24

Challenging Days

1, 7, 18, 23

Capricorn | November

Overall Theme

For a planner like you, Capricorn, your home has to be company-ready to celebrate the holidays, starting with the Thanksgiving feast you're hosting. Wait until Saturn goes direct in Pisces on the 4th before mailing invitations to the holiday dinner. Review your checklist to order food and supplies. Then tackle your gift list for December celebrations.

Relationships

Life is like a box of gourmet chocolates when guests dig in to the variety of treats you offer at one of your famous Thanksgiving dinners. Guests would help, but you usually like to run the show. Invite out-of-town and local guests, who arrive between the 20th and the 23rd. Break the ice around the table by asking guests to recall something they cherish from past Thanksgivings.

Success and Money

Shopping on the 20th produces ideal gift choices for those on your list and a few bargains. Shop online and look for free shipping to tackle the chore. Plan a festive dinner with your partner on the 2nd, visiting a new fine dining establishment. Donate to charities that provide meals for those without a home before the 16th.

Pitfalls and Potential Problems

Mercury and Mars conjunct in Scorpio and your solar eleventh house opposite Uranus in Taurus in your solar fifth house could uncover tension in a romantic relationship with either a child or a friend before November 10. Step in only if asked for help. The planets are restless on Thanksgiving Day. Light calming candles.

Rewarding Days
2, 8, 20, 22

Challenging Days
1, 4, 11, 23

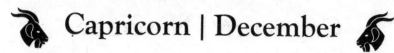

Capricorn | December

Overall Theme

In 2023 one of your most active houses has been your solar fifth, related to children, lovers, and social events. Another high-action house is your solar tenth, making moves to shift career priorities and elevate your life status. Are you ready? Process choices once Neptune in Pisces moves direct on December 6 in your solar third house.

Relationships

Your solar eleventh house of friendships has transiting Venus in Scorpio present almost all month, influencing the volume of invitations that come your way and the possibility of a friendship turning into love if you are unattached. Treat your family to a pre-holiday outing on the 22nd, and help children select gifts for charities to get them engaged in the spirit of giving. Attend a community holiday party on the 18th.

Success and Money

Charities benefit from your generosity on the 12th when the Sagittarius New Moon speaks to your love for humanity as you make generous donations to special causes. Enjoy reading, games, and a quiet night on this New Moon date. An unexpected gift from an old friend touches your heart.

Pitfalls and Potential Problems

When Mercury goes retrograde in Capricorn on the 13th, monitor scheduling changes in travel plans. Verify reservations. Protect money, security, and your feelings on the Cancer Full Moon of December 26. Jupiter in Taurus resumes direct motion in your solar fifth house on December 30 and inspires your intent to accomplish personal goals in 2024.

Rewarding Days

6, 7, 18, 22

Challenging Days

3, 13, 16, 26

Capricorn Action Table

These dates reflect the best—but not the only—times for success and ease in these activities, according to your Sun sign.

	JAN	FEB	MAR	APR	MAY	JUN	JUL	AUG	SEP	OCT	NOV	DEC
Move				20			12		14		8	
Romance	2		11		23			13			2	
Seek counseling/ coaching		22				11				4		
Ask for a raise	21			23		27			16			7
Vacation			24		18		17					6
Get a loan		18						18		24		

Aquarius

The Water Bearer
January 20 to February 18

≋

Element: Air

Quality: Fixed

Polarity: Yang/masculine

Planetary Ruler: Uranus

Meditation: I am a
wellspring of creativity

Gemstone: Amethyst

Power Stones: Aquamarine,
black pearl, chrysocolla

Key Phrase: I know

Glyph: Currents of energy

Anatomy: Ankles, circulatory
system

Colors: Iridescent blues, violet

Animals: Exotic birds

Myths/Legends: Ninhursag,
John the Baptist, Deucalion

House: Eleventh

Opposite Sign: Leo

Flower: Orchid

Keyword: Unconventional

The Aquarius Personality

Strengths, Talents, and the Creative Spark

One of the most intriguing signs of the zodiac is yours, Aquarius, and you enjoy keeping others guessing about who you are and what you're willing to share. You have so many interests that others wonder how you have the time to pursue them, since your conversations about them suggest you have considerable experience in multiple fields—and you often do. No wonder so many of your acquaintances enjoy talking with you and picking your brain to hear your take on politics, social interests, and world events. Yours is the sign of the Water Bearer, an air sign. Aquarius is the last of the four fixed signs of the zodiac and the natural occupant of the solar eleventh house of your employer's resources and your goals, hopes, wishes, motivations, groups, mutual organizations, friendships, new trends, unorthodox methods, humanitarian projects, and sudden revelations or change. Uranus rules your sign and attracts you to a variety of social settings and futuristic insights in your sphere of influence. As one of the most analytical signs, you're a natural problem-solver whose inventive style offers the universe effective discourses and tips for improving environmental, public, and social relationships.

In the work you choose and the talent you wish to display, you live up to the themes connected to the eleventh house, including joining forces with others for mutual gain, spearheading collaborative ventures, and working on shared causes that are multilayered and take time to implement for the greatest good of affected supporters. Expertise you demonstrate in the field of electronic technology improves through your innovative ideas and your problem-solving aptitude, resulting in outstanding operational practices. You represent the prototype of optimism, Aquarius, and excel at social networking. Most of you know an astrologer or two. Your many affiliations give you a feeling of pride and self-worth as you work to perfect conditions for humanity.

Intimacy and Personal Relationships

It's not unusual for you to become so involved in impersonal relations that you devote considerable time to group causes, long campaigns to bring about medical, political, and social change, or support enterprises where others need a helping hand. Personal relationships take a back seat to these urgent demands for your time. Your many interests influence your dating life and lead you to eligible prospects via your well-connected communication networks. Since you are known for being a member of the universal sign for friendship, it takes a very special person to capture your heart. With your independent spirit, you thrive with a partner who likes to talk with you and engage in mind play. You have been known to fall in love with a partner's mind. You'll find the best matches with Leos, your opposite sign, who can be quirky and match your love of the dramatic; the other two fire signs, Aries and Sagittarius, who enjoy gadgets, vehicles, and travel; and air signs Gemini and Libra, who usually match your love of communicating, partying, and intellectual pursuits. Less spontaneous signs like Taurus and Scorpio prefer fixed routines and can be more possessive, disliking having to share your time with members of groups you're assisting. Spend time with a loving partner who loves your creative mind and brings out your deepest romantic emotions.

Values and Resources

A fascination with unique people, organizations, and career choices leads you to experience an eclectic variety of adventures. You deeply enjoy the company of collaborators with inventive minds, ready to forge a new path and leave the stamp of originality on the intellectual properties you so skillfully develop. You like knowing where your next paycheck is coming from and seldom quit a job without obtaining a commitment from a reliable employer. If the work is monotonous and the conditions of career growth are not met, you will bail and move on to greener pastures. You are loyal to your employing organization and are protective of the assets and expenditures of the firm. You're usually willing to relocate for a choice position that makes use of your analytical and project management skills. Assignments in foreign countries appeal to you for the unusual work experiences they provide. Those who know you say you are all business, since you prefer not to divulge details about your personal life. Some of your friends disclose that they have never visited your home. When you do entertain, you leave others talking about the unusual menu and accommodations. Children in your life receive the most creative gifts from you.

Blind Spots and Blockages

Releasing conditions that no longer work in your life does not come easy for you, since you always hope for the best and fail to see the red light that pops up in front of you. At times circumstances you encounter call for a break and a change of scenery, whether it involves work or your personal life. You will leave a job a lot faster than you will a relationship. As independent as you may appear to others, you often stay rooted in difficult working and living arrangements out of fear of failure. When you accept a supposedly plum job that is a poor fit, your ego gets in the way and argues with your rational mind that this is a career coup. The bloom may be off the rose in the love department, but you hang in there until outside interference or a blowup occurs. Even then you may talk yourself out of leaving and have great difficulty saying goodbye permanently. Sometimes you just want to be friends but avoid telling your partner how you really feel. Internalize the meaning of closure.

Goals and Success

After the last few years of disruptions, you're ready to travel a more settled path that offers an innovative work environment, autonomy in managing your daily routine, and options that include exchanging information and technology with experts in other parts of the world. You could be especially effective in businesses that have seen the greatest loss of employees, leaving customers underserved. Exceptionally high numbers of employees sought new jobs in 2022, and that has left entire industries—travel, entertainment, food services including grocers and restaurants, hospitality, manufacturing, medical, retail, teaching, and transportation—devoid of qualified candidates. If you have experience in one of these areas, you'll be able to don your change-agent cap and figure out ways to build confidence in employees, develop and deliver training programs that respond to current industry needs, reorganize or pare down physical work space, and focus on analyzing skill sets to get the best mix of talent into the workforce. Some of you may desire to work in the family business and use your brilliant mind to channel energy into making it highly productive by revamping policies and procedures. Certain Aquarians lean toward starting a new business.

Aquarius Keywords for 2023
Election, exception, extraordinary

The Year Ahead for Aquarius

You'll experience the last visit from Saturn in your sign when the planet of restriction wraps up its two-and-a-half-year visit in your solar first house in March and moves into mystical Pisces. Your bag of tools includes extraordinary coping mechanisms and ideas for staying productive and upbeat. Jupiter starts off the year in Aries, occupying your solar third house of communication, contracts, education, neighborhood events, cousins and siblings, electronics, and transportation. Local travel may increase in this house, which is also the site of the first Solar Eclipse of 2023 that is sure to energize your mind with innovative ideas and the desire to take credential-building courses. Mercury has been retrograde in Capricorn since December 2022 in your solar twelfth house of healing, intuition, introspection, and sabbaticals. The communicator planet turns direct on January 18, opening the door to greater understanding of complex issues and implementation of projects you've had on hold since December.

Uranus stirs the pot in your solar fourth house of home with sudden revelations, shifts in behavior, movement into or out of your home, and a look at your home's physical foundation. The planet of chaos moves direct on January 22, restoring the stability you are seeking in employment arrangements and family relationships. Neptune in Pisces continues to move through your solar second house of assets, income, money you spend, and raises, giving you ideas about how to fulfill goals for self-improvement while simultaneously keeping an eye on managing expenses. Transiting Pluto in Capricorn occupies your solar twelfth house in the remaining years of this long transit, giving you a chance to recover from any health issues, care for others who are ill, deal with private matters, and nurture your dreams for the future. Think about which burdensome, critical issues you look forward to letting go of this year.

Jupiter

Jupiter starts out in Aries and your solar third house in 2023, renewing your passion for straightforward communication, outreach, increased local travel, contract terms, mental acuity, systems equipment, and cousins, neighbors, and siblings. This transit has a calming effect on complex detailed work and gives you a chance to find workable solutions to any post-pandemic issues that remain. Aquarius enjoys fixing problems and cutting the mental cobwebs loose. Change is in the wind, so look for future opportunities because Jupiter leaves Aries on May 16 and begins a rapid trip through Taurus and your solar fourth house, where it highlights your home and family dynamics. You'll have opportunities to demonstrate your excellent analytical skills as you continue to work from home, start a consulting business, or work on a remote assignment. While traveling through Taurus, Jupiter is going to pause for a few months by turning retrograde on September 4 and turning direct on December 30. Innovative accomplishments lead to greater visibility in your field and a raise in salary. Agreeable relationships with family members develop, leaving you content and inspired to continue the quest for meaningful causes. Those of you born between January 20 and February 6 see the most action while Jupiter is in Taurus.

Saturn

This is the final year that Saturn in Aquarius takes up residence in your solar first house of action, appearance, assertiveness, health, individuality, and self-promotion. The taskmaster planet has been creating tension and conflict on both inner and outer levels since the end of December 2020 and won't let up until you understand the source of the constant frustration over the pace of activity in your life. Saturn is one demanding orb and holds you to high standards of conduct when you are tasked with setting and meeting goals. In just a few months you'll be out from under the weight of delays and will be able to smoothly implement plans. Look for ways to strengthen relationships and build your brand if you run a business. Those of you born between February 11 and 18 see the most action while Saturn remains in Aquarius. Weigh personal priorities carefully. Are they in line with your goals and philosophy? Have you assessed the reasons that you feel stuck and how will you disengage from problem areas you've identified? Are you taking care of your health? On March 7, Saturn will move into Pisces for the next two and a half years in your solar second house of assets, income, salary, savings, and self-development plans. These matters affect your career and job status, your desire to move ahead in the work world, and professional relationships that influence long-term employment and retirement plans, including the innovation that gives you the most satisfaction. What is your current priority? While Saturn is in Pisces, Aquarians born between January 21 and 29 will experience the strongest impact from this transit related to earning power. Use the time to review your holdings, monitor your budget, and pay down debt.

Uranus

The year begins with Uranus in Taurus in retrograde motion and going direct on January 22, when it shakes up the energy in your solar fourth house of home, family, parents, base of operations, emotional temperature of residents, household activity, interior and exterior features of your home, and garden or landscaping features. With Uranus in a contentious angle to your Sun sign, you have seen how the disruptive planet affected family relationships, pushed you toward changing design themes for decorating your home, and instigated stricter rules for living in your home. Uranus arrived in Taurus in May 2018 and seemed to spare no one in the home from chaotic behavior, blowups, spontaneous arguments, and one surprise after another that affected stable employment. If you survived a layoff, reduced hours, or site relocation, you got off easy. Secure your home, replace old windows, and fix leaks. Uranus leaves its mark on buildings and grounds. Amid the disruption, you may have received an unexpected job offer or award for the exceptional solutions you suggested that affected the operation of the organization and kept it relevant. This year those of you born between February 4 and 14 feel the most activity from this shock-generating planet.

Neptune

Way back in April 2011, this mystical planet started putting moves on your solar second house, which has been the long-term home for transiting Neptune in Pisces ever since. Your solar second house represents assets, income, money you earn and how you spend it, and developmental opportunities that are qualifications builders. At times during this transit you have experienced unfavorable money deals, and the value of goods you purchased may not have met your expectations. Neptune is associated with compassion, healing, secrets, and psychological health and has the reputation for confusing issues by tossing a few curveballs and doubt your way when you're in the middle of solving decisions related to purchasing power. Anyone who's been there knows that wily vendors use false advertising and unsubstantiated claims about quality and durability of products, and limit the time you have to purchase goods and services. In 2023 review spending and resolve not to spend impulsively. Now Saturn in Pisces is moving into this solar second house, too, and this stern watchdog may help you guard against costly mistakes. Get out of the Neptune fog and see through the glitz. Dream realistic dreams and put an end to constant battles to pay off debt by adhering to your budget. Aquarians born between February 11 and 17 see the most activity from Neptune this year.

Pluto

No doubt you recall when Pluto in Capricorn first came calling in your solar twelfth house in January 2008. That's the year when you started hiding out from the baggage you were amassing in your private, secluded space, figuring no one needed to know about all this angst. In 2023 you'll see that this old pattern is going to be challenged. Pluto, the planet affiliated with psychological depth, arrived in your solar twelfth house of charity, dreams and nightmares, healing, psychic feelings, sabbaticals, secrets, and work done in seclusion years ago. Have you discovered issues associated with these themes that have imposed blocks on you? Eliminate a buildup of stress that affects performance, productivity, the quality of relationships, and how you take care of your health. The position of transiting Pluto in Capricorn creates stress for those of you born between February 15 and 18. Take an inventory of your unsettled worries and issues you procrastinate about to confront your real fear: failure. Ask for help if you're ready to let go of your fears but feel trapped. You hold the cards to engage in a more fulfilling life. Pluto is getting ready to make a brief entry into your sign, Aquarius, starting on March 23. It goes retrograde on May 1 in the first degree of Aquarius and returns to Capricorn on June 11 to complete the remaining months of its cycle, which officially ends in November 2024. Aquarians born on January 20 or 21 will feel a bit of a poke when Pluto moves into your sign on March 24 and occupies your solar first house of action, health, independence, personality, and self-image. You'll have a front seat to see how the transformational planet operates in the most personal arena of your chart. Be proactive about dealing with destructive habits, stubbornness, and excessive secrecy. Share the truth with partners, take the time to shed negative thinking patterns, and use your higher mind to attract a happy, inspirational life.

How Will This Year's Eclipses Affect You?

In 2023 a total of four eclipses occur: two Solar (New Moon) Eclipses and two Lunar (Full Moon) Eclipses, which create intense periods that start to manifest a few months before their actual occurrence. Two of the eclipse signs are changing this year. The first eclipse occurs in your solar third house, the second in your solar tenth house, the third in your solar ninth house, and the final eclipse in your solar fourth house. Eclipses unfold in cycles involving all twelve signs of the zodiac, and usually occur in pairs about two weeks apart. Don't fear eclipses—think of them as growth opportunities that allow you to release old and outworn patterns. They often stimulate unexpected surprises and windfalls. The closer an eclipse is to a planet or point in your birth chart, the greater the importance of the eclipse in your life. Those of you born with a planet at the same degree as an eclipse are likely to see a high level of activity in the house where the eclipse occurs.

The first Solar Eclipse of 2023 takes place on April 20 in Aries and your solar third house of communication, education, your mind, local travel, neighborhood, siblings, and transportation. Expect significant increases in calls and visits from neighbors, siblings, and cousins. Community matters may take on greater importance. Plans may revolve around purchasing a vehicle or educational pursuits. Set priorities related to work schedules and purchasing electronic equipment.

Two weeks later, on May 5, the first Lunar Eclipse of the year takes place in Scorpio and your solar tenth house of authority figures, career, ambition, recognition for achievement, and organizational conditions. If your birthday falls between February 3 and 5, the pressure is on to achieve performance goals and meet timelines while monitoring the quality of work in your area of responsibility. Celebrate success with your work group. Balance delivery of products and reports while maintaining healthy work habits to avoid burnout. Take a periodic day off to recharge, and schedule medical and dental checkups.

On October 14 the second Solar Eclipse of 2023 takes place in Libra and your solar ninth house of the higher mind, advanced education, foreign countries and cultures, in-laws, philosophy, publishing and writing, and long-distance travel. You could experience yet another postponement or cancellation of a cruise, vacation, or pleasure trip. Ride this one out until travel conditions stabilize. Focus instead on exploring a foreign assignment, a relocation offer for a different job, or temporary duty at a distant company location to experience job growth and a shift in responsibilities. Touch base with established networks.

The year's final eclipse is a Lunar Eclipse on October 28 in Taurus and your solar fourth house of home, foundation, family, parents, and your home's physical structure. Adapt an air of confidence and feel energized as you move in new directions, eagerly taking on stimulating projects. Show gratitude for the desirable changes that occurred in family relationships, and encourage loving rapport among family members.

Aquarius | January

Overall Theme
You're ready to get on with plans for 2023 and can't wait until the three retrograde planets shift into direct motion. With Mars in Gemini going direct in your solar fifth house on the 12th, you'll resurrect your social life by planning events with loved ones. On the 18th, Mercury in Capricorn moves forward in your solar twelfth house of seclusion, releasing stalemates. Unpredictable Uranus in Taurus could stir the ire of a family member on January 22.

Relationships
Bonding with visiting family members on the 2nd places high value on love and understanding. Special outings with children occur on the 3rd to extend holiday celebrating at a favorite entertainment venue. You and your partner share intimate moments and a delightful outing on the 8th, with plenty of privacy to talk and exchange information.

Success and Money
The New Moon in Aquarius on the 21st stimulates talks about upward movement in the workplace, with a welcome increase in salary. Gifts from friends and relatives were exceptionally generous during the holiday season. You bank the cash for vacation plans and use the gift cards for purchases and delicious dinners.

Pitfalls and Potential Problems
The Full Moon in Cancer on January 6 brings sniffles and lower energy than usual, indicating you could use extra sleep. Avoid confrontations at the workplace on the 16th, when lunar aspects show the potential for hostility over the spread of unfounded rumors. A meeting chair proves unreliable on the 18th when the agenda changes without notice.

Rewarding Days
2, 3, 8, 24

Challenging Days
6, 9, 16, 18

Aquarius | February

Overall Theme

If you were born on February 5, the Leo Full Moon is conjunct your Sun in your solar seventh house. Why not share a quiet outing with your partner by visiting botanical gardens to get some inspiration for spring planting? Then enjoy an early dinner, run a quick errand, and head home to catch an episode of a favorite TV program.

Relationships

Coworkers hold a birthday celebration for those born in February on the 6th. A long-distance trip on the 10th begins a pleasurable getaway that includes visiting relatives and early Valentine's Day bonding time with your partner. A neighbor calls on you to discuss concerns over a neighborhood safety incident on the 22nd, and you score points in problem-solving over coffee and cake.

Success and Money

The Pisces New Moon on the 20th highlights your solar second house of income and assets. You learn that jewelry you inherited is worth substantially more than you thought and make arrangements to discuss options to keep or sell it with your attorney. Working from home on the 18th gives you a chance to finish a critical paper that is due on the 22nd.

Pitfalls and Potential Problems

An auto show tempts you to preview next year's models to compare features on the 7th. Avoid a random purchase that increases your debt load, throwing you off course of your plan to reduce your budget in 2023. Prices are way too high.

Rewarding Days

6, 10, 18, 22

Challenging Days

5, 7, 12, 25

Aquarius | March

Overall Theme
The Aries New Moon in your solar third house on March 21 gives you ample opportunity to mingle with neighbors at a community event. The energy of the spring equinox on the 20th ushers in the Sun in Aries and has a congenial effect on participants, allowing organizers to enthusiastically receive suggestions for strengthening the spirit and commitment of residents.

Relationships
This month is all about work, when deadlines loom and your team and collaborators from diverse organizations gather to comment on project direction, new initiatives, hiring decisions, and strategies for meeting timelines. You and your colleagues gather on the 11th to dance and dine at a festive venue compliments of your generous boss. Save the 24th for game night with your children.

Success and Money
Venus and Jupiter in Aries and Mars in Gemini complement your plan to purchase electronic media equipment around the 11th. Your name is being tossed around work circles as a prime candidate for an upcoming position vacancy that fits your qualifications and could mean a generous raise.

Pitfalls and Potential Problems
On the March 7th Virgo Full Moon, a child pushes hard for an expensive toy. Use logic to encourage your offspring to contribute a portion of their allowance to the deal if this is something you'll approve. Mars and Mercury clash on the 17th, creating just enough tension to quash plans for a relaxing family outing that includes casual dinner plans.

Rewarding Days
2, 11, 15, 24

Challenging Days
5, 7, 17, 26

Aquarius | April

Overall Theme
The Aries New Moon on the 20th is the year's first Solar Eclipse and conjuncts Jupiter in late Aries in your solar third house, stimulating a growing interest in community affairs, your neighborhood, and landscaping plans.

Relationships
The first half of the month is a bit chaotic for you and your partner while finalizing home project details. Although you planned to travel late in the month, wait until your contractors finish the painting or other work so you have peace of mind. Attend a friend's engagement party around the 23rd.

Success and Money
Shop for new furniture after the 17th, when your raise comes through and your redecorating project is underway. Decide whether to replace existing floors or refinish them. You are leaning toward splurging on a bold new design with a nice touch of class. A mentor fields the announcement of a job lead that has promotion potential during the week of the 23rd.

Pitfalls and Potential Problems
Unexpected expenses emerge related to household matters on the 3rd. Pay for expedited shipment of materials to avoid project delays. The April 6th Full Moon in Libra and your ninth house of distant matters brings news about a relative's health. Good news arrives around the 21st.

Rewarding Days
15, 17, 21, 23

Challenging Days
3, 6, 8, 20

Aquarius | May

Overall Theme

Venus turns on the charm in Gemini and your solar fifth house of romance at the beginning of the month. Take the time to play if you're an eligible Aquarius. Meanwhile, Jupiter in Aries races to the finish line in your solar third house before turning over the baton of growth and prosperity to Taurus on the 16th, where it spends the rest of the year in your solar fourth house.

Relationships

The Lunar Eclipse of May 5 in Scorpio affects your career and advancement sector when opposing Mercury turns direct in Taurus in your solar tenth house on the 14th. Pending offers could mean a move to a new location, not something you're eager to do after recent household renovations. After the 18th, share work news with your family.

Success and Money

During the week of the 13th your boss discusses positions in the development stage, including supervisory ones that come about as the result of reorganizing teams. Stay alert and update your resume in case you're interested. You may find better options than a physical relocation. Money matters look promising after mid-month when Mercury goes direct in Taurus on the 14th.

Pitfalls and Potential Problems

Pluto turns retrograde on the 1st in Aquarius and your solar first house, emphasizing the need to eliminate personal habits and conditions that slow down productivity. What has been keeping you from performing at peak levels? Examine routines that don't work and shed these blocks. Poll colleagues for insight if you're stuck.

Rewarding Days

9, 13, 18, 22

Challenging Days

1, 5, 25, 31

Aquarius | June

Overall Theme
Your solar seventh house of partners has nonstop activity this month with Mars in Leo activating your social life and collaborative ventures. When Venus joins Mars in Leo on the 5th, your love life ignites and passion forces you to take a break and enjoy your lover's arms. Wrap up critical work on the 2nd before taking an enjoyable break.

Relationships
The 17th is a good time to begin a vacation with family. Schedule meaningful bonding time with them that includes their favorite leisure-time attractions. Playful, fun-loving Gemini on the cusp of your solar fifth house makes it easy to leave your work routine behind while you enjoy spontaneity and adventure that complement this welcome change of scenery.

Success and Money
From the 2nd through the 11th, money opportunities abound. A welcome raise hits your paycheck and gives you an extra cushion to cover vacation and household project plans. Your boss shows gratitude for your astute problem-solving skills that led to early project completion.

Pitfalls and Potential Problems
Friends are distracted during a special get-together on the June 3rd Sagittarius Full Moon in your solar eleventh house. Momentum fizzles fast. Saturn goes retrograde in Pisces on the 17th in your solar second house, alerting you to postpone approving large outlays of cash while managing a large household project. On June 30 Neptune goes retrograde in Pisces and your solar second house, prompting you to check the numbers on financial transactions.

Rewarding Days
2, 5, 11, 27

Challenging Days
1, 3, 22, 30

Aquarius | July

Overall Theme

This year's 4th of July holiday has mixed planetary aspects that accompany the Full Moon in Capricorn. If you understand astrology, you'll know why people prefer to stay home this year and pamper guests with delicious treats, fun, and games instead of traveling. Be the hit of the neighborhood by inviting nearby friends and family to a patriotic bash that embraces the American spirit.

Relationships

Family members gather to spend quality time together on the 11th. Steer clear of conflicts with partners or roommates on the 19th. Issues are sensitive and need immediate attention. Friends in high places invite you to a lovely party on the 30th. You meet congenial guests who immediately extend a dinner invitation for the next weekend.

Success and Money

Contracts and financial transactions get the green light around the 7th. The Cancer New Moon on the 17th energizes work teams who elect to pull together to resolve loose ends of a pending project to push for an early completion date. Management begins talking about performance awards to commend outstanding work.

Pitfalls and Potential Problems

Financial matters need a close look on July 21st if you've been contemplating refinancing a mortgage loan, especially if you or your partner experienced a recent job loss. When Venus goes retrograde in Leo on the 22nd, expect to spend the weekend poring over tax and earnings statements. Gather supporting documentation to strengthen approval options.

Rewarding Days

7, 11, 17, 30

Challenging Days

3, 19, 21, 27

Aquarius | August

Overall Theme

Money talks this month. The second Full Moon in August on the 30th in Pisces focuses energy on your solar second house of income and assets, spending, and self-development. Two of the five transiting planets in earth signs, Mercury and Mars, occupy your solar eighth house of joint funds, savings, and debt for most of the month.

Relationships

Plan an outing such as a hike, biking, or a volleyball game with your coworkers to give your body a workout on the 13th. Plan an event for the Labor Day weekend with friends, and take a vote on suggestions for celebrating the final summer holiday weekend of the year. Get romantic with your partner on the 18th.

Success and Money

Shop for school supplies and electronic equipment before the 23rd. Shop for loan rates if refinancing your home before Labor Day. Financial dealings favor your chart on the 18th, leading to successful transactions and purchases.

Pitfalls and Potential Problems

Two Full Moons occur this month, the first on August 1 in Aquarius and your solar first house and the second on August 30 in Pisces conjunct transiting Saturn in your solar eighth house, showing a need to act carefully in monetary dealings. Mercury in Virgo turns retrograde on the 23rd, while Uranus in Taurus stations to turn retrograde on the 28th in your solar fourth house.

Rewarding Days

4, 6, 13, 18

Challenging Days

3, 10, 17, 25

Aquarius | September

Overall Theme

The amorous feeling that comes over you after September 3 is straight from your heart when Venus in Leo goes direct in your solar seventh house. A neighbor sends you an invitation for the Labor Day holiday weekend to attend a congenial gathering with your partner. The event is warm and uplifting and you'll talk about it for days.

Relationships

Congregate with work colleagues on the 9th to celebrate the successful delivery of a high-visibility project. The executive team hosts a celebratory pizza party on the Monday after delivery. Plan a visit with relatives on the 16th, when siblings gather to honor an elderly relative's birthday.

Success and Money

Your reputation for delivering high-quality analytical work increases. Enjoy the limelight when your boss gives you a performance bonus on the 20th and names your team as most productive in the current contract cycle. Excitement abounds when your organization announces it secured the winning bid on a new two-year contract.

Pitfalls and Potential Problems

Jupiter goes retrograde in Taurus on the 4th, leaving you puzzled over why family members dropped the ball in finalizing travel plans scheduled to begin later in the month. Details about your availability were misinterpreted. Mercury turns direct in Virgo on the 15th, catching a few employees off guard with unfinished assignments. You'll find that your mind is sharp and so is your tongue on the Aries Full Moon in your solar third house on the 29th.

Rewarding Days

9, 14, 16, 20

Challenging Days

7, 12, 17, 29

Aquarius | October

Overall Theme

Mars in Libra is compatible with your Sun at the beginning of the month. When it moves into Scorpio and your solar tenth house on the 13th, you may feel an edge from aspects to other fixed planets in Taurus. Reunite with members of your team on October 4 to celebrate a successful outcome.

Relationships

Celebrate diverse groups and their talents. Promote accomplishments via Zoom broadcasts that link networks. Invite speakers from distant locations to deliver talks. The Solar Eclipse in Libra and your solar ninth house on the 14th highlights cordial relationships with professional colleagues in remote locations. Make plans to visit these sites in the coming year.

Success and Money

With Saturn in Pisces moving retrograde and guarding your wallet in your solar second house, keep an eye on funds you set aside for holiday spending. Continue to seed your retirement portfolio with the money from a recent raise and watch your assets grow. Treat children to brunch on the 11th.

Pitfalls and Potential Problems

As the only planet turning direct this month (on the 10th), Pluto in Capricorn occupies your private solar twelfth house of secrets and healing. What keeps you up at night and where do you feel stuck? Release irritating patterns by changing your attitude. Avoid an argument with your boss on the 16th. The final Lunar Eclipse of 2023 falls in Taurus and your solar fourth house of home on October 28.

Rewarding Days

4, 11, 14, 24

Challenging Days

1, 16, 18, 28

Aquarius | November

Overall Theme
You'll generate plenty of holiday spirit if you turn off your computer the week of the 19th and participate in donating meals to favorite charities, overseeing your Thanksgiving feast, and making sure your home is ready for guests. Enjoy a pre-holiday dinner hosted by your CEO around the time of the Scorpio New Moon on the 13th.

Relationships
You enjoy entertaining at home and surprising guests with favorite dishes and a variety of desserts, especially pies. This year, work colleagues, neighbors, and relatives all join you to celebrate Thanksgiving. Team up with your partner to serve the drinks, appetizers, and an elegant entrée while exuding a welcoming air to put every guest in a holiday mood.

Success and Money
Saturn in Pisces moves direct in your solar second house on the 4th, coinciding with the arrival of a holiday bonus or merit increase in your pay, a lucky break in the money zone. Start shopping on the 20th for early holiday presents and additional home decorations to enhance your home's beauty.

Pitfalls and Potential Problems
Mercury and Mars connect in your solar tenth house through the 11th, opposing transiting Uranus in Taurus in your solar fourth house. Expect a conflict between work and home demands that forces you to take charge of solving problems before the holiday week. The Gemini Full Moon on the 27th in your solar fifth house favors staying close to home to recover after the holiday rush.

Rewarding Days
2, 4, 20, 22

Challenging Days
10, 11, 23, 27

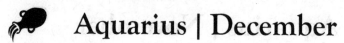

Aquarius | December

Overall Theme

You'll get a boost from compatible Mars in Sagittarius in your solar eleventh house all month that increases the number of invitations you receive from friends and professional groups to attend cocktail, dinner, and lunch buffets that put you in a festive holiday mood. Be sure to mail gifts and holiday cards early and look for free delivery offers from online vendors.

Relationships

Ask close relatives to join your family for pre-holiday festivities to embrace the spirit of togetherness starting December 9. Guests from a distance start arriving on the 22nd, warming your heart and sharing the awe-inspiring miracles of the season. Savor the love while you enjoy these holiday treasures.

Success and Money

Neptune in Pisces goes direct on December 6 in your solar second house, highlighting practical and spiritual insight while accelerating plans to allocate earned raises and bonus money to cover holiday and household expenses. Saturn in Pisces is on board, too, and keeps you watchful of impulse spending. Make the season bright for a favorite charity by mailing a contribution on the 18th.

Pitfalls and Potential Problems

Two other planets shift direction this month. Mercury goes retrograde in Capricorn on December 13 in your solar twelfth house and could delay the execution of plans you've had on the drawing board until next February. Jupiter in Taurus neutralizes an edgy rapport at home base when it goes direct in your solar fourth house on December 30.

Rewarding Days

6, 7, 18, 22

Challenging Days

3, 8, 13, 26

Aquarius Action Table

These dates reflect the best—but not the only—times for success and ease in these activities, according to your Sun sign.

	JAN	FEB	MAR	APR	MAY	JUN	JUL	AUG	SEP	OCT	NOV	DEC
Move		10		23					16			7
Romance	8	22	24				30	13	14		2	
Seek counseling/ coaching					9							
Ask for a raise	24		15		13	27	7			11		18
Vacation				17		11				14	22	
Get a loan								4				

Pisces

The Fish
February 18 to March 20

$\mathcal{H}$

Element: Water

Quality: Mutable

Polarity: Yin/feminine

Planetary Ruler: Neptune

Meditation: I successfully navigate my emotions

Gemstone: Aquamarine

Power Stones: Amethyst, bloodstone, tourmaline

Key Phrase: I believe

Glyph: Two fish swimming in opposite directions

Anatomy: Feet, lymphatic system

Colors: Sea green, violet

Animals: Fish, sea mammals

Myths/Legends: Aphrodite, Buddha, Jesus of Nazareth

House: Twelfth

Opposite Sign: Virgo

Flower: Water lily

Keyword: Transcendence

The Pisces Personality

Strengths, Talents, and the Creative Spark

Pisces, you have the distinction of being one of the most complex signs of the zodiac. Your signature symbol is the dual Fishes, swimming up and downstream and adding texture to your water sign element. Who realizes that behind your dreamy eyes is a mind that values personal privacy while you probe the mysteries of what makes others tick? When you need to share most, you often swim in the opposite direction and retreat until you come up with a new perspective. Freedom means a lot to you, and you shun confinement even though it is closely affiliated with your sign and the solar twelfth house of seclusion, retreat, and regrouping. As a Pisces, you own a generous spirit, love a mystery, take pleasure in journaling to give voice to important goals, and appreciate theater, film, art, and music. Yours is the last of the four mutable signs of the zodiac, and the only mutable water sign, with Neptune as your ruler and the natural occupant of the twelfth house of charity, healing, meditation, psychic experiences, loose ends, and secrets.

Currently you are enjoying both increased spirituality and notoriety with transiting Neptune in Pisces occupying the heavens through 2026. What fun you'll have using your intuitive insight and expanding your metaphysical side. Be sure you don't disappear into the fog that Neptune spreads or get confused about priorities during this long journey. Your colors are lavender, mauve, purple, sea green, violet, and soft royal hues. You bring your creative gifts to the world and look for ways to launch a new enterprise, especially with Neptune, your ruling planet, entering a late-degree cycle. Yours is the sign most affiliated with liquids of the earth (including oil and gas), aromatherapy, alcohol, medicinal drugs and illegal drugs, and ether.

Intimacy and Personal Relationships

Pisces can often be a flirt who dances, sings, or charms the audience. Your role model in the love department might be Cinderella, because you often visualize the perfect partner walking into your life one day and stealing your heart. As a bona fide soul mate seeker, you want the bells and whistles that include love at first sight and a happy ending. You bubble over with love and kindness. When you make a deep connection with a partner, you're in it for life, even if the "music" stops playing. You hang on too long to a lost cause, but when you're gone, you're gone, and aren't hesitant to remarry when the next sublime partner comes along. Possible partners are the other two water signs, Cancer and Scorpio, who resonate to your sensitivities. Attraction to your opposite sign of Virgo can be magnetic and keep you mesmerized. Other suitors are Taurus or Capricorn, who compete to hold your interest as a date or a good friend. Stability could be absent with a Gemini or Sagittarius and make you doubt, early in the game, that the relationship will last. Vary your routine when you are ready to find romance, and you're likely to meet your match. With your compassionate heart, you can be a kind and loyal friend and supporter of your cherished family.

Values and Resources

You do best when you listen to your inner voice and then follow with questions when information seems to be missing or needs clarification. Even though you like to see the best in others, taking what you hear for granted when you have doubts leads to confusion. In a work setting, you value the option of telecommuting, unless you are one of the Pisces group who dislikes using electronic technology. You might also prefer physical gardening and shrub maintenance to any other type of exercise because it allows you time to think. Many of you were born with a lucky streak thanks to your affiliation with Jupiter, your sign's former ruler before Neptune's discovery. Playing the lottery can be your jam, and you use favorite numbers to bring in winning results on a hot ticket. The home of your dreams includes big closets and abundant storage. You spend time and money on your wardrobe and especially splurge on shoes. Coordination of accessories is a must to define your strong fashion sense. And if your psychic sense keeps you busy, tune in, because those strong vibrations you're getting are on to something big.

Blind Spots and Blockages

Certain Pisces spend too much time on games, hobbies, or daydreaming until you realize that you are off track in meeting goals, a habit that annoys your boss. Supervisors dislike when you take too long to complete assignments, blow them off when they question the status of a task, or you seem to misunderstand the point of the work based on the content of material you submit for their review. Some of you are gamblers and enjoy playing the lottery or making trips to Atlantic City, Reno, and Las Vegas. These excursions can be fun as long as you don't forget to set a limit on how much money you have available for gambling without hurting your financial assets. Bosses call you stubborn when you refuse to sign up for developmental training courses designed to acquaint you with new technology or provide systems support. Although you're normally good-natured, those who work with you claim that you sometimes give defensive responses when you're asked for unanticipated information or requests, giving you a reputation for being uncooperative.

Goals and Success

Many Pisces are drawn to service professions that cover a wide spectrum of options. If your job provides you with privacy, a good salary, and behind-the-scenes activity, you willingly put in long years of service. Employment could include work in charitable or healing institutions; work at government agencies; the role of a secret agent, an intelligence officer, or an analyst who digs into confidential matters; healing and metaphysical arts; therapeutic practices like psychology; or writing novels, mysteries, and poetry. You have the classic makeup of one who can be gainfully employed in your own business or who attracts work-from-home jobs or freelance assignments. The more athletic among you find work as swimming instructors or have a desire to compete on a team in swimming and water sports venues. Those of you who journal or keep a diary raise your success probability by keeping goals in front of you and taking the right steps to fulfill your dreams.

Pisces Keywords for 2023
Afterthought, aid, approval

The Year Ahead for Pisces

In 2023 you'll have two outer planets in your sign and several planets making an aspect to your Sun based on when your birthday falls. Jupiter in Aries makes a mild semisextile aspect in your solar second house through May 16. Then it moves into Taurus and your solar third house, making an easy sextile aspect through the end of the year. Saturn challenges your solar twelfth house of solitude in Aquarius until it moves into Pisces on March 7, while Uranus makes a compatible connection to your Sun while in Taurus all year. Neptune conjuncts your Sun if you were born in the later degrees of Pisces, and Pluto nears the end of a harmonious cycle for those of you born in the last few degrees of Pisces.

Mars in Gemini is the first planet to go direct in 2023, in your solar fourth house of home and family on January 12, giving the go-ahead to implement plans that were put on hold related to household movement, projects, and relationships. Mercury in Capricorn goes direct on January 18 in your solar eleventh house, encouraging you to make decisions related to friendships, memberships in professional groups, and goals. Pluto in Capricorn is still plodding through your solar eleventh house of groups and goals until March 23, when it transitions into Aquarius for several months.

Uranus in Taurus, transiting your solar third house, will turn direct on January 22, clearing a path for resumption of contract awards, communication enhancements, and neighborhood activity. Transiting Saturn in Aquarius finishes its two-and-a-half-year tour of duty in your solar twelfth house, where you juggled assignments, worked on your resume, and possibly recovered from illness. On March 7, the planet of restriction moves into your sign and your solar first house, where you'll assess personal strength, energy, individuality, and innovation. The taskmaster planet will meet up with transiting Neptune in late degrees of your sign, allowing you to analyze confusing aspects of puzzling circumstances and relationships that are affecting your life.

Jupiter

In 2023 while Jupiter in Aries dashes through your solar second house of assets, bonuses, income, and new employment opportunities, you'll develop a solid financial plan. On May 16 Jupiter moves into Taurus and your solar third house, allowing you to make decisions related to education, electronic equipment, neighborhood ventures, siblings, and vehicle replacement. Market your resume to potential employers if employment has been sporadic. Assignments related to the pandemic may call for you to prepare status reports for analysis of key conditions, especially those that continue to have an effect on the public or private sectors, medical breakthroughs, or food services. You may receive offers to launch a new enterprise or start your own business. When Jupiter begins its rapid trip through Taurus, it pauses for a few months by going retrograde on September 4 and turning direct on December 30. The planet of opportunity occupies your solar third house for seven months in 2023, looking for ways to connect with community matters, siblings, cousins, neighbors, and transportation. Find options to create inspiring products using your fine mind. Individuals born between February 19 and March 7 see the most action this year while Jupiter is in Taurus.

Saturn

At the start of 2023, the planet of restriction continues its journey in Aquarius and your solar twelfth house of charity, healing, planning, privacy, regrouping, and seclusion. You explore new opportunities that include a search for a new position or the start of your own business, or you may ponder whether to retire or enroll in a certificate program to expand skills in newly evolving markets. Aid for others plays a big role in your employment future. Those of you born between March 12 and 20 see the most action while Saturn wraps up its cycle in Aquarius.

Saturn moves into Pisces on March 7 in your solar first house of action, appearance, assertiveness, health, individuality, and self-discovery. What you decide to do is in your hands and works best if you adapt to changing environmental conditions. If you have a partner, you may have to assess what conditions must be accommodated and work out details. During the remaining nine months of 2023, Saturn most affects those of you born between February 19 and 27. Enjoy the benefits of harmonious relationships with work colleagues and with your partner. If you've been pushing hard to hold things together, take a break and relax to clear your head before you accept a position in a new organization. Share goals with your partner and get an opinion on your vision for the future. Transiting Neptune in Pisces shares this solar first house, giving you the intuitive insight to assess the strength of your decisions and relationships and the intuition to implement your dreams.

Uranus

Transiting Uranus in Taurus starts the year in retrograde motion, going direct on January 22 and shaking up the energy in your philosophically oriented solar third house. With this activity, you have probably had your share of miscommunications, delays, or setbacks for a variety of reasons. That's because the planet of disruption and surprises has been occupying this house since May 2018. Although it is in a sign compatible with yours, the Uranian energy conflicts with your more relaxed demeanor. Uranus in Taurus has been residing in your solar third house, overseeing the comings and goings of local events, contracts, communication, siblings, cousins, neighbors, transportation issues, education and schools, electronic equipment, and your state of mind. Have you felt the chaotic energy resulting from the unpredictable planet's explosive nature? One more Taurus eclipse lands in your solar third house on October 28 and stays relevant through the spring of 2024, opening your eyes to new networking channels and a positive mental outlook. A job search or enrollment in coursework could bring increased local travel. If you were born between March 5 and 15, Uranus has the greatest impact on your impressionable mind. Get ready to experience a series of encounters that influence your career or residential choices, and consider life-changing opportunities. Let go of the worries in your sensitive psyche and let in a ray of optimism.

Neptune

Your solar first house of action, assertiveness, innovation, passion, the physical body, personality, self-image, and temperament is the site of considerable activity in 2023 as Neptune in Pisces reinforces the role it has been playing since April 2011. Reflect on what you've experienced with this ephemeral yet inspiring energy that brings you hazy moments when you would rather concentrate and distracts you from the organized life you're trying to pursue. You're quite familiar with how Neptune tempts you to daydream rather than take a pragmatic view of the issues that show up in and complicate life. Saturn in Pisces arrives in this same solar first house March 7 to aid in validating your feelings of self-worth and substantiating the entrance of an eclectic and inspiring group of people. Single Pisces may meet a new partner or two to date or share business interests. Tap into your humor and stimulate your deep Neptune compassion in your exchanges with others, many of whom want to cultivate your friendship. Use your intuition to understand the depth of your feelings for others. What is working and what is not? Be a good listener and study body language. Let what you desire fall into place, allowing you to develop meaningful relationships. Neptune aids in validating feelings by putting you in touch with your inner vision, using your intuitive, probing mind to understand others. Trust your psychic gifts. Pisces born between March 12 and 19 see the most activity from the conjunction of Neptune in Pisces this year. Embrace the forces of your brilliant, mystical mind.

Pluto

In 2008 Pluto in Capricorn first entered your solar eleventh house of associates, friends, club members, professional organizations, and peer groups. While Pluto winds up this long passage, the slow-moving planet urges you to address old issues you've held on to in this goal-oriented house. Identify contradictions in how your subconscious mind evaluates initiatives and relationships connected to this sector. If you have identified unyielding leaders who want dynamics to stay the same, regardless of the impact that changing circumstances identify, then say goodbye. Examine any baggage still affecting your memberships and group goals. Invite the Pluto-driven karma cleaners to dispose of any remaining anxiety. Don't treat problems as an afterthought when you can easily release the hold those with stubborn mindsets may have over you. If Pluto has identified relationship power struggles, assess them and have a serious talk with key people. Further confrontations mean you are hugging your blind spot. Let go and live. Release painful issues and master the hurdle.

Pluto enters the final degrees of Capricorn in late 2024. The transformer makes an easy trine aspect to your Sun this year if your birthday falls between March 17 and 20, the most affected dates. Pluto makes a brief entry into Aquarius starting on March 23. It turns retrograde on May 1 in the first degree of Aquarius and returns to Capricorn on June 11 to complete the remaining months of its cycle, which officially ends in November 2024. Pisces born between February 18 and 20 feel the impact of a brief encounter when Pluto occupies Aquarius from March 23 through June 11. Explore intuitive messages that focus on upcoming decisions that have not yet been announced.

How Will This Year's Eclipses Affect You?

In 2023 a total of four eclipses occur: two Solar (New Moon) Eclipses and two Lunar (Full Moon) Eclipses, which create intense periods that start to manifest a few months before their actual occurrence. Two of the eclipse signs are changing this year. The first eclipse occurs in your solar second house, the second in your solar ninth house, the third in your solar eighth house, and the final eclipse in your solar third house. Eclipses unfold in cycles involving all twelve signs of the zodiac, and usually occur in pairs about two weeks apart. Don't fear eclipses—think of them as growth opportunities that allow you to release old and outworn patterns. They often stimulate unexpected surprises and windfalls. The closer an eclipse is to a planet or point in your birth chart, the greater the importance of the eclipse in your life. Those of you born with a planet at the same degree as an eclipse are likely to see a high level of activity in the house where the eclipse occurs.

The first Solar Eclipse of 2023 takes place on April 20 in Aries and your solar second house of assets, income, and spending habits. You'll be examining your salary, determining whether you can live well on what you earn or should start searching for a better-paying job. Among your goals are seeding savings and retirement plans, reducing debt, and purchasing real estate. Invest in educational programs that build strong credentials for competing in new positions. Show flexibility.

Two weeks later, on May 5, the first Lunar Eclipse of the year takes place in Scorpio and your solar ninth house of the higher mind, education, foreigners and foreign countries and cultures, in-laws, publishing, and long-distance travel. Although you are tired of the unexpected jolts that interfere with your plans because of the opposition of Uranus in Taurus in your solar third house, be proud of how well you were able to communicate, provide training, and solve problems for employees at a distant location using remote technology. Consider work details to build credentials in lieu of moving. Share experiences with others to help them cope with social and work changes and steer them toward situation-specific experts. Maintain a positive attitude as you take bows for current achievements and explore new beginnings.

On October 14 the second Solar Eclipse of 2023 takes place in Libra and your solar eighth house of joint income, savings, and debt, as well as karmic conditions, psychological matters, investments, estates, wills, sex, birth, death, and regeneration. If you have planets in this house in your birth chart, expect surprises related to these themes. Matters that were escalating in April could come to a head, requiring a joint decision. A partner may bring in a raise in salary that will benefit you if you plan to pay off a mortgage or increase monthly payments. Seek assistance from financial specialists if warranted.

The year's final eclipse is a Lunar Eclipse on October 28 in Taurus and your solar third house of communication, education, local travel, neighbors, siblings, your mind, and transportation. With Uranus also in this house, the power of this eclipse could result in a high volume of mental chatter and pressure to sign contracts. Neighborhood safety and welfare are important to your family and neighbors. Circumstances may lead you to a new employment venue that maximizes your talent in communicating and solving problems.

Pisces | January

Overall Theme
Several planets shift direction this month. The first to move is Mars in Gemini and your solar fourth house on the 12th, calling attention to the tenor of family relationships. On January 18 Mercury goes direct in Capricorn and your solar eleventh house, an indicator that you'll experience stepped-up communications from friends and members of professional groups. Approval for a community event arrives after the 22nd, when Uranus turns direct in Taurus and your solar third house.

Relationships
Relatives vie for your attention on January 2 and 3, when visitors and immediate family continue the holiday celebrations with outings, shows, and festive dinners. After the 8th you'll be fully engaged in critical tasks at your workplace, collaborating with teammates and assessing priorities with imminent dates for completion. As an afterthought, your boss adds another report to the pile. By the weekend you're ready to chill on a quiet Sunday.

Success and Money
The Aquarius New Moon dawns in your solar twelfth house on the 21st, giving you a chance to work on goals for 2023, assess your healthy financial picture, and pay off the balances on holiday gifts. Purchase wardrobe additions with holiday gift money.

Pitfalls and Potential Problems
Check on the cost of a music venue on the January 6th Full Moon in Cancer before you purchase expensive tickets that increase the price by several hundred dollars. Double-check documents on the 18th—they may not be ready for your boss's signature and need a closer look.

Rewarding Days
2, 3, 8, 21

Challenging Days
4, 6, 18, 20

Pisces | February

Overall Theme

The Full Moon in Leo on February 5 lands in your solar sixth house, allowing time to catch up on work you brought home to give it a fresh eye and assess viability. Go to bed early to be your sharpest on Monday. With Venus in Pisces occupying your solar first house for the first few weeks of the month, love for your partner dominates your thoughts.

Relationships

Children, friends, and lovers occupy your heart and leisure time in this special month that also includes Valentine's Day. Bond with children on the 2nd with attendance at school activities they enjoy. The 10th is perfect for romance with your partner. Schedule a Valentine's Day dinner with your partner and favorite friends on the 17th, toasting love and admiration.

Success and Money

Your money picture reflects an optimistic beat on the 10th when you learn you're at the top of the list to win a high-profile assignment. Make sure your resume has been updated and talk to mentors. The New Moon in Pisces on the 20th stimulates gratitude toward coworkers who show support.

Pitfalls and Potential Problems

Winter storms may lead to a canceled business trip on the 12th. Neighbors are at odds with community issues and ask residents to choose a side on the 25th. Request more details before agreeing if you are on the fence. A friend may offer a flimsy excuse for canceling a lunch date on the 16th.

Rewarding Days

2, 10, 17, 22

Challenging Days

7, 12, 16, 25

Pisces | March

Overall Theme

Venus transits Aries and your solar second house through the 16th, along with Jupiter, activating deep discounts on home furnishings. Your solar second house of income and values is the site of the Aries New Moon on the 21st, which helps you negotiate terms for a home loan when you meet with a reputable mortgage lender offering favorable interest rates.

Relationships

Recreation is on your mind when you treat your children to a special game or event on the 2nd. During a romantic weekend getaway on the 11th, you and your partner bond in love by sharing feelings and dreams.

Success and Money

Positive lunar aspects in your solar tenth house of career and employing organization on the 15th lead to insightful discussions with your boss about your role in an upcoming staffing makeover of work divisions. The discussion whets your appetite for doing a creative analysis of positions, and your intuitive mind tells you the job is yours. Buy a lottery ticket on the 22nd.

Pitfalls and Potential Problems

Business partners or collaborators are edgy on the March 7th Virgo Full Moon. Pull away when discussions get volatile and pick another day to discuss work procedures. Don't bring complaints to your boss on the 14th or your intentions may be misunderstood.

Rewarding Days

2, 11, 15, 22

Challenging Days

7, 14, 16, 26

Pisces | April

Overall Theme

When the assertive Sun, Mercury, and Jupiter in fire sign Aries show up in your solar second house favorably aspecting the Moon in Leo in your solar sixth house on the 1st, you could be ready to spend some of your hard-earned cash on a pricey item like a new car, engagement ring, or vacation home. Compare prices first.

Relationships

Bond with siblings on the 21st, laying the groundwork for upcoming spring invitations. Have dinner out with family on the 23rd to discuss projects, children's interests, and dates to put on the calendar. Attend a social event on the 25th with your partner that includes seldom-seen friends or former classmates.

Success and Money

How fortunate to have the very first Solar Eclipse of the year falling in your solar second house on the 20th, joining prosperity-minded Jupiter in Aries and encouraging you to initiate a job search, a new financial plan that includes investment and savings accounts, and creative ventures with your partner. Prepare your vision board.

Pitfalls and Potential Problems

The April 6th Full Moon in Libra opposes the Sun and Jupiter, warning you away from impulse spending and unplanned travel. Keep a clear head and work on taxes instead, especially if you haven't yet filed them. Mercury in Taurus turns retrograde in your solar third house on the 21st, highlighting safety matters in your local environment.

Rewarding Days
1, 20, 23, 25

Challenging Days
3, 6, 8, 27

Pisces | May

Overall Theme

The energy of the May 5th Lunar Eclipse in Scorpio and your solar third house of communication aligns with transiting Uranus in Taurus also in this house, resulting in unclear messages or confusing phone calls. Retrograde Mercury in Taurus in your solar third house goes direct on May 14. Make phone calls to clear up misunderstandings.

Relationships

Colleagues recognize contributions you've made to a humanitarian cause at a luncheon on the 9th. An invitation to chair the group may be close behind. Your heart swells with pride when a teen child receives an appealing offer of a college scholarship after mid-month. Congratulate your offspring and celebrate with family on the 23rd.

Success and Money

When Jupiter in Taurus arrives in your solar third house on the 16th, activity in this sector picks up steam and talk turns to planning a summer vacation to begin after the delivery date of a key assignment. Work connected to an insightful assessment of business and policy practices gets rave reviews from peer groups after the 28th.

Pitfalls and Potential Problems

Pluto in Aquarius, at odds with the Moon, goes retrograde in your solar twelfth house on May 1. Ignore a Monday morning grouch who wants to make waves over trivial matters. By evening, harmony returns to your home. The Scorpio Lunar Eclipse on the 5th highlights strained long-distance communication. Set up a Zoom meeting on the 19th to discuss and resolve the tension.

Rewarding Days

9, 19, 23, 28

Challenging Days

1, 5, 14, 31

Pisces | June

Overall Theme

Be sure to resolve contracting issues for both personal and business enterprises this month, especially before Saturn goes retrograde on June 17 in Pisces and your solar first house. Concerns about a long-distance work matter are likely to involve an interactive Zoom meeting to look at specifics on the 2nd.

Relationships

A scheduling conflict prevents you from attending a work-related social invitation on the Sagittarius Full Moon of June 3. Meet a close friend for lunch on the 6th who asks you to be a sounding board over a difficult decision to leave the current job. A sibling contacts you on the 5th to coordinate July holiday plans. Clear dates with your partner before committing.

Success and Money

On the 17th you begin an overnight trip that extends through the June 18th New Moon in Gemini. You and your family enjoy fun and recreation featuring swimming, a picnic, or water rides. A work contract deserves a second look with its tempting offer of a salary increase near the 15th.

Pitfalls and Potential Problems

On the 30th, Neptune in Pisces turns retrograde in your solar first house until December 6, creating confusion over plans to implement a new system to streamline processes. Clarify details thoroughly.

Rewarding Days

2, 6, 15, 28

Challenging Days

1, 3, 22, 30

Pisces | July

Overall Theme
Even though the Capricorn Full Moon on the 3rd makes a harmonious aspect to your Pisces Sun, lunar aspects are unfavorable for travel over the 4th of July holiday. Connect with community residents to plan a holiday celebration to honor our nation's birthday. A patriotic-themed menu and sparkling cake will put neighbors in a festive mood.

Relationships
When the Moon is in your sign on the 7th, lunar aspects offer a compatible time to enjoy a short getaway with your partner and family. Bond with those you cherish and enjoy time with your significant other. Schedule travel the week of the 17th, starting with the Cancer New Moon that day. Accept a friend's invitation for a day at the beach on the 31st.

Success and Money
Uranus in your solar third house greets you with surprising news that your parents are treating you to a weeklong adventure trip to a place that has been on your radar screen. The New Moon in Cancer on the 17th favors enrolling younger children in swimming lessons before an August vacation.

Pitfalls and Potential Problems
When transiting Venus in Leo turns retrograde in your solar sixth house on the 23rd, you may have to cancel plans with a friend because of a health concern. Keep your wallet hidden on the 10th or you'll pick up the lunch check for unexpected work visitors.

Rewarding Days
7, 12, 17, 31

Challenging Days
5, 10, 23, 27

Pisces | August

Overall Theme

The first of two Full Moons in August shows up on the 1st in Aquarius and your solar twelfth house of introspection, giving you an opportunity to ponder developing plans you have with family members. By the second Full Moon, which occurs in Pisces and your solar first house on August 30, you're ready to implement your choices in September.

Relationships

Children claim the family limelight on the 13th, excited to be starting their last vacation of summer. The venue is resort-oriented, with multiple activities that please every age. You and your partner are ready for a Friday night dinner and dance on the 18th to nurture your spirits. Invite friends for a casual meal and a movie on the 27th.

Success and Money

Involvement with a favorite charity on the 4th sets the tone for an elegant gala in late fall. Look for entertainment bargains from the 10th through the 13th. Enjoy your finds and the surprises you'll share with your family. Consider booking a Broadway show in October.

Pitfalls and Potential Problems

Friction between family members on the 1st involves the opposition of Mercury and Saturn. Address conflicts before they escalate and put a damper on vacation time. Mercury turns retrograde in Virgo on the 23rd, affecting pending partnership decisions. Uranus in Taurus goes retrograde on the 28th in your solar third house of local interests and complicates your meeting schedule.

Rewarding Days

4, 13, 18, 27

Challenging Days

1, 17, 23, 28

Pisces | September

Overall Theme

Since several planets shift direction this month, pause before tackling any major decisions. First, Venus in Leo goes direct in your solar sixth house on September 3, followed by Jupiter in Taurus turning retrograde in your solar third house on the 4th through December 30. Routines get back to normal when Mercury turns direct on the 15th in Virgo and your solar seventh house.

Relationships

Accompany your sibling or cousin to an event on the 6th. Attend a birthday lunch with members of a professional group to honor a long-time colleague celebrating a milestone on the 23rd.

Success and Money

Jupiter favors deals you are setting up, such as work contracts, educational pursuits for you or your children, and home decorating projects. Notice the enjoyable relationships you're cultivating with cousins and siblings. Put a dent in credit card debt on the 16th.

Pitfalls and Potential Problems

If you're shopping for household remodeling estimates, don't bother to meet with contractors until after the Labor Day holiday. Line up at least two more companies to compare prices before selecting a well-qualified firm. A couple pieces of office equipment could fail on the 12th, necessitating a call for prompt repairs.

Rewarding Days

6, 14, 16, 23

Challenging Days

7, 12, 17, 29

Pisces | October

Overall Theme

This month brings invitations for invigorating outings from relatives, friends, and traveling partners looking to share an adventure with you. Single Pisces receive their share of attention from flirtatious friends, especially when the Moon and Venus visit your solar seventh house on the 10th.

Relationships

On October 14 the final Solar Eclipse of 2023 occurs in Libra and your solar eighth house. You and your mate could be feeling amorous and take advantage of beautiful fall weather to schedule a two-day stay at a popular spa or other venue. Friends invite you to a much-touted concert on the 20th.

Success and Money

Jupiter in Taurus and your solar third house for the remainder of the year gives you an advantageous position for expanding your communication and writing skills well into 2024. Your boss likes your style and the reliability you demonstrate in completing assignments. Look for a salary boost after the October 14th Solar Eclipse in Libra.

Pitfalls and Potential Problems

After a six-month retrograde period, Pluto turns direct in Capricorn on October 10 in your solar eleventh house. You've been mulling over terminating your membership in a political or social group this year and feel justified in breaking ties over uninspiring leadership qualities. You may experience disappointment when the management team reneges on a revised work policy on the 18th.

Rewarding Days
10, 14, 20, 24

Challenging Days
1, 7, 18, 23

Pisces | November

Overall Theme

You're into solving puzzles—crosswords, anagrams, and the good old-fashioned practical kind—which need your intuitive touch when the Moon is in Gemini on the 1st. You'll want to get a head start on pressing chores this holiday season. Make finishing work assignments a priority to allow plenty of time for gift shopping.

Relationships

On the 17th children start migrating back to home base to share the Thanksgiving feast. Invite extra guests who live far from their families to your dinner. While the food roasts in the oven, keep the kindness going by asking your family to serve an early meal at a local shelter. Offer invited guests an array of festive dishes and desserts.

Success and Money

An unusual gift from relatives at a distance arrives on the November 13th New Moon in Scorpio. You receive a bonus award shortly after Saturn goes direct in Pisces on the 4th. Share part of your bonus money with a charitable group that provides holiday meals to those in need. Buy extra supplies to make the holiday season brighter around the 17th.

Pitfalls and Potential Problems

A mini mutiny in mutable signs takes place this month when the Sagittarius Sun in your solar tenth house takes a hard hit from Saturn in Pisces in your solar first house on Thanksgiving. The Moon in Aries and your solar second house opposes Venus in Libra and your solar eighth house later that day. Keep politics out of the Thanksgiving table discussions.

Rewarding Days

1, 4, 8, 17

Challenging Days

11, 23, 25, 27

Pisces | December

Overall Theme

Right after Neptune goes direct in Pisces on the 6th in your solar first house, holiday invitations for the next three weeks fill your mailbox. Party season seems endless, with special events filling your calendar every week, including parades, cocktail parties, dinners, and brunches.

Relationships

Attend an event with your partner on the 5th to celebrate their achievements. Accept an invitation to a holiday dinner sponsored by a professional affiliation on the 14th. Buy raffle tickets to support a children's charity and purchase an extra toy. Guests begin to arrive on the 22nd, kicking off the holiday celebrations.

Success and Money

Jupiter in Taurus transits your solar third house for most of this month, reminding you of the prosperity that has come your way this year—caring neighbors, a lovely community, loving siblings and cousins, and the brand-new car that is sitting in your driveway. Work perks arrive in the form of a fascinating new job, a raise, or a bonus.

Pitfalls and Potential Problems

Planets boldly shift direction this month, starting with Neptune's direct motion in Pisces and your solar first house on the 6th, followed by Mercury turning retrograde on the 13th in Capricorn and your solar eleventh house. Jupiter goes direct in Taurus on the 30th in your solar third house, suggesting that your expertise in communication will be a focus in 2024.

Rewarding Days

5, 7, 14, 22

Challenging Days

3, 8, 13, 26

Pisces Action Table

These dates reflect the best—but not the only—times for success and ease in these activities, according to your Sun sign.

	JAN	FEB	MAR	APR	MAY	JUN	JUL	AUG	SEP	OCT	NOV	DEC
Move			11			2						
Romance		10			28		17	13		10		5
Seek counseling/coaching	2				19			27			17	
Ask for a raise	8		15	20		15			23	14		
Vacation				25			12				1	
Get a loan		22							16			7